Messed-Up Choices

We make the choices, and then the choices make us!

MOIRA DARRELL

Written by a real, live human.

MESSED-UP CHOICES

Moira Darrell

Written by a real, live human

Copyright © 2024 Moira Darrell

All rights reserved.

No part of this book may be reproduced, stored in any retrieval devices or passed on in any form or by any means, electronic, mechanical, photocopied, faxed, recording or otherwise, without express written permission of the author.

ISBN: 978-1-7781408-3-9 (ePub)
ISBN: 978-1-7781408-2-2 (print)

This is a work of total fiction. Any familiar names, characters or events are products of the author's imagination.

Some character names may be similar to actual people; however, the character names do not designate real people, living or dead. Any names or event similarities are entirely coincidental. All the characters live in the author's mind, not in life.

Moira Darrell Wiley original quotes:
　"Instead of worrying about what was or what might be, rejoice in what IS."
　"If you don't laugh, you cry."
　"Forward and onward."
Original Poem:
　"BE KIND BECAUSE YOU CAN'T REWIND" – written by Moira Darrell Wiley

Cover Photo by the author
Could I Have This Dance as sung by Anne Murray was written by
　Wayland Holyfield
Book cover and layout by Human Powered Design

Find me at: facebook.com/moiradarrellbooks

Contents

PROLOGUE Matthew's Journal — 1
PART ONE
One Hurdle at a Time — 7
Back In The Day — 10
Matthew's Journal — 18
Trust — 25
The Fun We Had — 31
The Wedding — 35
Phoebe and Leonard — 40
Matthew's Journal — 43
RV Resort — 46
Confiding — 54
Matthew's Journal — 59
For Sale — 61
Where Did Matt Go? — 66
Resort Stories — 70
Matthew's Journal — 80
What Can I Do? — 82
PART TWO
Matthew's Journal — 87
At That Moment — 90
Day-To-Day — 91
Matthew's Journal — 98
What Is Matthew Hiding? — 101
Awake — 107
Matthew's Journal — 112

That Is So Selfish	116
Matthew's Journal	121
Girls' Night Out	124
Matthew's Journal	129
Life In Pictures	133
Desertscaping	138
Matthew's Journal	145
Still Hurting	148
Matthew's Journal	152
Memories	156
Family Situations	161
Menacing Telephone Calls	169
Matthew's Journal	171
Painting Sheep	174
Sherlock & Watson	178
Snickers!	183
Matthew's Journal	190
I Usually Aim Higher!	193
Mothers	197
Retirement	204
I Sprained My Freaking Ankle	208
Did Matt Do It?	214
PART THREE	
Matthew's Journal	219
Words	221
Attitude Adjustment	226
A New Beginning?	228
What the Hell?	234
Travis And Ashley	236
Matthew's Journal	245
Louie and Dewie	249
Quandaries	251
Turning Against Matt!	258
Matthew's Journal	264

The Beat Goes On	267
What Next?	275
Success	282
EPILOGUE	288
Thank You	294
Overview for *Selena and Her Mysteries*	296
Note from the Author	299
About the Author	303
Research	305

NOTE: This book is a family drama - recommended 18+

Book mentions attempt at suicide.

Check out this website:

https://www.mayoclinic.org/diseases-conditions/suicide/symptoms-causes/syc-20378048

For help, telephone: 988 in USA // 911 in CANADA

Dedicated to

Nancy and Joel Carlson
I value their never-ending friendship, as well as the absolute pleasure of knowing I was always welcome.

Thank you to those amazing people from our own RV Resort for being exactly who they are.

No particular person or RV Resort is portrayed in this book. It's a fiction!

Locations in *MESSED-UP CHOICES* include:
Palm Springs and area, California
Portland, Oregon
Calgary, Alberta

Also written by Moira Darrell:
SELENA AND HER MYSTERIES

Palm Desert, California

PROLOGUE

MATTHEW'S JOURNAL

When I'd regained consciousness as if from a dream, I had peculiar and unsettling recollections. Had they been real?

I'd had a vague memory of experiencing panic, realizing I was hovering at the corner of a room – on the ceiling!

What the hell? If that wasn't mind blowing enough, I had seen myself below lying on a cot. No, not a cot – a hospital bed. No! No! No!

Jenna had been beside my bed – then a memory returned of the earlier event, a memory of what I had done before. Déjà vu. But this couldn't be happening. Or wait – this meant I didn't die. I felt that I was going to be all right. Wasn't I? Medical personnel had been scattered about, and machines hooked up. Travis and Ashley stood behind Jenna. Her hands were clasped in prayer. In prayer? Then I noticed the clergy at the foot of the bed. Oh God! Oh Jenna!

Jenna had whimpered, "Matthew, Matthew, can you hear me?"

I had heard her as I lay there. Correction, as I had hovered on the ceiling looking down. Memories had flashed back to me – the events of last night, the events from this morning. Or had it been longer? I didn't know. I didn't think I really wanted to die that night. I'd just wanted something. But what had I wanted? I'd wanted Jenna and the children; I'd wanted things to be easier.

Once I had acted on that choice to end my life by overdose, the scenario could've gone either way. I'd wondered "Have I survived? What did all this mean?" Seeing all the tubes and machines, the fact I was on the ceiling(!), not awake in the bed, and our minister standing there, I was on a two-way street. Which way was I going? I had been vaguely aware of a beckoning light appearing at the end of a long grey tunnel. I remember wondering as I peered through that tunnel, "Should I stay here, or should I surrender to its unmistakeable pull?"

I had attempted to get to the light, but I'd stayed at the ceiling for a long time watching myself below. I'd wondered what would happen to me. I'd tried to move to comfort Jenna and the children, but I had been trapped on that ceiling with no ability to move.

I'd heard Jenna's frantic voice, "I have to call Mom and Dad and Clara and Jack – right now. They need to know."

I recall thinking, "Why am I up here? I want to be with my family." I hadn't understood what I was seeing. For that matter, I hadn't understood why I was seeing anything. I'd decided that I must be alive. I'd watched, aware of the clearing of my airway, insertion of a breathing tube, being administered some sort of medication. I'd felt no pain. Should I have felt pain? I'd watched helplessly as intravenous fluids were put into me. "What was happening? Were they saving me? I loved my wife. I loved my children. I had let them down."

I'd felt faintly cognizant that sometimes I'd been on the level of the bed, but not being aware if I was in my body. I recall that I'd felt emptiness as though a lot of time had passed. Events and people came and went.

From the ceiling, I had seen my mother and father enter the room, Mom crying. They had been alone with me, holding hands. I couldn't think clearly, but that had seemed special to me – my mother and father holding hands.

Then Jenna, Ashley and Travis had been with me at another time. I'd felt hazy, maybe dozing off and on. Was that when I was in my body on the bed?

Then I'd blanked out (again).

And then light shone in my eyes. I felt awareness. I was in the hospital bed. My mind was so sketchy. Those memories haunted me. My eyes randomly opened and closed, but I didn't have control over their function. I commanded my eyes to open.

PART ONE

Instead Of Worrying What 'Was'
Or What 'Might Be,'
Rejoice In What 'IS'

Palm Desert, California

1

3 Months Before

One Hurdle at a Time

❖ JENNA ❖

WHAT DOES IT FEEL like to be depressed? Matthew and I've been married for so many years, I felt I knew Matthew inside and out, but he's changed before my eyes – He changed years ago, in fact.

Long before, prior to being fired from his job, his interest in work had done a flip-flop from happy and excited to go out the door for work to hesitating and leaving late, making excuses to delay going. Worse yet, it developed into not wanting to go at all once he became ill. "I'm not feeling good, Jenna. I can't go today."

I hesitantly offered one day, "Just get ready for work, have some breakfast, and you'll feel better once you're out the door." I said this as he pulled the covers over his head.

"No, leave me alone."

His once sand-toned blond hair no longer lush, laying damp and flat against his head, the lop-sided smile non-existent – his face often empty of emotion, unsure of what we'd just been talking about, hopeless, exhausted. He had headaches and digestive issues, not really caring about eating what I prepared. He used to love to cook various meals. His mood swings are unmanageable. He is not the Matthew I fell in love with, nor the Matthew I've known all these years.

Who is he? And then who am I? Those two thoughts struck me smack in the gut.

And the drinking.

Agitated, I asked him, "Where are you hiding the booze?"

Groggily, "What?"

"You've been sneaking drinks for weeks."

His friend, Aaron, had told me about Matthew's drinking a couple of weeks ago, but I knew anyway.

From under the covers, I heard a groan, and he heaved a sigh that turned into his perpetual cough before saying, "I know you want more from me. I can't give it. I have nothing to give you or anyone else."

"You've been ill with that bloody cough for over a year." I worried about him and about us. Thinking maybe a reality check could be in order, I bravely stated matter-of-factly, "They could fire you."

Another deep sigh, another racking cough as he stuck his head out to give me a sad, despondent expression. Then he'd turned over, away from me. "I don't care if they fire me. I can't even make myself work from home. Now they want me coming into the office. I already said, 'Leave me alone' – Get out of here!"

Matthew had withdrawn from me, from our friends and distanced himself from our children. Not that he had been an angel before. His temper was frightening.

I've been watching his moods these past few years – more than I ever had to. He'd changed then into someone dark, and, now with his illness and depression, he's changed again. This time he's physically ill as well as emotionally. *I don't want to say even to myself that he's mentally ill.*

When he was promoted to Business Manager in Acquisitions, we were ecstatic. Corner office, large windows. Matthew had led the administrative and management side of *Smooth Image Surgery* for decades, the promotion an expected reward. When the pandemic came, no one in the 'plastic' surgery business was prepared. Accounts fell away; people stopped coming. Depression invaded Matthew's psyche. Even though business was slowly recovering, it had been slumped for two years.

My anxiety levels had risen exponentially. His pal, Aaron, had covered for Matthew at *Smooth Image Surgery* as best he could, coming over in the evenings and weekends, even reading books to Matthew. That was when I noticed something about Aaron. *Don't go there!* I chastised myself. But there it was again. I thought about Aaron holding the book. *Aaron has big hands.* So, I mentally slap myself, and I mentally slap myself even harder at my next thought, refusing to acknowledge it.

What am I doing? I'm a married woman. And that's my husband's best friend!

I sighed with longing, a longing of knowing what I really needed and wanted – to have my husband back – the real one.

The wind wailed outside as I rushed to close the windows. *Another day, another windstorm. Will it at least rain today?*

I resigned myself to yet another day of him staying in bed half the day. "I'll bring you coffee." I left, leaving the door open in case he called.

"Maybe tomorrow," I whispered to myself hopelessly.

—⚘—

Unwanted memories of the past years crowded into my brain.

The man I had fallen in love with dramatically changed two years ago. Matthew became moody – black moods, emotionally unstable. I thought it was me – that he could love me for only so long and then he couldn't because it was my fault. Maybe I did something or said something wrong, and he'd turn on me. For 27 years of our marriage, I'd been a self-confident woman, loved by my husband. But I lost that self-confidence, slowly. I no longer felt I knew him. *I don't know who I am, don't know when it's safe to comment.* Sometimes if I kept quiet, he'd yell, "What's the matter with you? Are you playing the victim again?" When these episodes took over him, he looked wild.

He hasn't been physically aggressive toward me, but he slams doors, cupboards. Once he punched a hole in the wall.

Portland, Oregon

2

Before

Back In The Day

❖ JENNA ❖

THIRTY YEARS AGO, MY family had travelled from Calgary, Alberta, to Portland, Oregon, for a holiday in July – the whole crew. Mom had picked Portland.

"I want to visit the 'City of Roses,'" she'd insisted.

I deemed it cool to be going to the United States for a trip. I wondered if it would feel different from Canada. In the past, we'd holidayed in Vancouver for a week every couple of years, staying with relatives. I don't actually know how Mom and Dad swung the money for the six of us to stay for two weeks in Portland. We were on the 9th floor of the Portland Sheraton Hotel located on Multnomah directly across from the Lloyd Center. What a blast for us with one room for the parents and one room for the kids, although we weren't kids by a long shot. My younger siblings, twins Joan and Ruby, were 19. At 17, already showing signs of becoming muscular, Robert scowled with displeasure about having a cot brought in.

"For crap's sake, I'm not a kid. I'm not sharing with you."

Joan responded, equally as loud, "Shut up, dipshit. You'll do as you're told. It's not your money we're using."

Dad walked in through the adjoining doorway, "Robert Barnes! Is there a problem?"

"No sir."

"Good. Settle it quietly and politely. No more nonsense!"

"Yes sir." Contritely.

As Dad strode back through the doorway to their room, Joan stuck her tongue out at Robert and gave him a sneer.

Robert pulled the sheets off her bed and whispered, "Settle it quietly and politely."

We were celebrating my having graduated with a teaching degree. Did we head out after our parents were asleep? Damn right! The swimming pool was where the action was for those under 21. *Twenty-one is the legal drinking age! What the hell?* At home, it was 18. Since I was 22 years old, I could have gone to the bar, but this was a family holiday, and I was enjoying the time with my siblings.

University had been gruelling – I'd put my nose to the grindstone and missed out on opportunities to be with my family. Thankfully, even with Calgary having half the 1.5 million population it does now, I could still live at home, but I spent a huge amount of time studying. I'd proudly graduated with Distinction from the University of Calgary.

Down at the pool, there were really hot guys my age. They noticed Ruby, Joan and me quickly. We each had long auburn hair and bodies that attracted their attention. Ruby made eyes at the guys. Joan tired of them being super silly. She picked up Ruby's book by mistake, then unceremoniously tossed the Shakespearean tragedy aside and jumped into the pool to do laps.

There were young girls posturing for our Robert who was wearing his coal-black hair long to his shoulders. The guys, along with Robert, showed off by strutting around while the other boys laughed and pushed each other into the pool. One guy stood out for me with his long sandy blond hair falling over one eyebrow and a smile curved up more on one side than the other, exceedingly captivating – not strutting, laughing or pushing. He was working as the lifeguard, one seriously cool looking lifeguard – tall, well-built and handsome – sexy.

Three evenings into our family vacation, one of the times my siblings and I were at the pool without our parents, I strolled past the lifeguard station. Well, I strolled past the lifeguard station for the fifth time that evening, lingering. The lifeguard came down from his little perch. I spotted his name badge, MATTHEW HANSON.

"Hi!" He smiled and bowed his head, an arch to one eyebrow as though he'd asked me a question, blue eyes flashing.

"Hi back, Matthew," nodding at his badge. "I'm Jenna Barnes from Calgary."

"I've noticed you here at the pool, wondered if you'd want to catch a drink?" That smile again, higher on one side than the other, the arched eyebrow. Then concern appearing. *Was he worried I'd say no? He must be able to tell I'm legal age.*

Not shy and used to guys hitting on me, I decided in the affirmative. He had a great body, muscles right where they should be. He looked terrific, swimsuit included. I let him stew for a few moments more.

"Yeah, that'd be cool. Never had a proposition from a lifeguard." I grinned, "When?"

We met after his shift. I'd changed into a blue cotton sundress, thin straps and sandals. He watched out for traffic as we crossed the street. Matthew had a quiet way of speaking, yet he had a lot to say about his lifeguard gig, his university studies and what he expected out of his future.

Leaning in, grabbing my hand, he asked, "Where'll you teach?"

"I have a Special Ed position lined up in Calgary. Not a school that's top of my list, but I can move as positions open. It'll work out fine."

On the same evening that would have been our third date, my parents arranged for a proper family supper at *Clyde's Prime Rib Restaurant*. Once the decision was made about the time we'd be leaving for the restaurant, I swallowed any hesitation I had and perkily announced, "I've someone I want to bring along. We met at the pool. Matthew Hanson, and he's the hotel lifeguard."

My siblings gave me knowing glances and chuckles, and Robert made a *smooch, smooch* noise.

"That's not helpful, Robert." That from my father. Dad's strikingly handsome, chisel-featured face appeared annoyed. He stood there, all 5'11 of him, strong build, physically fit. He planted himself in front of Robert to study my mother who had been looking at me. She'd turned to send Robert an 'I'm not impressed' stare.

Now rotating his head slightly to inspect me, my father asked, "Has he been a gentleman with you?"

Oh, lord, some fathers! "Really, Dad. I'm 22. Remember? You shouldn't even be asking me that! We've just been hanging out. We like each other. Nothing will come of it. We're only here for another week."

His gaze fell on my mother. He spoke quietly, as though just to her, "It only takes once."

"Leonard! Not in front of the children." Mom stood up, stretching her 5'5" frame to full height, her shoulder-length blonde hair tied back with a clip, green eyes switching from displeasure to fury.

"Sorry, Phoebe. I wouldn't have married anyone else, but we both know the reason for our hasty wedding."

Dad's voice had become fainter, and Mom appeared to calm down as my dad whispered, "I didn't mean anything, and they're not exactly children."

"My point exactly!" I declared.

After they had moved across the room, still having an intense conversation, my dad turned his head toward me, his arms surrounding my mother. Then he spoke over the chatter of my siblings, "We'd be delighted to meet Matthew."

Letting go of Mom, but taking her hand, Dad glanced sideways toward Robert, saying in an admonishing tone, "Robert."

"Yep, no biggie."

My father shouldn't have asked that lame question – whether Matthew and I were sexually active. At 22 years old, he should have known we weren't simply holding hands!

The next week raced by. My parents had watched with approval as Matthew pulled out my chair at the restaurant, saw he was incredibly attentive and that his manners were as good as any of ours, superior to Robert's. Robert liked to tackle his meal similar to when he was on the football field, full speed ahead and 'don't reach for anything he might have his hand out ready to grasp'. No mercy! Joan and Ruby couldn't have failed to see the light in our eyes as we assessed each other at the pool. However, tonight they were especially demure all evening.

Dad, of course, got to the point. "What do you do, besides being a lifeguard?"

Matthew said, "I'm working toward an accounting degree."

"What are your prospects for afterward?"

Third degree! I wanted to tell Dad to stop, but I also had an interest in his response.

"Good jobs, enough to get by."

We'd already talked about his degree, and that he was taking classes at Portland State University. *Matthew downplayed the possibilities in his career to Dad. Playing it cool.*

Late at night following a stroll around Portland, hand in hand, or after an hour or so at the bar, Matthew and I'd go into the lifeguard locker room and find an out-of-the way nook. It's amazing what little space one needs to make out in! A little kissing led to a lot of kissing and a little petting led to a lot of petting. By the sixth night, I think we steamed up the mirrors. I always wore simple clothing, a dress that could be easily discarded.

―⚚―

When Matthew could get away, he accompanied our family to our tourist attractions. He'd suggested various sites that Dad gratefully acknowledged would be enjoyable.

"Phoebe, you mentioned gardening. I hoped you'd love the Rose Test Garden," Matthew had ventured during the excursion.

Looking quite pleased with the extra attention, Mom responded warmly, "It's marvellous. The brochure says all the roses are named after Shakespearean characters. Thanks for suggesting it." Peering over the top of her sunglasses, she said thoughtfully, "Ahhh, I can hear Ruby going off on a poetry tangent."

Matthew turned questioningly toward my mom. "What?" Glancing where my mom was looking, then listening, "Oh, I see some of the real Ruby, I suppose."

"Indeed," I said, "this is our Ruby."

Ruby's auburn hair flowed behind her as she sauntered through the Shakespeare Garden, having read the sign that the garden originally featured flowers mentioned in William Shakespeare's works. William Shakespeare was someone she didn't ever tire of reading. She had memorized numerous long soliloquies. With both arms outstretched, she exuberantly proclaimed from *A Midsummer Night's Dream*:

> "But earthlier happy is the rose distill'd,
> Than that which withering on the virgin thorn
> Grows, lives and dies in single blessedness."

As she walked along, reciting more Shakespeare, I heard Joan laugh and say in an overly dramatic, long-suffering voice, "Come on Robert, let's walk over to the Queens' Walk."

"Yeah, I'm outtie."

Joan said, "What?"

"Outta here, out of here. What rock have you been under? That's cool talk."

After snickering, she said, "Right! You're one real cool guy."

Matthew and I tagged along to the Queens' Walk area and found Joan studying the bronze plaques honouring the Rose Festival Queens. Robert peered at the sky, sighing deeply. He quickly turned when he saw us and pretended to be studying a rose. Sliding closer to Matthew, he muttered out of the side of his mouth, "What the hell have you gotten us into? What's next on your agenda – a doily museum?"

"How did you guess?" Matthew smirked and added, "I arranged it just for you."

"Ass!"

"I like you too," stated Matthew, unfazed by Robert's remark.

After Mom and Dad joined us, Mom said she wanted to go to the Pittock Mansion. They were outvoted by us. Instead, we decided to go to the Oaks Amusement Park where Matthew regaled us about his past exploits with his brother, Neil.

Dad appeased Mom by saying, "Phoebe, I'll take you tomorrow. I want to see the architecture. We'll enjoy it more without these five muppets!"

Near the end of my family's holiday time, Matthew asked, "Would you consider teaching in Portland?"

"What?!" I was stunned! For a moment. Then I'd surrendered to the image of being with Matthew long-term, living with Matthew, continuing to enjoy what we'd found in each other. *Move to the United States?* I sensed it would be an awfully strange experience moving countries. *Would I lose my identity?*

Replying, "Maybe." And then, "Yes." *I must not be reasoning clearly.* I quickly became hesitant about leaving and going back to Calgary, smitten as I was with this man. That evening, Matthew and I researched the possibility of my teaching in Portland. The outcome wouldn't be straightforward. I couldn't easily get a job in the USA.

My next visit to Portland meant it was time to meet his parents. I don't relish re-visiting that scenario. Matthew's father seemed fine – strict, but friendly. His mother, however, seemed to have a dislike for me as soon as I entered the home. There were remarks about the length of my dress, my hair not being the right style for me, and then, "It wouldn't be that hard to shed that extra weight. Think how much better you could look for Matthew."

Her attitude as the years went by didn't change. I wouldn't change my life to garner her good opinion. I did, in fact, shed a couple of pounds only because working in the classroom with children gave me more exercise than sitting in university classes. I told myself it was zero to do with a mean-spirited mother of a boyfriend. The fiancé part came one year later.

We'd talked about it. In fact, five months into our relationship, Matthew whispered, "If I was ever going to marry anyone, it would be you, Jenna Barnes!" After laughing, I said, "I hope that wasn't a proposal because we're not anywhere near that yet." I left with Matthew believing it wouldn't be long before there was a ring on my finger. I wasn't certain what I believed.

"Just not yet." I reiterated to myself as I boarded the plane, but a tell-tale smile lingered on my lips, still swollen from his good-bye kisses, and feeling the heat in my lower abdomen at the thought of his hands on me.

Palm Desert, California

MATTHEW'S JOURNAL

There was unlimited time to think during my hospital stay between physio, occupational and Life Counsellor therapy. As I sat propped up in my hospital bed, I thought. And I thought.

That's why I started this Journal. Writing down my past and present experiences will help me sort through events leading up to where I am now. Maybe help me know where had I gone wrong!

I had the guilt of what I attempted to do, but that's behind me. I have a magnificent life that I almost threw away. My attitude has changed now that I'm awake and aware. It's as though I am now awake in many ways. While I sit here initially, I'm wildly giddy that I lived!

As I thought back, my parents were the best they could be when I was growing up though my mother was controlling, and my dad had a police officer attitude. "Watch your step, Matthew."

Some of my best childhood memories are of my brother, Neil, and I. The Shore Trolley, Aerial Tram and Oaks Amusement Park seeped through my thoughts. We'd gone with our parents prior to us being teenagers, but we went on our own many times afterwards, without our parents knowing where we were. They were busy doing all the stuff parents did. Neil, being four years my junior, followed me around like a puppy.

One time as the Willamette Shore Trolley was arriving near the Marquam Bridge, Neil leaned over the side, giving me a leer, testing my resolve to let him be himself. He'd told me earlier I wasn't letting him grow up because I always told him what to do.

"Hey, watch out! You nut, you're gonna fall!"

"That's half the fun, Matt!"

At the Amusement Park, he leaned over another railing. God, what a kid!

"Get back here! Mom and Dad will have my hide if you get hurt. They don't even know we came here. If you want to follow me around, you better listen!"

"Free Willy" was filmed at our Oaks Amusement Park. We both loved The Screaming Eagle ride which was featured in the film. When he was younger, Neil cried during half of the movie, yet wanted to watch it over and over. When we went to the Amusement Park, he walked around the ride area picturing the whale from the movie, pondering how the movie was made. I supposed he'd grow up to be a film producer or an actor, not a veterinarian. And yet, his profession is perfect for him. He developed a love for animals from a young age. Mom and Dad weren't into pets, but he had goldfish and a hamster, as well as numerous cats he "adopted" from around the neighbourhood, none of which were allowed in our house. Neil was always putting scraps of lunch or supper in his pockets and, years later, he'd bought dried cat food with his own money to feed these feral cats.

Maybe his being four years younger meant I didn't ever get to know the growing-up version of him. Sometimes I shake my head and realize he's a grown man. Sharyn, his wife, has the same zany, carefree outlook, even though she's an Administrator at a Chiropractic clinic in Portland. Their personalities really came out after I recovered. Jenna told me at first Neil and Sharyn were deeply distressed. However, by the time I was aware enough to visit with them, they were both mocking me, lightening the situation.

It shouldn't have been surprising that three days after I regained consciousness, Neil smuggled a Beta fish in a bowl with a stick of bamboo for it to hide behind and placed it on my side table. Sharyn lay down four books and a sign in Neil's handwriting. I moved closer to read what he'd written. The sign read: "BETA YOU A DOLLA YOU WON'T SWALLOW THESE BOOKS". They were all Tall Tales – "Paul Bunyan," "Davy Crockett," "Johnny Appleseed" and "Chicken Little".

I managed, "What? Um, thanks..." Then it twigged. "Tall Tales. Swallow. That I won't believe these books. Okay, you're an idiot," as I laughed. "You got me this time."

Just then, my parents came into the room, Mom displaying a horrified scowl.

"What are you thinking, Neil... Sharyn? How is this funny? How dare you make fun of this situation? Sharyn, this was probably your idea."

Neil, defending Sharyn, replied, "Mom, this was my brilliant idea."

But I still chuckled so heartily that Mom stopped talking, a small smile slowly forming on her lips. Dad's cop sense of humour had already kicked in, and he was belly laughing. The situation defused, and Neil and Sharyn seemed proud of themselves for accomplishing this unthinkable act and obviously lightening up my day.

"I beta I couldn't get a laugh out of Mom, but I'm glad I lost this bet," Neil mumbled as he handed Sharyn a dollar bill.

My best pal had been and still was Aaron Smythe, usually suggesting something when Neil wasn't with us – something we shouldn't do. Thinking of Aaron, I reiterated my dad's old comments about Aaron while we were growing up. "Aaron will get into real trouble some day. You should not hang around with him." Yet Aaron was my best friend. He was thrilling, always into things he shouldn't be. Girls, drugs.

That memory abandoned, my mind snapped to Jenna – Jenna Barnes, the one girl-woman who had snatched my attention from my lifeguard duties long enough for me to fall in love with. What would my life have been without her? I'd been madly in love with her for the past three decades.

I acknowledged sitting here that I'd had emotional issues before covid. I realized now I'd been a real bastard to her for two years prior to my depression. I conceded it now – the bad part, the part I had no excuse for. Two years prior to my depression when I felt work stress, I took it out on Jenna.

"Where the hell do you think you're going?" as she headed off to bed. "You can wait until I'm ready."

I'd developed black moods, scowling at everything she did. Sometimes they'd last for days.

"Quit playing the victim," when she'd give up and cry, or if she became silent.

I firmly decided to make my life over again not just for myself – for her. I now felt disgust for that period of time.

An unbidden and shocking thought came to me, though. What could I do to make it better for everyone? I whispered, "Hell, I'm so messed up, I can't even kill myself properly." Damn it! No more thoughts like that. I have to keep to the straight and narrow for me, for Jenna.

I am coming back from my depression and suicide attempt, but I'm lying to everyone by not telling them that I have self doubts and some bad thoughts that I should have succeeded in my suicide attempt.

Thirty years ago, I'd seen her at the hotel pool. Usually girls found me irresistible – a magnet. So, I figured Jenna would react the same as all the others. I guessed this would just be another summer romance, but it wasn't. She was stunning. Even more than that, I realized after we had spent time together, she was stunning on the inside as well.

I had known what I wanted – Jenna! We had the most wonderful 11 days. Hell, the thought of meeting her parents back then – scary. Could I pass their judgement? I'd known a few Canadians through university and as a lifeguard. I certainly hadn't met any Canadian parents of a current and, hopefully, long-lasting girlfriend. This mattered! After mulling over how

I'd behave, I'd decided just to be myself. Apparently, it worked because I was on their good side. As Leonard shook my hand, mine felt insubstantial compared to his massive, calloused work hands, his grip firmer. Her mom, Phoebe, was extremely kind and thoughtful; her dad, Leonard, stern, but loving toward his children and his wife. I lapped it all up.

It'd taken awhile for Jenna to feel fully the way I did. She was contemplative, insightful and didn't give her heart away lightly. During our dating time, I'd wondered if she had been in love with someone when she'd been younger – something that affected her in an appalling way.

The sex was great back then, unrestricted. We both had experience. It wasn't just the sex though. I loved Jenna. I hadn't ever felt this way before. There had been girlfriends throughout high school and university, one or two steadies. Definitely a few flings brought about by my lifeguard gig. But my feelings toward Jenna were different, permanent. I longed for her to be with me forever. I felt bereaved each time she left to go back to Calgary. I missed her smile, her upbeat nature, even her frown. I'd grab for her at night, but she wasn't there. I wanted the warmth of her body curved next to mine. I'd think I saw her shadow coming from the kitchen, but a cloud had passed under the sun. She'd taken my sun away when she left.

At that time, Jenna was considering a move to teach in Portland and leaving the winter cold of Calgary behind. She'd miss her family and her friends. She'd said, "I'm prepared for the bleak, cloudy winter season of Oregon." Calgary summers were sunny and warm; whereas, Portland took getting used to – cloudy, misty, rainy.

My mother would be a hard sell. For a few years, Jenna confided to me things my mother had said to her, but I reasoned even my mother wouldn't stoop that low. Jenna must be overreacting. Some heated discussions followed, and our marital arguments mostly comprised dialogues about my mother.

I came home from work unexpectedly one day to surprise Jenna at lunch time. Strangely, my mom's car was parked out front. My plan was not to call out I was home so I could surprise both of them. As I walked toward our kitchen, I overheard my mother speaking to Jenna, heatedly. I prepared to defend my mother. Even with Jenna almost facing away from me, I could see she was attempting to sooth our crying baby, Ashley, in her arms. Two-year-old Travis was fingerpainting with ketchup and making patterns with his peas on his lunch plate.

"You aren't looking after Ashley properly. You shouldn't be nursing. She's obviously hungry. Breastfeeding is disgusting. Get some formula for her."

I tentatively took a step forward but realized that from my mother's position behind the top cabinets, she couldn't see me. I stopped myself, feeling hot – perspiration had collected under my armpits. I was glued to the spot, disbelieving, yet deep down recognizing I knew this. I had been a jerk, ignoring the fact the episode playing out before me had been inevitable.

As I stood motionless, sunglasses in hand, considering giving my mother a blast about her own parenting skills, weighing how to approach this inappropriate behaviour, I heard Jenna say, "Mom, I'm doing the best I can. You and I should be friends."

By this time, my mother appeared to be on a roll. "I keep telling you, don't call me Mom. I'll let you know if you're ever even part of our family, and, another thing, you have dust bunnies everywhere."

I internally kicked myself. How could I have let down so badly the one woman I loved? I'd been on the receiving end of these motherly "pep talks" many, too many, times not to know the toll they took.

Instead of announcing myself, I went to the front door, opened it and then closed it, tossed my sunglasses on the hall table, braced myself by taking a deep breath. I needed to fortify myself – to face my mother. I walked over to Jenna, ignoring my mother for the moment and took Jenna into my arms, gazed into her eyes, did a little headshake toward my mother and kissed Jenna's cheek. Looking surprised at my being home, Jenna blinked a few times, her glasses askew on her face, Ashley's little fingers entwined around them. Was she worried she'd be in trouble, that we'd have yet another argument about my mother – me blaming her?

Still ignoring my mother, I exclaimed, "Jenna, I missed you. You must be tired from cooking lunch and caring for the kids. You're an amazing mother. I'll hold Ashley for a bit. I'll meet you upstairs after I visit with Mom for a few moments – before she leaves."

As Jenna tentatively smiled and handed Ashley to me, I touched her shoulder, saying, "I'll bring the kids up in a few minutes". I whispered in her ear, "And eat crow for lunch." She gave me a rueful smile at that, straightening her glasses. She patted Travis' head and went out of the kitchen. I could hear her footsteps moving away on our living room floor.

Then I acknowledged my mother, saying, "Hi mom. I bet helping Jenna with the kids and the housework has kept you busy. But, if by chance you don't agree with how Jenna handles our household, perhaps you could keep it to yourself."

A defiant stare crossed my mother's face. She was trying to stare me down. I managed not to blink first. She glanced away. Inwardly I sighed with relief. Not only did I not want a scene, but my mother could still scare me.

She'd stood there – in our kitchen, in our home – telling my wife how to run her own home, how to mother her children – when she hadn't been much of a mother herself. I didn't need a response, but I wanted her to know Jenna came first.

Now, after my attempt to end my magnificent life, I needed to show Jenna she truly didn't ever need to doubt me. Did she doubt my love for her? The life we had together? Could I keep that promise with those unwanted thoughts of suicide crowding in?

Calgary, Alberta, Canada

3

Before and After Matthew's Attempt

Trust

❖ JENNA ❖

WHEN I WAS IN high school shopping with friends at the Sunridge Mall in Calgary where I'd grown up, I saw my long-term boyfriend sitting in the far corner of the Food Court. I grinned and waved when he glanced my way. Immediately his usually pale face had reddened, but he waved back. Slowly, my gaze caught someone sitting beside him – a girl. She'd smirked at me, a smirk I felt told me a story of their relationship. It was a sneer of the conqueror, and she wanted me to know I was the vanquished.

I turned and walked away, but Samson caught up with me.

"Who. Is. Your. Friend?" I hissed trying not to grit my teeth.

Pointing toward the girl who was tossing her long dyed blonde hair over her bare shoulder – then straightening a thin bra strap, he answered in an innocent tone, "That's Cherise, my cousin visiting from Saskatchewan."

Then switching his facial expression to exasperation and accusation, Samson stated in a mocking voice, "Did you think we were on a date right here out in public? Don't be foolish! I wouldn't do anything to let you down."

He'd talked to me this way before. Superior. Then he changed his tone again, touching my arm. Warm tingles ran through me, his immaculately smooth fingers moving up my arm. I glanced back at Cherise, and it satisfied me to observe her expressions of annoyance and impatience.

I swung my eyes to Samson as his fingers brushed against my cheek. Gazing deep into my eyes, he said, "You and I, Jenna, we're a couple. You should trust me."

Sure, I felt somewhat mollified, but I'd been told by two of my good friends, Lynda and Marilyn, twice over the past year that Samson was seeing other girls behind my back. I'd taken Samson's word against theirs, and they felt betrayed by me. I hadn't wanted to believe them. I told them that, and they remained my friends, but more distant toward me. Even my twin sisters, Ruby and Joan, told me their friends had seen him with another girl. I wouldn't believe them either. Samson assured me he was only with me. At 18 years old, I wanted so badly to believe him, to believe in him, to believe in *us*, to believe this dark haired, good-looking boy was mine alone.

"I'll catch up with you later. I promised Cherise I'd take her somewhere special while she's here visiting."

He caressed my shoulder, moving his thumb to the inside of my arm, brushing against my breast as his hand travelled down to my hand and his fingers lingered on my hand for a moment before he turned away – turned away back to his cousin. *To take her somewhere special, he'd said.* I spun away with my insides still tingling from his touch.

I'd met Matthew four years after finding out that Samson had indeed been cheating on me. Matthew and I dated long distance with telephone calls, hookups when one of us could get a weekend away and fell madly in love. After Samson, I'd had a hard time trusting men. There had been a handful of boyfriends throughout university, but Matthew was different. I was drawn to him. However, Samson's treatment of me had taken its toll.

Matthew and I were walking toward his car after a supper out. Once we were driving in his older model Jeep Cherokee, I told

Matthew about the encounter with Samson at the Sunridge Mall years before and, afterward, that I'd found out Samson had definitely been cheating on me with various girls over a period of time. Without taking his eyes from the road, he snarled, "Where is this Samson now?" His anger startled me as he declared, "I'll teach him a thing or two."

"Well, you won't need to teach him a fricking thing. I already did."

It had been four years since my high school sweetheart of three years had publicly humiliated me at a party for his 19th birthday. His sister, Wendy, had called to invite me. I wondered at the time why Samson hadn't issued the invitation himself. *Maybe it was a surprise party?*

When I arrived at his south Calgary home, I had to park Mom's Chevy Malibu over a block away because of the number of other cars on the street, presumably for his birthday shindig. It was a sprawling ranch-style home, red-bricked façade, massive in size, money oozing out of it. I'd previously been in Samson's home with its extravagant interior, lavish in style.

When I snuck a peek through the side window, people I knew were grabbing bowls of chips and fancy hors d'oeuvres to bring outside. As I strode toward Samson, planning to plant a kiss on his 'happy to see you' lips, his back was facing me. Turning to see who was clicking on heels in the distance behind him, he swung around toward me, then showed me his back again, ignoring me. Shocked, I witnessed him holding someone's hand – the same girl I'd seen him with in the mall a few weeks prior. I didn't say it out loud, but inside my head, I was screaming *Cousin! Bastard! Bitch!*

He hadn't invited me to this dance party in his backyard, and now I could see the reason. *Why had his sister invited me?* I stood stock still at the corner of their massive backyard, not going forward as I'd intended. I was hesitating, deciding if I should just leave when I heard footsteps scurrying behind me.

"Jenna," Wendy said as she caught up to me, panting a little from running, her black hair curling around her oval face, "I wanted to catch you before you saw them." She pulled me around so I was facing her, not her jackass brother. "You've believed every lie Sammy's told you, but he's been seein' other girls. This one isn't the first. I tried to talk to you last week."

I started to turn back to Samson. "Wait, the only way you were gonna believe what's happening is to see it. Samson isn't nice. He only thinks of himself. He doesn't care for this girl either. He's just like our father."

That I'd believed, visualizing their father's leer as he checked me out when I'd come over to Samson's home. Everyone talked about his father, a womanizer who couldn't keep his pants on. Turning around again and seeing Samson with this "cousin" had me steamed. I wasn't a shrinking violet, and I showed that part of me.

"Samson!" I called to him as I marched forward, while he squirmed, letting go of Cherise's hand. I then rushed the 20 steps separating us and slammed into him with my full body weight almost knocking us both down. At 5'10" and physically fit, my time on the volleyball A team was paying off. I held onto the pool handrail, but I didn't let go of Samson. The day had been 85F, but the coolness in the Calgary September night air meant the pool wouldn't be inviting. Still holding his T-shirt, I took another lunge toward him, letting go as I knocked him clear over the edge into his backyard pool.

"You got him, Jenna! Good for you." I heard Lynda's voice.

But I wasn't done. Cherise, when she first saw me, had a smug "Fuck You" expression on her face. Now she stood there transfixed, and I grabbed her and shoved her in the pool with him. One of "Cinderella's" slippers remained, alone, beside the pool, so I kicked that in as well. Then I heard the sound of applause. Lynda and Marilyn came up to me and each took me by an arm, guiding me away from the turmoil in my mind and the turmoil I had left behind me.

Lynda whispered as I stumbled through the crowd, excusing myself absent-mindedly, "Wendy told us to come. She said she'd invited you and asked us to escort you away after you saw Samson and that bitch."

Pausing to let several people pass us, I felt numb, maybe cold from the splashes of water permeating my clothing. The Bastard and the Bitch weren't the only ones wet, although my spirits weren't as dampened from that encounter as I would have expected.

Marilyn hugged me and wiped away a tear from my eye, and said knowingly, "We're sorry you had to go through this."

After another set of people walked past us, I trudged forward. Stopping abruptly, I glanced over at my friends. I realized even though I was crying for something that could never be, I felt the loyalty and love of these two friends. No – three friends, including Samson's sister.

We stopped at the front step, each seeming to need to catch a breath, finally away from the crowd. I felt flustered, yet victorious. "I apologize for not listening. I didn't want it to be true."

"We knew that. It was hard, though."

I didn't want to go home, so we spent two hours at Dairy Queen eating, well, cake. Ice cream cake, not birthday cake.

I dawdled between bites and said bitterly, "I wish I'd stayed to throw his cake in his face!"

Marilyn dampened that vision, "You did enough. Cake in the face wouldn't have been adequate for that bastard!"

We laughed, but I was actually devastated. I'd been a fool. A lovesick fool, depending on a guy to make me feel whole. I'd made a pledge I believed I could keep. *It will never happen again – cuz guys aren't dependable.*

Samson's sister, Wendy, told me the next day the party broke up right after my splash event and she'd been grounded for two weeks for inviting me. "My father was *not* happy with me, but Mom persuaded him not to issue an entire month's grounding."

"I'm sorry."

"It was worth it. Sammy still hasn't spoken to me, but Cherise has been over. She gave me a piece of her mind. I doubt she had much to spare in the first place."

"Oh, for the love of…," Matthew said with a chuckle in his voice. He hadn't laughed outright at first. He had taken my hand and squeezed it, sympathy on his face. However, as I progressed in recounting what had transpired, he laughed and laughed throughout the remainder of my retribution toward Samson. In fact, an hour later, he laughed again. When I peeked at him questioningly, for we were at a movie and he was drawing attention to us during a tense climactic scene, he said determinedly, "That's my girl! I love you."

I turned and took his face in my hands, moving forward and kissing him tenderly. "You're my guy, and I love you too."

I hadn't verbalized my love before with such feeling. I did love Matthew, but I'd held back. Something in how he'd handled this entire emotional story had twigged the sentiment that had been lacking on my part. He's my guy!

After that, Matthew and I hadn't slowed down in planning for my teaching in the United States and moving in together. We persisted in checking for employment opportunities for me in Portland. Matthew had copied school information and an article he came across from another state with regard to recruiting Canadian teachers to fill openings for which qualified Americans were not available. I checked out all ads and stored that information in my head for future reference and deliberation. We continued to check for availability in Oregon.

Voilà! Months later, we found classes that were open in Math, Science, English, Spanish and Special Education. That was the decision maker. I'd already been teaching English and Special Education in Calgary!

After a year-long employment process, I began an entirely new episode of my life with a new husband, a new job, a new school, a new country. My parents were happy for me, trying not to display distress I was leaving Calgary. Clara basically didn't accept my arrival in Portland at all.

Palm Springs, California

4

27 Years Before Matthew's Attempt

The Fun We Had

❖ JENNA ❖

Two years after our wedding, Matthew walked into the house and asked, "What'd you think of moving to California?"

"California?! Wow."

"I have a job I want to apply for in Palm Springs. Check out this posting." As he handed me the sheet of paper, he added, "It's spot-on for me. I checked. There's a job available for you if you're interested."

I squealed before he was done his sales pitch. Jumping up from the couch holding the job description, I shouted, "Yes!"

We danced a little jig. I loved this idea. It was a typical dreary November day in Portland, and the idea of sunshine and heat thrilled me. Three days later, we flew to Palm Springs, and I indeed became enamoured with the entire Coachella Valley. Matthew's parents wouldn't be at all happy he'd be leaving Portland. At this point in our lives, our happiness was what was important to us. Of course, moving away from Clara was going to be mentally and emotionally healthy for me.

—⚋—

We walked off the down escalator at the Palm Springs airport. This area led into an enclosed part of the airport, an expansive area and open to the sun shining from above. Passengers were walking on the sidewalk to get to the Exit area to pick up their luggage. We walked past dogs on leashes lazing on the lawn; suitcases were beside benches as other passengers awaiting the next flights took a break in the sunshine prior to going up the escalator to catch their flight home – back to some much cooler climate – stalling the inevitable.

"Matthew, this is Heaven! How could anyone not want to move here?" I had stopped, mesmerized by the scenes playing out in front of me. Matthew stopped beside me, took my hand and squeezed it, obviously pleased with my response.

Coming from a wet, cloudy, morose day in Portland, rain streaming from the sky and all Portland weather stations forecasting cloud for the next ten days, this warm (well hot) day was heavenly.

"It does get hotter in summer. It's 90 degrees right now. That's pretty warm, but I mean really, really hot – 120 above."

"What do people do? I mean, I think it'd be hard to live in 120. Obviously, everyone here does." As a joke, I inquired, "Do they hibernate in the summer?"

We resumed walking, inhibited slightly as other passengers jostled past us, giving us a glance of irritation that we were slowing down their progress as they hurried to their holiday.

"Yeah, not hibernate. In Calgary winters, you'd plan for a blizzard. You wouldn't go out at minus 35. You'd live your life around the cold, the snow and dress for the weather."

We had only packed a carry-on suitcase each requiring no wait time in the luggage area. Walking straight out into the day, I stopped again, taking in the clear, sunny skies and trembling with anticipation of a life here.

"Indeed, it's hot, but I could get used to this, the palm trees swaying, the sun on my face in November!"

Moving out of the way of other departing passengers, I said, "So, maybe shop early morning and late evening. We get lots of days in the 80s during the Alberta summer. It's best to get everything done when it's not *wow*, 120 above!"

I added with a suggestive wink at Matthew, "I'd dress skimpily."

"I'll expect that. That's why I want to move here."

I grinned and smacked him, then kissed him.

After spending a few days searching for our first Palm Springs home, an apartment somewhere between my new job at Palm Valley School teaching English and Special Ed and *Smooth Image Surgery* where Matthew would be one of two CPAs on staff, we were lucky to find a delightful two-bedroom near Baristo Park within our price range.

Smooth Image Surgery was a well recognized name in the all-encompassing reconstruction/altering, cosmetic surgery business spread over several locations. There was a huge staff of mostly young professionals, all friendly. Matthew had been told there were sundry after work get togethers. He was exceedingly happy to be employed there as a CPA. My mom's first inquiry was, "Can I get a discount?"

While admiring the apartment we had just rented, I opened a window to the view of blue skies, letting in a small draft of wind scented with orange blossoms. I caught my breath as a large striped, long-legged, long-necked bird scurried toward the nearby bushes.

"What the heck?!!"

The realtor, standing beside me, laughed and then said, "A roadrunner."

Matthew had rushed into the room and said, "Did you see a roadrunner?"

"Like Wile E. Coyote?" I asked the realtor.

Matthew and I got the rundown of a real roadrunner. She explained, "A roadrunner can't outrun a coyote. You see them perched on rocks or running as we just witnessed, probably chasing something to eat."

Matthew and I were enthralled with seeing a real roadrunner. I was less excited to find out roadrunners ate snakes and particularly not impressed when I realized there were snakes available for them to eat.

Once we were settled in Palm Springs, we already had a multitude of places we wanted to go. We'd been amassing a substantive list for weeks, so excited to get involved in the nine cities and what they had to offer.

"I can't go another day without a Sherman's Restaurant Grilled Reuben with Pastrami," proclaimed a thrilled Matthew.

It was slathered with Swiss cheese, sauerkraut on rye with fries. Being a little more restrained, I'd ordered a superb Western Scramble – eggs, ham, peppers, onions and cheese. We both felt like little piggies, oh my!

Off to Cabot's Pueblo Museum. The eccentric 1941 building didn't disappoint. It was always meant to be used as a museum, along with being the residence of Cabot and Portia Yerxa.

Matthew surmised, "My new workplace is steel and glass. It's intriguing to compare that with this house built into the rock."

"You're right. It's breathtaking. How hard to build, collecting old telegraph poles and 'found' panes of glass for windows." When we were leaving, I knew I had to come back.

—∞—

Matthew had been overjoyed with his career at *Smooth Image Surgery*. At the time, he'd been correct in his view this was a great experience for him. His base pay was very good and after his performance bonuses were factored in, the compensation was first rate. He felt connected to his colleagues and his company, and I relished my teaching career at Palm Valley School.

No one knew exactly what people were really like – down in their core. Were they work friends or was there anyone among them who was darker than they let on?

Multiple locations

5

The Wedding

❖ JENNA ❖

I WAS WEARING A sun dress which I'd bought in San Diego when Matthew and I'd been on a holiday, just the two of us – a flowered and flowing dress, with a lace bodice – a silly holiday beach dress. Adorning my face were square, pink-rimmed eyeglasses. My necklace was made of seashells, and, in my hair, I wore a wreath made of green string beans. My feet were decked out with bathroom slippers, also pink. *I hate pink!*

Matthew was wearing his tattered bathrobe, cufflinks somehow embedded in the material at the wrists, a flowered tie gracing his neck. On his head, he wore a pink cowboy hat. The idea floated through my mind, *to match my slippers*. Flowered rubber boots were on his feet.

My siblings, Robert, Joan and Ruby, had on matching purple sun visors with sunglasses strung around their necks on a rope, creating necklaces. On their wrists were flowers laced together with elastic bands. Each of the three wore a lime green tuxedo and paisley shirt. Joan and Ruby wore pink high heels, Robert pink cowboy boots.

Matthew's brother, Neil, and Neil's wife, Sharyn, had on flowing white robes tied with what seemed to be fronds from palm trees. Their hats were of bougainvillea flowers.

Mom was in a gaudy fuchsia bathing suit, hair done up in curlers, barefoot and, oh my God – she was pregnant!

My dad's attire was just as outlandish – he wore a woman's bikini, nothing else!

Clara pranced in on the back of a black stallion, with Jack being pulled behind on a wheeled cart. Clara, in a dazzling fuchsia overcoat, purple leggings, with red runners and Jack in a monk's robe, a police hat hanging crookedly from his head.

The church, shockingly, was a bar of some sort, gaudily and peculiarly decorated with streamers made of a thousand pink cotton balls and large sunflowers, a pink Cadillac parked smack in the center.

Matthew's friend, Aaron, his usual skimpy beard gone long and pointed, was the minister, adorned with tie-dyed T-shirt and flowered denims. Aaron's chin-length hair was no longer dark brown but dyed blond and in an Afro.

Off to the side was a table displaying the Wedding Cake covered with dog biscuits.

As the moment of the service arrived, Matthew and I couldn't understand a word because it was in French!

I jolted awake because of a cramp in my neck, feeling confounded about the whole event. *My mother's pregnant* – at our wedding. I laughed out loud, snorting.

The woozy sensation of sleep dissipated. I groggily realized I was in our own bed, and our wedding had been decades prior. I glanced at my watch, noting 5:32 a.m., and I cringed with the agonizing realization this was day 4 of Matthew's hospital stay, and I was alone in our bed. "Matthew, Matthew…"

I knew I couldn't attend at the hospital yet. They had been lenient, but I'd need to wait until at least 9:30 to let morning staff care for Matthew. The doctor would have done his rounds by then, and I'd get an opportunity to quiz Dr. Masood again today.

No chance of more sleep. With my thoughts centered on Matthew and the dream I just had, I marvelled at the outcome of our actual wedding. It had been a larger affair than either Matthew or I wanted. We advised our parents we wished for a simple wedding – both sets of parents, our siblings, friends, a couple of aunts and uncles to attend our ceremony – and then go to a quiet restaurant to celebrate. Mom and Clara got to talking about what they wanted.

"No, not every relative and friend," I asserted.

"Exactly!" said Matthew.

Clara exploded with, "This is as much for us as it is for you. If you want to get married, we get to show you off."

Matthew quietly said, "We don't want that. If you want to show off, throw a party later."

The fathers stepped in with Matthew's father, Jack, saying, "Whose day is this Phoebe, Clara?"

Matthew and I both affirmed, "Ours, not yours."

Clara, not backing down, declared obnoxiously, "We have a right to our ideas for this wedding."

Mom appeared abashed, maybe at herself, maybe embarrassed about Clara's raucous outburst. I think she had realized she and Clara were being unreasonable. This was confirmed in her next statement.

Mom took a miniscule step away from Clara and said, "Well, I do see I'm attempting to have the wedding I missed by encouraging you both to have a large wedding. Let's talk more about it after we cool down."

Clara shook her head at my Mom and gave her and then me a withering look, saying, "That leaves me wanting more than these two."

"I put my foot down here." My dad had inserted himself into the fray. "Jenna and Matthew should do what they want for their own wedding."

Jack also took a step back, stood next to Dad and said, "I agree. Matthew and Jenna should have the day they want to have."

Clara stormed out of the Portland hotel room where Mom, Dad and I had been staying this weekend to discuss Matthew and my wedding plans, supposedly a happy occasion where both sets of parents could meet and enjoy each other's company. *Fat chance!*

So… Our wedding took place in the Norman-styled St. Barnabas Anglican Church situated north of the Bow River in NW Calgary – the church my family attended. My siblings and I had each been baptised and confirmed here. We had a lovely service with both Matthew and I sanctioning the number of relatives and friends to be invited by each set of parents.

Of course, my good friends, Lynda and Marilyn, as well as Wendy (Samson's sister who'd become close to me), and all our other friends were invited. Ruby and Joan were bridesmaids; Matthew's best friend, Aaron, and Matthew's brother, Neil, were the groomsmen. Robert was the usher, and he did an excellent job. He loved telling people where to go. We invited our grandparents and close family, as well as some of our parents' friends. Everyone could invite their spouse or partner.

The weather co-operated with no rain, no wind – or snow for that matter. In Calgary, located beside the mountains, snow could magically appear even in the midst of roses blooming, robins in their nests and squirrels scampering through the green-leafed hedges.

As we entered the church, the sun shone down on us, a smattering of clouds in the west, temperatures at 25C/80F. My dad escorted me into the church, with my mom coming up on my other side. Once in this beautiful old church, my attention pivoted on Matthew – nothing else. My dad stopped my forward movement with a little squeeze to my arm, and I realized I must wait while the wedding party found their spots at the front. We had rehearsed this last night, before the rehearsal party. All I wanted to do was to sprint forward to Matthew, but, thanks to Dad, I caught myself and took a steadying breath.

I wore a floor-length wedding gown with satin and lace Mom and I had picked out, a short train and beaded bodice. I even wore a flowing veil. Matthew wore a deep blue tailored suit with a light blue shirt and a deep blue tie. I felt like a Queen with Matthew as my King that day.

Ruefully allowing myself a small smile, I thought of the difference between the clothing worn by attendees from my dream and the guests' attire at our wedding. Dad's own deep blue three-piece suit, white shirt, striped, blue tie; Mom's light blue floor length layered fringe dress with a beaded top, scoop neck, a hint of sleeves, wearing this with her best sapphire and gold jewellery; Clara in a bronze taffeta evening dress with a wrap, Jack in a dashing navy-blue suit, light blue shirt and navy tie.

Joan and Ruby had picked out mid thigh, cinnamon rose chiffon dresses with a ruffle at the bottom, and the groomsmen wore rented faux deep blue tuxedos with blue and cinnamon striped ties. The minister wore his regular robe. Grinning outright, I recalled *No pink anywhere.*

I'd given Matthew a man's wooden jewellery box to keep his watch collection organized. He had gifted me a gold heart necklace and matching bracelet.

I fondled them now.

Tossing the remembrances aside for a moment, I turned over and moved closer to Matthew's side of the bed. I hugged myself, fretting about Matthew's health and state of mind.

"But he'll recover!" I told myself in a calm, assuring voice: "He's going to be fine. This has to be the start of our new beginning, has to be. It's been a bleak road lately."

Palm Desert, California

6

2 Years Before Matthew's Attempt – November

Phoebe and Leonard

❖ PHOEBE ❖

LEONARD SHOUTED TO ME through the open window, "Phoebe, that's the last of the suitcases!"

He stepped in the door with Charlie, our tri-coloured King Charles Cavalier Spaniel, scampering behind him. As we unpacked at our Palm Estates RV Resort park model a couple of years ago, Leonard screwed up his only slightly lined face and speculated, "We forgot to pack the electric toothbrushes."

I sauntered past the bathroom holding a small suitcase and muttered, "Leonard, I can pretty much live without an electric toothbrush. They make my whole face vibrate. You may love them, but I'll enjoy the reprieve."

"Catty wife!"

I rearranged clothing in a drawer and took a long, critical scan of myself in the closet mirror, saying confidently, "Ahhh, but you love me anyway."

"I do, always."

That made me smile and my green eyes sparkle. Then I noted in the mirror that my smile brought out all sorts of little laugh lines. My hair still had some blonde intermingled with the grey, and I twisted my face to make my hair swing a little, ignoring the little jiggle of my tummy.

Interrupting my mirror critique, I sighed and said, "Glad we got Juanita to come in to clean. I don't relish dust everywhere when I'm on vacation."

"Vacation for five months? We're retired, dear. This is a vacation from a vacation."

Smiling again at our mutual teasing, I replied coyly, "We are retired, but you stay involved with your construction business!"

Smacking me on the bum as he sidled into our small bedroom, squeezing past me, Leonard attempted to imitate my mocking expression, then said, "Hey, let's get to the pool while the rest of the gang's still there. I'll take Charlie out for a wee, then we'll go. I saw Thaddy and Martha head that way before we began unpacking. The bags can wait. It's 3:30 – perfect timing."

As I glanced around our winter home away from home, I thought about our five months ahead.

Excited, I said, "I love coming back to be with our winter friends. I miss them all summer. Aren't you happy to be back in our second home?"

"God yes. It's tiny, but it's our home as well."

Our little park model is 600 square feet, including an added sunroom. Our front door opened into the living room/sunroom, beside the dining area. We had a two-bum kitchen which meant if you were friendly, two of you could prepare the meal. The bathroom stood just off our bedroom, with a backdoor a few feet away, leading to a confined backyard. But, oh, that backyard! It was our retreat and alive with hummingbirds, bees, finches, doves and an occasional roadrunner.

I sighed deeply.

Standing beside me, Leonard asked, "Is something wrong?"

"No, Leonard. It's a sigh of contentment."

"Good, good."

Sitting in the resort hot tub hours later, an evening still warm after a hot day, we were reminiscing. I said, "It's so quiet at night." I noted hardly a breath of wind through the acacia and palm trees and quiet voices in the distance of people having get togethers on their lots.

I asked Leonard dreamily, drink in hand, "Who would've thought all those decades ago that our daughter would marry a boy from Portland, that we would get a motorhome, come down to the Coachella Valley for an occasional holiday and then we'd decide to buy a place and stay every winter?"

He grinned, took another sip and said, "Who'd have thought we'd have any money when we first started out? Man, oh man!"

"And having Jenna a few months after we got married."

Staring off into the palm trees beside the pool and then back at me, "But you got your Nurses' Aid Certificate. Never thought I'd be anything but a labourer on minimum wage. We both worked hard for 35 years to get to this spot."

Getting into the conversation we'd had several times over the decades of our marriage, I agreed, "We did."

Smirking at me from under his ballcap he didn't even need at this time of day, he said, "You give me jabs about still keeping my finger on the pulse of our construction company, but I've always known you love being involved yourself. Darn it, you helped me paint those houses on your days off. *LP BUILDING & CUSTOM HOMES* was your idea for a company name."

Responding as I pulled his *Calgary Flames* ballcap off his head and set it on the edge of the hot tub, "Yeah, it's always been our company, Leonard and Phoebe Building & Custom Homes." Wiggling my feet in the water thoughtfully, "We did it, and now here we are – a dozen years of enjoying a life we didn't dream of."

"But it *is* our life now."

I slid into his raised arm and said, "It feels terrific to acknowledge what we accomplished."

Holding our glasses up high above the swirling water, we brought them together.

Smiling at each other, "To us and our life and our love."

Clink.

Palm Desert, California

MATTHEW'S JOURNAL

During the two years I had the black moods – during the time I was a Diablo, I couldn't stop yelling at Jenna and picking at her. I felt she deserved it. She was always a victim – People called her Sweet Jenna. I needed to hurt her verbally to put her in her place. At the time the moods struck, I couldn't stand her. Even if she'd look at me, I found fault with her expression. If she didn't look at me, it made me even more angry.

My hard work and promotion to Business Manager became the noose around my neck. The bosses expected me to conjure up business even though there was a pandemic happening throughout the entire world. Our thriving company fell onto hard times. The boss, George Alphonse, needed someone to blame. Crap! It couldn't be thought to be his fault. His insults were an hourly occurrence, said in front of staff. It became commonplace for other staff to pick up on his vibes toward me and make derogatory remarks.

When I started to have actual depression, I couldn't shake my despondency even though Jenna tried hard to help me through it. I couldn't make myself care about anything. I hated everything, and I started drinking – hiding it – I thought.

During my depression, all our family had been tediously patient with me. I'd angrily said many times, "Leave me alone!" I hadn't cared about what they were saying when they attempted to involve me in their day-to-day activities or how they were going to do such and such. I couldn't get interested in listening to

Ashley relate what courses she was taking in her next semester or Travis talking about his job. I loved my family, but I couldn't be around anyone without wanting to scream like a banshee or cry like a baby. Stomping from the room, I'd slam the door. "Just stop!"

Jenna put on a good front. She went to work each day, perhaps some days glad to be away from me and my gloom; however, she texted me twice each morning and twice each afternoon. Often her texts went unanswered.

Or I'd text "Stop bothering me."

We had spent a lot of time at the Palm Estate RV Resort in the pool, hot tub or sitting around firepits and drinking beer which didn't go well with my depression. There were times I just up and left for awhile saying I was taking their Spaniel, Charlie, for a walk, but I'd just slump down on the couch.

Jenna was more contented when her parents were here. I tried. I may have even fooled them some of the time. Phoebe and Leonard are good people, accepting me as Jenna's boyfriend from the onset, ecstatic about our engagement and marriage. When each child was born, they were over the moon with excitement for us, standing back as they watched us grow into parents, not judging. I honestly felt they were the parents that I had missed growing up. Sure, my mom and dad were okay. My mom tried, not successfully, to be a decent mother and grandmother. My father was fine in his own way, but he was a police officer at heart, and he had a very uncompromising exterior. When my mother wasn't around, his fatherly side came out, but they seemed to feed off each other to get me to do their bidding.

There was a point when Jenna reported my illness in detail to her parents. I could tell. Jenna had previously always covered for my moods.

Jenna made doctor's appointments I refused to go to. While her parents were here last year for their stay at the resort, Jenna and her parents escorted me to a doctor's appointment, her dad taking my arm, "Come with me, Matthew. We're going to the doctor."

Following that reveal by Jenna, the Happy Hour scenarios changed. Leonard would silently pick up my third beer and have it as his own. That bothered me. If he missed that third beer, Jenna would wander by and put it off to the side. Suddenly, they understood my issues. I think it made life easier for awhile until the depression advanced again – when I stopped taking my meds.

We visited with Phoebe and Leonard and their buddies during their RV Resort months, and we had them back at our home for suppers some Sundays. What I did enjoy about these visits after my depression had worsened was my other best friend, Charlie. That dog always came and sat by me. He'd curl up right beside me, lick my hand and put his head on my lap. Those times I'd had enough of the social interaction, I'd flop down on the couch with Charlie beside me, doing nothing, seeing nothing.

It reached the point when I couldn't do it anymore. Jenna curbed her parents' suppers at our place. Their visits were shorter and mostly involved hovering in the kitchen. At that point in time, I pondered if they were discussing the Smooth Image Surgery accusations surrounding me – that I stole files regarding a prominent client and then blackmailed her? Maybe they believed that.

Palm Desert, California

7

19 Months Before Matthew's Attempt – March

RV Resort

❖ JENNA ❖

WHILE MATTHEW'S DEPRESSION, SENSE of gloom and melancholy were beginning, I still endeavoured to keep things normal. *No use sitting at home with Matthew not communicating. His illness wasn't his fault. His previous horrid behaviour was.*

I attempted once to share my dissatisfaction about Matthew's verbal abuse with my mother. "Matthew has started to say awful things to me." I didn't want to get into it all, but I felt dreadfully upset.

"All marriages go through change. He's just stressed from work."

Even my mother couldn't believe that Matthew, the gentle persona he could portray to everyone else, would be unpleasant to me. *If not my mother, who can I turn to?*

Infuriatingly, he could control his black moods with everyone else, even his mother. She was not a nice woman, and he withered in front of her. With me, he'd be his sweet self, and, in a blink, he'd verbally attack me, scaring me. I told myself he'd had a nasty childhood, thinking I could show him that I loved him no matter what. I took what he dished out, shrinking within myself each time, every time a little more, but still reaching out to him, to comfort him, to make him better. It was an abysmal two years. It was two years of hell. There were times I wished I was a violent person – I would have punched him in the mouth.

Late in the day, the sun was sinking down behind the San Jacinto Mountains, its glow still visible from where I stood. I felt small. Matthew had told me I was useless, that our children didn't even like me, called me the victim again, his words echoing in my head, the turmoil still reverberating, even though it had been two hours before.

Now I heard him come in the front door. As he closed the door behind him, I had no idea if his black mood was still on him, if I should pretend I hadn't known he came home and skulk away, not drawing his attention to me – so he wouldn't verbally hurt me again.

He walked toward me. I took a deep breath, waiting.

"I love you," he whispered, eyes diverted.

Walking away was hard for me, but what could I say? I had lied once in a while. Maybe I did love him, but I didn't like him very much, not so close to his nasty words spoken to me two hours ago. I'd be able to say it later, wouldn't I?

I loved the man who Matthew had been – the real Matthew – with all my heart, the heart that was now forming a protective shield around it – sadly protecting myself from *him*.

—⚍—

Surprisingly, weeks later, on a beautiful day with the sun shining and a tranquil breeze blowing, Matthew suggested going to the RV Resort.

"Let's go see your parents and Charlie. And the gang."

"Fantastic."

He'd wanted to sit and watch television or spend time in bed before getting on some medications for his depression. *Is this medication the beginning of something better?* He was the love of my life, so handsome, but my knight in shining armour had eyes not as bright or interested as they used to be.

My mom and dad have wintered in Palm Estates RV Resort, a gated community in the Coachella Valley, for the past dozen years. Matthew and I resided in Palm Desert, one of the nine cities visitors simply call Palm Springs. Most of these cities are side-by-side with only a street in between. The Coachella Valley is almost surrounded by mountains – the San Jacinto, Santa Rosa and little San Bernardino. Sitting beside Palm Springs to the east is Cathedral City, Rancho Mirage, Palm Desert. Moving a little south, Indian Wells, La Quinta, and then north to Indio and Coachella. On the north side of the I-10 is Desert Hot Springs.

Even though there are frequently times the people in the Resort, being a generation older than Matthew and me, drive me batty with their opinions, I still love hearing all the intricacies of their relationships with each other. They get along, but there are hiccups. The various accents from different parts of the United States and Canada intrigue me. I've always found accents fascinating.

I tended to think of their friends as where they were from:
New York Thaddy and Martha Bartlett,
Omaha Owen and Trudy Dougherty,
British Columbia Bruce and Eileen Livingston.

That day, we discovered my parents and their friends were right on schedule – pool time.

Thaddy wasn't in the pool. He was standing by a table with two drinks – one in each hand – his greying helmet of red-tinged hair peeked out from under his fedora hat. He walked to the pool, down the steps and handed his wife, Martha, a can of spritzer.

She reached for it and said, "Thanks, Thaddy!"

"Hi, Mom, Dad, Martha, Thaddy, Trudy, Owen. Knew where you'd be. Got our suits on. How's everything?"

Trudy replied for the group, "Been here since November. Lots of new people. Five of our friends couldn't come this year – health or financial reasons."

I nodded as Trudy continued. I'd heard the same thing from Mom and Dad. "Some places for sale, others for rent. People expecting to be able to come back next year. We're hoping we can come back next year. I don't think Owen can …"

Retreating to my own thoughts, I knew my mom and dad loved coming down to the Palm Estates RV Resort. Dad had ranted several times, "It's a little presumptuous for the RV Resort to call it Estates. We all live in Park Models or recreation vehicles – zilch estate-like at all." I loved the mixture of greenery, palm trees, acacia and ficus trees, bougainvillea, lantana and oleander bushes everywhere. I envisioned my own yard, in desperate need of a revamp. Here, if you wanted a grapefruit for your breakfast or an orange for a snack and didn't have your own tree, just walk a couple of lots over and someone would have a basket of them out front.

Matthew had brought a beer over to me, and I noted he had one as well. I tuned back into their conversation to hear Thaddy chuckling, then saying, "We can go to Bingo tonight, see how much moolah we can win, eh Lennie?"

Dad didn't appreciate being called Lennie, but he didn't ever comment. Martha had called our son, Travis, 'Travie' once. Travis had replied, "Well, Marthie, my name is pronounced Travis. No 'ie.'"

I'd speculated how that comment would go over, but Martha had simply continued on as though this burly young man had not said anything. Burly resulted from his usual 'workout' being extremely physical where he laboured in the construction trade just outside of Los Angeles, his muscular build and trim waist a testament to his hard work. Tattoos adorned his arms: the word *CALIFORNIA* snaked up his right arm within the shape of our state; our State orange poppy on his left inside wrist; a double set of palm trees on his left arm. He tells me he is restraining himself until he knows what else he wants. *Hopefully ROBIN.* Ashley's long-time friend, Robin, fit quite well into our lives. I had an inkling there was a chemistry between Robin and Travis. I hoped so.

Travis was meticulous in his profession; however, I marvelled he could leave a trail of messy debris behind him whenever he left a room in our house. He reminded me of my brother, Robert, not simply because Robert also was a construction worker, but both were messy, boisterous, tell you as it is – no nonsense, yet good humoured. It always gave me a tender reaction to see the similarities. Robert's only tattoo were the words *CALGARY FLAMES,* Alberta's hockey team.

But Travis is somewhat unhappy with his labouring job. He told me not to tell Matthew or Ashley until he figures it out.

Ashley had said upon Travis getting the *CALIFORNIA* tattoo, "You embarrass me with all those tattoos. What's the point? I'd never let anyone put those on me."

To end her critique, he'd said, "Ash, it's my body."

To which she replied, using Martha's nickname, "Yes, Travie, if you want to look cool, then those abominations work well."

"Don't call me Travie."

"Don't call me Ash!"

Matthew and I took our canned beers, entered the pool to enjoy the interaction of my parents and their friends. Trudy and Owen, even though they were a few years older than Mom and Dad, had been their best buddies for probably 10-11 years. Trudy—grey hair streaked with slashes of burgundy, petite, a little on the plump side, feisty, friendly, and Owen—tall, lean, full head of grey hair, quiet, slightly bent over—were from Omaha, Nebraska. Both preferred clothing from Marios, Glossy or Costco.

Owen repeated on a number of occasions throughout the years, "If Costco doesn't have it, I don't need it!" Everyone habitually chuckled at that.

The banter between these seniors stimulated my own thoughts. I wondered if Matthew and our friends would sound like this in 25 years. *Or did we sound like this now to Travis and Ashley?* I moaned inwardly.

Most of the discussion as I listened today centered around the activities my mom and dad would be enjoying in the camaraderie of their neighbours. Everyone was welcoming and sociable, anticipating the season's events.

Mom nodded at me and said, "This week, there's Spaghetti Supper and a Sunday Breakfast."

"You love dressing up for that and seeing everyone."

We'd been with them to various events and saw the enjoyment everyone had. The food tasted delicious, prepared by owner and renter volunteers. All the attendees sat, visited, ate their meals, usually had a glass of alcohol supplied or brought their own. The mood was regularly festive, embracing new people to their park.

I glanced at Matthew, and his smile seemed genuine. I mouthed, "Should we go?" He walked over and touched my hand, acknowledging he felt fine to stay awhile.

As I did my usual gauging of how Matthew was doing, I could see him lean toward Owen to catch the conversation. That brought a smile to my face, thrilled to see him involved. *Thank God for the meds.*

I'd lost the mental and emotional support of my husband. I'd become used to not having Matthew for companionship or friendship, even when we were in the same room sitting together. I'd turned more and more to my parents, hanging out with Mom, Dad and their crowd. Many of our 'couple' friends had turned away from us as Matthew became more despondent with his depression. Matthew spurned social activities and dissuaded many of our friends in the past several months.

Being a gregarious person, I craved friendship. My parents filled that gap. When they were here each winter, I spent more and more time with Mom. I brought Matthew as often as he felt willing to visit, and I worried about him when I was away.

Mom turned to me, took my hand and gave it a squeeze.

"Are you okay?"

"Yeah, just thinking. You visit with Trudy. I'm enjoying your conversation."

I squeezed her hand back, and she gave me her reassuring smile. As my mind wandered, she returned to her conversation with Trudy. They met up every day for a walk, to play mahjongg, pickleball, dance class or just shoot the breeze. Owen had always hiked and golfed with Dad, until recently. When I asked Dad how his golf game was lately, he'd admitted to me he didn't feel like golfing these days. *Why?*

Sitting on lawn chairs at Thaddy and Martha's a half hour later, having changed into dry warmer clothing, munching on the chips and appies provided, I mused about what I had been doing as a 20-something and what I'd be doing in 25 years. *What were Travis and Ashley doing now? Getting ready for supper in their respective apartments? Travis out somewhere with friends? Ashley finishing up an assignment?*

Jolted back to the current conversation, I heard a loud voice. "Eileen bought tickets for the Jersey Boys tribute concert. Who else here is going?" queried Martha, adding, "I am, for sure."

Thaddy said, "That's sissy stuff. Yeah, nah, I'm not goin.'"

Martha, big-boned, average height, once again wearing something that didn't suit her figure, was always friendly. Giving Thaddy a smirk and shaking her chin length blonde bob, she then asked again, "Who else is going? I'm buyin' my ticket tomorrow. Jenna, Mattie, you coming?"

Mom turned back to me, questioning me with her eyes. I glanced at Matthew. He nodded.

"For sure, Matthew and I would be interested."

"That's great," said Martha.

Everyone else said they were going, and Thaddy relented, "Nah, yeah, I'll go, but I'm takin' scotch in my carry mug."

"You're such a tool, Thaddy," said Trudy. Her sunglasses were now worn on the top of her head, and her bright blue eyes shone as she grinned.

"Yeah, I know and proud of it." His eyes held a glint of satisfaction.

Matthew nodded 'all's well'. I noted the second beer. The chirping of birds had subsided now as the sun sank early behind those huge San Jacinto Mountains. I mulled over what life would be like if Matthew didn't get over his cough? What if his depression remained? If he dodged going to work more often? What about his drinking? *I can't worry about everything. It's got to be all right.*

I studied Mom and Dad, noticing the energy in their expressions and actions. Good on them for still being so vibrant, recollecting for a moment Dad didn't feel like golfing any longer, but letting the thought evaporate. I had enough distress with Matthew. Dad would be fine. I concluded they were both fine as I again watched them with their friends. Matthew and I would work out his ongoing issues. *I hope.*

I wondered aloud, "Where are Eileen and Bruce?"

"They'll be along about 6:00. Eileen's getting a big meal up. We helped this morning," explained Mom.

Owen got out of his chair, but he got out of his chair slowly, almost painfully. He obviously favoured the use of his arms and winced sharply as he moved.

Mom queried, "Are you feeling all right, Owen?"

"Oh, just a twinge. I'm fine." Trudy appeared anxious, but immediately smiled when Mom glanced her way. "Let's get over to Eileen's to help. Owen, you go on home. I'll be back in a wee bit."

"Yep, I'm done this hootenanny," Owen stated with a slight grimace. "I had a rooty-tooty time."

"Love your way of describing things, Owen," said my dad. Charlie scampered out of Owen's path, gave a little "Woof" as if hoping to go for a walk.

"I can't shake the Nebraska off of me." He gave Dad a pat on the back, resting his hand there for a moment as he walked past.

"See you, Owen." Dad leaned over to give Charlie a gentle scratch behind his ear. "I'll take Charlie for a walk now." Obviously, Charlie heard the 'walk' word. Another very hopeful "Woof."

Trudy glanced at me and said, "You're both to come to supper. We're all invited. We booked the community room,"

I examined Matthew's body language where I perceived the familiar expression of his being tired with hopelessness etched on his face. *We've been here long enough.*

Rotating my heart bracelet on my wrist and knowing what I needed to say, I responded, "We'll pass on supper for tonight. But thank you for the invite."

Palm Desert, California

8

19 Months Before Matthew's Attempt – March

Confiding

❖ JENNA ❖

I ANSWERED THE LANDLINE on the second ring. I sat outside, enjoying the scent of heavenly fresh rain, rain that rarely comes to the desert. Dew lingered on the grass and plants. The hummingbirds were all over the yard.

"We're off to sit with Trudy at the hospital, the Eisenhower. A fire truck and the ambulance came for Owen 15 minutes ago."

"Oh my God! What happened?"

I surmised Dad must've been driving since Mom had called, and I could hear traffic. They were on speaker. Sounds were coming from outside of their Kia Soul, rushing past as though they were on the I-10.

Mom almost yelled, distressed, "We don't know!"

"Phoebe," Dad replied, more calmly. "It must've been his abdomen. He's been complaining for a few days."

"Dad, why are you on the highway? You don't go that way to the Eisenhower." I hoped he hadn't been distraught enough that he had taken a wrong turn. "I can hear the traffic."

"We were coming back from the Cabazon Outlets when Trudy called to ask your mom to come sit with her while she waited. Jenna, can you drive over and pick up Charlie? I'm not sure how long we'll be."

"Absolutely, I can leave right now. Anything else you know?"

Mom said, "Trudy told me he's been ignoring pain in his stomach. He lifted something a few months ago, something dreadfully heavy. He'd picked it up at an odd body angle. Said he's been in more pain the past few weeks."

Dad offered another insight, "He's being a man. But he should've gone to a doctor. We're turning onto Bob Hope now."

"Call me when you know anything."

"We will, darling. We'll call right away."

"Please give Trudy a hug for me, Mom."

"Of course."

Hours later, Mom called on their way back to the RV Resort.

Trudy shouted from the back, "Hi Jenna." Then, lowering her voice, she said, "Owen's gonna be fine for now. Eisenhower did tests, and Owen had a weak spot in the inginal canal. He should have surgery, but there's no opening for surgery here until well after we usually leave for home."

"Inguinal, Trudy," corrected Mom.

"That's right," offered Dad, "But, Trudy, the doctor told you that later in life muscles deteriorate."

Trudy cut in, "The nurse said these hernias develop when muscles weaken. But Owen keeps himself in good shape. His muscles shouldn't have weakened. It's that damn bag of rocks he moved."

I asked, "They kept him?"

"The doctor just said for precautions they were keeping him overnight. I'm concerned about that, but I'll drive back first thing in the morning. And we'll yak on our cellphones tonight. He better not discharge himself. He's done that before."

Dad asked, "Why?"

"Jeez Louise, you'd be surprised at what he's done before. He didn't trust the care he received at our home hospital, nor did he trust the doctor. It was for, well, men stuff. He can tell you if you ask him – if he wants to tell you. I'm just saying I hope he doesn't end up home tonight before they observe him properly."

Mom and Dad inquired about Charlie. "Oh, you guys, he's fine. Matthew and Charlie have been snoozing on the couch. I'll bring him now if you want, but you know Charlie feels at home here. Matthew and I love that dog."

One week after Owen's visit to the Eisenhower Emergency, Mom teared up in the restaurant during our lunch date.

"What? Mom?"

"Trudy and Owen told us last night they are going home at the end of the week."

Mom cried outright now.

"Shall we leave Lulu's? You can't want to be here."

"No, I'll just run to the restroom. I'll splash ice cold water on my face and be right back." At my commencing to stand, she ordered gently, "No, you stay here. Hold our table." Tears streaming down one cheek – one lovely, worn cheek. My heart wrenched for her.

We didn't fit into the atmosphere of Lulu California Bistro right now. I glanced around me. Lulu's was a fascinating place. The décor put people into a party mode, multi-level seating arrangements, the huge photos of Lucy and Desi, wrap-around bar, colourful hanging lights, large outdoor dining with heat lamps – all meant for a light-hearted eating adventure. Laughter rang out from various tables.

The waitress came, looking questioningly at me.

"My mom will be right back. Could you bring two iced teas, one with no ice? Thanks."

Would she really prefer a glass of wine? That would be unusual, but this was an unusual circumstance. Trudy and Owen leaving!! Thankfully, Mom and Dad had other close friends and dozens of other friends throughout the park. As a whole, the park residents were kind and helpful. If someone became ill, there were always offers and follow through with driving, getting groceries, bringing meals, always giving a shoulder to cry on. I understood from listening to my parents and their friends that when they came down to the Resort, they felt like their friends here were almost as close and sometimes closer than their own friends or family at home. It felt reassuring to know if Owen and Trudy stayed in the resort that there would be people upset about Owen and willing to do anything to help. *If they came back.*

Disturbing me out of my reverie, Mom said as she sat down, "It's the worst. They might not come back next year." That confirmed my assessment of what might come.

"What changed since Owen's hospital stay?"

"Partly this hernia thing. But when Trudy announced they might not come back next year, I recalled she'd been interrupted by Thaddy one night. She had started to say something about 'Owen might not...' It bothered me, but the subject changed quickly. Now they've talked with their own new doctor at home – one he apparently likes and trusts!"

"Yes?"

"This Doctor Abbot says they should come home. Eisenhower sent results to him. The surgery can't be done here soon enough. Their home doctor has ordered an MRI for Tuesday next week, settling this issue immediately. Owen knew more than he conveyed to Trudy. She's furious about that, but mostly just wants Owen to get treated.

"She and Owen talked about selling their place – the whole kit and caboodle. If they could come back, they'd just rent so there wouldn't be a commitment to come. They didn't want their park model to sit for another year like it did during the pandemic."

Lunch became a gloomy affair. I watched as my beautiful mother trifled with her Lulu's Classic Cobb Salad, moving the rotisserie chicken, bacon and ham around with her fork. She picked at the egg, then ate it. It appeared delicious. I put my hand out toward her, and she put her hand on top of mine immediately. I turned my hand upward, and we held hands that way.

"I'll miss them both," muttered my mother.

"I know you will. But they might rent..." I continued lamely, "You'll keep in touch even if they don't."

"Yeah, small talk, chit chat, 'how are the kids?' Not the same."

"I know."

A piece of rotisserie chicken disappeared into a frowning mouth. Chewing, she said, "Real friends are hard to find."

Again, lamely, I declared, "I know."

I toyed with my Chinese Chicken Salad, putting the odd wonton or mandarin orange into my mouth. The scallions, cabbage and peppers were outstanding.

Confessing, "We've lost a lot of friends because Matthew isn't as outgoing as he used to be."

"I didn't realize that – about the friends. It's obvious he isn't as sociable."

"Thankfully, Cynthia and Milena are still my friends, and Matthew has Aaron. We don't ever see anyone else. I'll tell you more on the way home. Maybe it's time you and Dad knew the score. I didn't mean to take away from what you're telling me. It just slipped out. I felt sorry for myself is all."

Finishing up our salads, something clicked with Mom and me. She scrutinized me and got hold of herself to concentrate on me. That hadn't been planned. *Maybe it's a good thing.* I looked away, conscious of her inspection.

She patted my hand in earnest, saying, "I'm sorry, sweetie. When you drop me off, come in. We'll chat."

It could be good to take her mind off Trudy and Owen for a half hour or so. *Definitely it's about time I confided more to them.*

"Sure, I'll come in for a much-needed conversation." As we walked out the restaurant door, I called Matthew to tell him my plan to stay at my mom's place, that I'd be another hour. This tactic of calling or texting a couple of times every day also allowed me to check on him, just to hear his voice and to 'see' what he was up to.

Palm Desert, California

MATTHEW'S JOURNAL

    I could now look back at how my depression had escalated. Before I attempted to kill myself, I'd spend all my mornings in bed, afternoons on the couch and evenings with my eyes glued to the television that I didn't see. Jenna would often snuggle beside me, watching, waiting. Oftentimes, I just wanted to be alone, and I would shrug her off.
    "That's all right, Matthew. I've got something I need to do now, anyway." She'd say it with a conviction that didn't touch her eyes, eyes she shaded from me with her hair that had fallen over them, but I caught the sorrow, yet didn't make myself care.
    As my depression had progressed, I got it into my head everyone would be better off without me. Jenna was still working full time – texting or calling me four times a day to chat, coming home and making supper, as well as tending to me, doing everything she could to draw me out. My kids were walking on eggshells around me. Her parents, when down in the Coachella Valley, also tried, but there was nothing they could do to get through to me. I had no life. I had no career. I was pulling everyone around me down. I was on three prescriptions from when Jenna, Phoebe and Leonard strong armed me to attend at our doctor's office. That doctor recommended therapy, but I balked, saying, "I'll try the pills first." I was deeply concerned any therapy would mean I'd be forced into some sort of care.
    Prior to their intervention, I'd created a terrible scene inside our front door when Jenna thought she'd tricked me into going to see a therapist. When I realized she must be planning something of that sort, I braced myself in the doorway, screaming for her to

leave me alone. "Stop," I yelled and pulled away from her, slamming the door almost in her face. I didn't care if I was out of control.

I just wanted to be left alone. I took the pills for awhile, along with a few drinks. Several weeks later, I muttered to myself, "They're really wasted on me. No one cares about me. I'm just in the way. Everyone would be better off without me."

Well before my suicide attempt, I decided to save my pills. I had no actual plan in mind, but I liked alcohol, and it helped more to dull the depression and fatigue anyway.

Calgary, Alberta, Canada

9

14 Months Before Matthew's Attempt – August

For Sale

❖ JENNA ❖

"The 'For Sale' sign was put up today by their listing agent. And they're not going back to the Resort – not going to rent."

I was having a Zoom call with my mother. They were back in Calgary. Mom stood by her kitchen counter, the same kitchen counter where I'd grown up helping her make meals and baking. Moving up to her lips was her favourite coffee cup, "BEST GRANDMOTHER". Her hair was clipped back, and she had on one of the tops we'd bought the past winter.

"What happened?"

I had just finished icing Matthew's birthday cake for tomorrow. He was out getting some groceries and running errands. I could get this out of the way before he returned home. When he returned home, he'd be exhausted. He had a hard time doing these errands, and he really had reached a point where he didn't want to interact with other people, in particular when it was business related. We talked – well, I talked. He would fade out, and I would let him rest. Sometimes I'd try to chat him out of his gloom, but he'd walk away. Sometimes I felt glad he'd walked away. *His depression's affecting me.*

Mom said something, and I realized I hadn't been listening. Quickly, I caught up with what she was saying. She seemed drained of emotion. Her gorgeous face revealed red eyes tearing up.

"Owen finally got his surgery in Omaha as I told you a couple of weeks ago. He suffered quite a bit waiting, a lot of pain, couldn't bend over, all that. It had been more complicated when they discovered he had hernias on both sides of his abdomen."

At this, she sat down on a kitchen stool, defeated.

"And?" I'd asked because I could see there was more.

"He had a bladder injury during the surgery. Something about 'port placement', dissecting something, maybe something to do with a sliding hernia. I can't recall, and I didn't understand her in the first place. I'm certain she didn't get it all either." Mom appeared uncertain, as though trying to recall what Trudy had told her.

"They won't come back?"

"The surgeon should've caught the problem at the time of surgery. Now they have to go back in to repair it." Again, she appeared uncomfortable, I presumed because she didn't appreciate the issue enough to explain it to me.

Then she went on, "There's more she isn't telling me. I think the surgeon found something when doing the surgery. Of course, I'm concerned it's cancer. But she denied knowing what it was. She said the children have told them it's time they stayed closer to home in Omaha."

"Oh no!" I could see the stress, hear the stress in her voice. "Mom, do you want me to come to Calgary to spend some time with you?"

"Not in the least. Of course, I want to see you, but Matthew needs you, and I'm just being a whiner. Eva called me this morning, and we chatted. She and Robert are coming over tonight for supper."

I could see she had perked up, envisioning Robert and Eva coming over with their children, Kimberley and Darren.

The Zoom camera showed her beaming expression when she did say good-bye.

"Love you, Mom. I'm sorry."

"Me too, love you. Say happy birthday to Matthew from us."

"For sure, I will. Bye."

In reflecting back to my brother, Robert, and his family visiting Mom, Dad, Matthew and me here in Palm Desert this past March, I felt glad to have had the chance to see them all. It was the first time they had come to the Valley. All these years, and the first time. I only went back to Canada sporadically. We texted often, and we conversed on the telephone once every couple of months. When Robert came to visit, I saw he appeared healthy. It was a hard job – construction. He still had the trim waist, thick neck. I was surprised to note his once black hair showed a lot of grey at the sides – my little brother turning grey! His eyes were clear chocolate brown, exhibiting the happiness he felt seeing me.

We'd been to a few places, but the second week Robert didn't want to go anywhere touristy. Their stay at the Renaissance Hotel downtown enabled them all to do their own thing. In an emphatic voice, Eva had said, "I really enjoy the location – ideal for us to just knock about downtown."

Robert and my nephew, Darren, checked out the hockey rink, played pickleball at the resort, went on hikes on their own while Eva and Kimberley traipsed around downtown Palm Springs.

At our place one day during their visit, the squeeze Robert gave my arm allowed him to flaunt his muscles like when he was a kid. I punched him in one broad shoulder to show who was still boss.

He had yelled as though our mother were here, "Ouch, mommy, she's picking on me again!"

I chuckled at his nonsense before I retorted, "Cry baby. What are you guys doing today?"

"What have you got planned, big sis?"

"Considering going to The Living Desert. I gave you the pamphlet last night. I hope you want to come too."

"Matthew," Robert glanced toward Matthew who sat on a kitchen chair, a resigned expression flowing over his face. "Are you interested in going to the zoo?"

At Matthew's miniscule head shake, Robert faced me and announced, "Nah, Matthew and I are gonna hang out here today."

I felt disappointed as my time with Robert dwindled each day, and he wasn't very keen to do what I wanted to do, but I felt appreciative Robert sensed Matthew simply wanted to stay home, and he wanted to hang around with him. Frankly, it was a good call. I loved my brother, and I felt extremely glad he'd come down. Eva was a remarkable person, so patient to put up with my brother's peculiarities, his pattern of building them a home, then moving, and building another one.

I contemplated everything Eva and the kids were getting out of their visit down here, the sightseeing, the museums, taking in a couple of shows at the casinos, and how Robert mostly wanted to stick around and visit at the resort with Mom and Dad, enjoy the happy hours and hang out with Matthew. Now, the part about hanging out with Matthew was terrific. I saw in Robert's expression after I'd asked him about coming with us, that he gave a slight head tilt toward Matthew to let me know he wanted to be there for Matthew. I admired that. I just wish he'd wanted to see more of the Valley as well. I sensed if he ventured out more, then he would want to come back other years because it did have a tremendous number of activities to offer, and the fact I lived here.

Eva, their children and I had an excellent time, though. They were smitten with our home and the entire Valley. My kids took their cousins to some night spots, to downtown Palm Springs, to Village Fest – even, I think, to some more questionable venues. They were all adults, and I wasn't concerned with what they did. I also knew Travis and Ashley were cognizant of what was more or less acceptable and where not to go. Good lord, they lived in LA!

"You'll come back, will you?" I'd questioned Eva on one of our outings, this one to Joshua Tree National Park.

Robert had said before, "Maybe in a few years, when my work settles down, maybe then I'll come back. Ask Eva and the kids."

Swinging her eyes from the view back to me, she replied, "Now I've been here – finally, I plan to come back with or without Robert. You wouldn't mind, would you?"

Seeing her standing there, tiny, yet strongly built, strong-minded, hair pouring around her shoulders and fluttering in the wind, she felt like a sister to me.

"Eva, that's exactly what I had hoped. Robert works hard and has indicated he'll wait a few years to come back. He's more than welcome, but you and the kids can come any time. I'd love to have you. I think on this vacation, we got to know each other more than ever."

"Thank you, Jenna. This has been the best vacation we've ever been on. Robert doesn't appreciate vacations. You knew that. When I've persuaded him to go somewhere, it's not that he makes it miserable for me. He simply doesn't enjoy it. This, really this whole two weeks, has been busy, but relaxing."

"Then it's a date! You come back next year. Okay?"

Brown eyes flashing with happiness, she'd replied enthusiastically, "Deal! With or without him."

Palm Desert, California

10

12 Months Before Matthew's Attempt

Where Did Matt Go?

❖ AARON ❖

WE GREW UP ON the same street, attended the same schools. We managed to convince ourselves we both wanted to be Certified Public Accountants. We were going to make our fortune while living in Portland. I felt beyond disappointed – maybe even betrayed – when Matt moved to Palm Springs, leaving me in the rain, mist and cloud for six months of Portland's winters while he went to work in the warm sunshine and blue skies all year round.

Several years later Matt had texted me:

> Smooth Image Surgery is
> hiring. You'd be perfect.
> Sending info in email

My reply:

> I read your email. Hell
> yeah, I'll be applying!

I updated my résumé and sent it in that morning. Matt may have known I got the interview before I did, but I whipped him off a text.

> Got an interview Friday. Can
> I crash at your place?

Yes! I'll pick you up at the
airport. I know the flight time.

Jenna appeared thrilled with the idea of my moving to the area. I found a place near work. Everything was going well for the 18 years I've lived here – before Matt's depression became noticeable.

Matt had always been my best pal, but he'd displayed a dark side occasionally. In two years or so prior to this depression, I'd noticed a slight shift in Jenna's adoration of Matt. I couldn't put my finger on it, but I'd perceived an underlying wariness in her when she said something – nothing to cause upset – but she'd glance apprehensively at him, I believe gauging his reaction. It indicated that her sense of self – her confidence had slipped. It pained me to see her react in that manner. I wanted to comfort her. It bothered me because I felt protective of Jenna – maybe even something more.

Since his depression and covid, I had Matt's back and covered for him multiple times when he couldn't finish a project. While he worked from home, I'd stop by evenings to help out. Then he attracted the notice of the Director of Human Resources. I think he'd been called into the office three or four times about his performance before he acknowledged it all to me, but I knew. Everyone in the department knew.

When Matt had been stressed during university, he'd drink a lot. He started using pot during exams, something I perhaps shouldn't have suggested we use. I didn't know he'd have a problem with it, that he'd do it so often.

I owe him big time. He took the heat when an undergrad saw a few joints in Matt's room. They'd been mine, the ones I'd encouraged him to smoke before he started smoking pot on his own. The undergrad became a pain in the butt thereafter, asking for joints repeatedly, saying he'd report Matt if he didn't give. Matt did me a solid. I'd already received a reprimand from the university. It would have been two strikes against me if Matt had reported the drugs were mine. Yeah, I owed him.

During Matt's deteriorating depression this past year, he'd started drinking again – at first only a couple here and there throughout the day. He hid the bottles from Jenna, and I didn't say a word until it got out of hand – I was his friend – I needed to protect him. Thank God we'd made a pact not to do drugs after university. I became concerned he'd renege on that one.

At work, the Director of Human Resources, George Alphonse, decided to place the blame that the company was suffering during the pandemic onto Matt. Work stress contributed to his depression; his workload suffered. I did all I could to help him in the Acquisitions area. George made countless derogatory remarks about Matthew being a problem. I couldn't help him at that point. It was a heart-wrenching experience to observe my best friend and colleague go through that turbulence in his career.

I rode over on my motorcycle to visit in the evenings and on as many Saturdays as I could. Matt barely even responded to tales of the outside world, what was happening in the sports world, the stock market and in my life. My life! I went through three girlfriends during his depression, confiding in an unresponsive friend. Jenna talked me through two of my own short episodes of despair over lost love, as well as my having moved to Palm Springs and yet still lost my friend, Matt. I continued to go to his home, and he must have noticed I was there. When Jenna and I were immersed in conversation, I was sure he'd been aware. Glancing his way, I saw a glint in his eyes before they closed again.

Being an avid reader, I showed up with three books one day: *Jack Reacher* by Lee Child, *Kidnapped* by Robert Louis Stevenson and *Hunt For Red October* by Tom Clancey. I asked him to point to which one I should read aloud. When he ignored me, I chose *Kidnapped* with him not acknowledging any interest. His brain hopefully registered something going on, something getting his attention. The reading gave me a reprieve from having to find things to chat about. He appeared to be sleeping, but, once in a while, he'd open his eyes, a tiny spark deep in them. Then his eyes would close.

It was obvious to me his depression and maybe the meds allowed him no interest in anything. Jenna came in on a weekend to listen, telling me Stevenson's *Kidnapped* had been one of her favourite books years before, along with its sequel, *Catriona*. I hadn't known about a sequel. She listened avidly when Matt could only give the book fractured attention.

I'd never seen Matt depressed before – anxious at examinations, sure, but not this. Jenna looked so fearful and agonized. I hesitated to comfort her because I didn't want it to turn into something more. We'd exchanged a few glances, and she'd quickly turned away. It had been me that told Matt to go for the chick in the skimpy bikini at the hotel. I couldn't help but notice her when dropping off a package for Matt one night. I was *very* impressed. I told Matt she looked hot. He'd given me a look and said, "Yeah, I know. Stay away!"

Palm Desert, California

11

7 Months Before Matthew's Attempt – February

Resort Stories

❖ JENNA ❖

I'D GONE TO THE resort to drop Mom off after an afternoon bumming around for a few hours and having a cup of tea at the mall.

"Come in and say hello to your father. Visit a bit."

"Of course!"

When I came in, Charlie jumped up to greet me. I loved this dog – a cutie and affectionate. The dog snuggled up beside Matthew when we were both visiting. "Whatcha' up to, Charlie?"

After a hug and a peck on my cheek from Dad, I opened the fridge and grabbed a soda. While sitting on the couch, Mom started the conversation of neighbours.

"Some of the antics Thaddy and Martha relay happened in their Arizona RV Resort sound far-fetched. Neighbours were texting them to ask who visited, why their water fountain was turned off, where had they gone in their car that afternoon because they were dressed up."

Dad spoke up, "We think our resort is the best. The others lacked community."

Mom resumed her subject of the other resort, "What else did those neighbours in that Arizona RV Resort do with their days?"

I surmised, "I'm certain that happens everywhere."

"Speaking of happenings, it's our turn for Happy Hour. We have lemon shrimp and appies in the freezer. Will you BBQ them?"

"Yeah, that's the only way to go."

"There's a case of Modelo, other beer, and soda. Most will bring their own."

Looking my direction, Dad said, "Call Matthew. We'll probably be outside. Such a gorgeous afternoon. I didn't get a chance to see you this week."

"Yeah, I'll call." There was a chance Matthew would prefer not to come if he'd had a tiring day, mentally or emotionally. As it turned out though, he picked up on the first ring.

"Hey, you. Yeah, I'd really like to. It's been a couple of weeks."

Yes! His new medication allowed me to feel hopeful for his mood.

I rang off, told Mom and Dad, and settled in, anticipating a nice time with their park neighbours. The RV folk were a lot older than Matthew and me, but somehow, we all got along fine, probably because Matthew and I didn't have a real social life. Mom and Dad had all the preparations done, just a few odds and ends to assemble. Charlie tucked himself beside Mom on the couch, eyes watching my father. Dad bent over toward Charlie. With his hands weathered from all his outdoor construction work, he slipped Charlie a piece of salami. He stared at me, and said, "Shh-hh, don't tell your mother."

Mom turned her head toward Dad and glanced suspiciously at Charlie. "Leonard, what's he chewing on?"

Not getting involved in that conversation, I stood up, saying, "Mom, your place is tidy. Nothing for me to do." I did see the makings of a sandwich on the cutting board, cleaned it up and wiped that area. "The sunroom is bright and cheery if we need to come inside."

An hour later, their friends had assembled in my parents' back yard. Matthew had arrived, looking tired, but relaxed.

Mom said, "Martha, I told Jenna about your Arizona park neighbours…"

Dad groaned, rolled his eyes and interrupted, "Does anyone want more lemon shrimp, a beer, iced tea? Anything?"

Their neighbour, Ralph Helmsing from Montana (earning my title Montana Ralph), a new owner this year in Palm Estates RV Resort, winked at Dad. His white fringed mustache moved along with his wide mouth as he grinned and said, "Yep, more shrimp."

I saw Mom give Dad an annoyed glare, and he grinned at her. She walked past him and slapped him on the arm.

Eileen (whom I still called B.C. Eileen), her mass of vibrant red hair swaying along with her as she stood up, giggling, "Anyone else want me to grab a beer while I'm at the cooler?" She was outgoing, always trying hard to fit in. She had on one of her muumuu-style, loose-fit bohemian dresses, her oval blue glasses, a matching shade.

The resort yard crew must've cleaned up the site today. There had been a frenzied wind the night before up to 41 mph in Palm Desert and 46 mph in Palm Springs. Palm branches lying throughout our own neighbourhood, and sand piled up along the street. I could smell the dust in the air. Indian Canyon and North Gene Autry had been shut down again because of sand build-up. Studying the area, I couldn't see any sign of that here.

When no one answered Eileen, she asked again, "Anyone want anything while I'm up?"

"I'll have another Versace," replied her husband, Bruce, his tall, willow-thin frame bending away from his wife, Eileen, as he moved to make a path for her. The gap between his front teeth was displayed as he smiled a tormenting smile toward Eileen.

Ralph's wife, "Montana Betty" Helmsing, swung her blonde-streaked auburn head toward Bruce as he spoke, probably weighing if he was fooling. She asked, "Versace?"

I knew this old story from having it mentioned in numerous exchanges over the years. Moving his ballcap backward on his head, he smiled at Betty in a conspiratorial manner. Both the new owners, Betty and Ralph, turned their chairs toward Bruce. In an impatient manner, Ralph prompted Bruce, "What's this? Versace? Isn't that clothes?" The rest of us stopped talking and gave Bruce the time to tell his story.

Gleefully continuing a story about their first trip to Mexico, Eileen attempted to stop him from embarrassing her in front of the new residents. Staring with annoyance at her husband, then seeming to resign herself, she said, "What the hell? I'll tell it this time." She explained about ordering a Versace for four days and always receiving the beer she thought she'd ordered. Her husband had finally told her on the fourth day the word was Cerveza.

Betty had risen up and given Eileen a pat on the back as she nudged her slim frame past. "I'm off to the washroom. Back in a jiffy. Eileen, you're a real treat. I'm going to love coming down to California."

Martha stated abruptly in her New York lingo, "Grimy, Bruce, I woulda smacked you for real. Betty, we love this park, and you will too. Something happening a few times each week. It's an amazing resort. Everyone's friendly."

I glanced at Matthew, and he seemed to be enjoying the lively discussions. My dad got my attention with the word 'pickleball'. I had been learning how to play, and I knew pickleball was a big thing at Palm Estates RV Resort.

"There's a pickleball tournament, the men's event, coming up. Last year Alfred Burkhart won, and Dan from Regina came in second."

Mom said, "The women's tourney is two weeks after. Trudy won last year."

Once pickleball was mentioned, the conversation swayed to some serious plays, shuffling, drills and the best paddle. Most of this was beyond my capabilities, for sure.

My mind zoned away from pickleball as I watched Betty's body language. She looked at Mom as though she wanted to say something to her. Moments passed, her expressions seemed to swirl, until she couldn't keep still. *She's getting ready to speak.* I could see it in her eyes through her incredibly cute cat glasses.

Realizing Betty was now speaking, I listened, "I'm going to floor shuffleboard tomorrow."

Betty seemed to be waiting, pushing her glasses up toward the bridge of her nose, looking hopeful. Since she was the new park resident, it occurred to me she might not be comfortable coming right out to ask if anyone wanted to play with her. This seemed similar to being the new kid in school. I felt a kinship with her, hoping it would work out.

Mom didn't take the hook right away, simply saying, "I've never played. The indoor courts appear professional."

Getting brave, Betty said, leaning toward mom, "Anyone can play. Phoebe, why don't you come?" Braver still, "Eileen, Martha, would you come?"

Eileen said, "Bruce and I always play pickleball at the same time as shuffleboard."

Glancing toward mom, Betty looked apprehensive, about to say more just as Martha announced, "Let me check my crowded schedule. I usually head to quilting. Then there's dancercise, yoga…" and she trailed off. It seemed she obviously wasn't interested.

Betty waited, I think holding her breath, for Mom's response now. I wanted to step in, but knew I couldn't interfere just as Mom said, "I'd like to go with you." She took a long breath. I think she'd made a momentous decision weighing her feelings of betraying the friendship she'd had with Trudy for all those years.

"Yes, I'll come with you tomorrow," Mom sighed, then nodded her head at the decision she knew was the right one.

My happiness soared for Mom. It was time she stopped grieving for her lost friendship. Betty would make a good friend, not taking away from what Mom and Trudy had.

After Mom went in to get some dessert for the group, she then sat down beside Betty. She smiled a wistful smile, and said to Betty, "Maybe we could play Hand and Foot at the library some afternoon."

"You betcha, that would be very nice," Betty said while beaming.

It was then I felt a tear trickle from my eye, sliding silently down my cheek, followed by another. As I turned to furtively brush them away, checking to ensure no one was paying attention, I felt a catch in my throat. *What?* I had been happy for Mom, and I truly was. *Why was I emotional?* I had friends, good friends, Milena and Cynthia. I still saw Milena daily at work, spending recess and lunchtime together, talking, chatting. Cynthia was my other good friend. We all used to get together regularly, the rendezvous less often of late. We hadn't been out for an event in several weeks, but I knew I could count them as my friends. However, I hadn't ever confided in either of them regarding Matthew's depression issues or his black moods. *I'm ashamed to tell them what has become of our marriage.*

And Matthew had Aaron, thankfully, but I knew I couldn't disregard the wave of loneliness for myself and for Matthew. Most of our friends had given up on us because Matthew didn't want the trouble of going out or having people in. His illness, his irritability would not endure that social contact. *So now I'm a suck, and cry at someone else's happiness.*

I knew I'd missed some of the conversations while acknowledging these emotions. I felt a sense of release. I rubbed again at a tear, pretending to swat away a fly, smiled as I thought again of my mom and Betty becoming friends.

Thaddy yelled, "Hey, did you know Alfred sold his BBQ? About time he got a new one. The steaks were delicious, but the appearance of that thing! Totally black soot inside and out. I can't reckon who'd buy it. They'll need a sandblaster to get the grease off."

Dad said definitively, "Well, it sold!"

Mom turned to Betty and chuckled while saying, "Alfred is the best host in the park. Happy Hours begin at 11:00 in the morning and go until 6:00 when someone decides it time to get home."

Betty inquired, "Something regular?"

"Totally," said Dad in a manner of wonderment.

"This is an excellent park," said Ralph, glancing over at his wife. He had a gratified smile, his eyes moving back and forth between Betty and Mom. He seemed especially happy about Mom and Betty's possible friendship.

Martha jumped in with, "You'll love it here, Betty. I never lock my doors."

Matthew looked a trifle askance at this, interjecting, "We keep our doors locked all the time."

Thaddy announced, "Well, nice evenin'. Leonard, I'm heading home. I got that shed to finish paintin' tomorrow. Are yous guys up to workin' in the morning before it gets hot?"

"It's time for us to disperse as well," ventured Eileen. "Bruce and I hike in the morning. Phoebe and Leonard, you both used to hike. Coming tomorrow?"

My dad glanced at Mom as he answered, "Not tomorrow. I'll help Thaddy paint his shed."

As they reached the edge of the park model, Eileen said, "Yeah, I wasn't thinking about the shed. We'll stop to see how you're doing after." She chuckled, and said, "Maybe it'll all be done by the time we pop over."

"I've got lots of help. Great park for people helpin.'"

The evening was ending on a high note. Mom, Dad, Matthew and I had gone inside to tidy up. As I watched my father walk away with Charlie, my dad seemed to favour one leg, something I realized I'd noted earlier.

I faced my mother, "Why is Dad dragging his left foot?"

"It's not up to me to say."

My father turned and replied with a noticeable grimace, "Man, oh man. Not the left hip – the right one. Need surgery."

"Oh no!" I exclaimed. "Why haven't you said anything? We need to know just as you'd be interested in our lives," I added, purposely not singling out Matthew.

"Exactly..." sighed my mom.

Sighing, then butting in, "Okay, here's the scoop," my dad began, then paused.

"What?" inquired Matthew, a little impatient. "What's going on that you won't share with us? You've asked me innumerable times over these months how I'm doing." Then seeming to realize he sounded curt, he continued, "We appreciate everything you do for us. Perhaps we can reciprocate by helping you." That thought seemed to exhaust him, and he slowly sat down on the arm of the sofa.

"Okay, okay. It's just this hip has been a problem building up for some time now. I can't hike, I can't ride my bike properly. I haven't been golfing. I go with the guys in the cart sometimes just to be sociable."

Moving closer to my dad, I put my hand on his arm, near his elbow. "I wish you'd told me."

"I don't want it to be real."

"That makes sense to me," muttered Matthew. "I hate it when things get real." I gave him a sharp look, actually hoping he would divulge something of his ongoing depression directly to my parents, but he skipped over that. "When's surgery?"

"Leonard went to the doctor last fall, a year before we came this time. The GP sent a referral for an orthopaedic surgeon in Calgary."

"What! What the hell, a year ago, and you didn't tell me?"

"Yeah, it took a year to get an appointment with the surgeon. I hear some patients are waiting well over two years to get in for hip surgery. I went to the ortho guy before we came here, got an MRI, and I have a follow-up appointment with the surgeon the end of March."

Mom clarified, "We'll be leaving early this year for that appointment. His cardiologist at home wants to see him for a change in heart medication."

"Dad!"

Swinging around toward my mom, Dad said, "Phoebe!!"

Mom blinked at the rebuke, but gave him a glare and said, "Well, if we're telling, then let's get it all out there."

Grabbing and holding onto my lucky necklace, I gasped, "You've been on the same medication for ten years. Why is there a change now?" *What else has happened?*

"Fine! I couldn't change medications prior to coming to the US cuz my health insurance cost would've gone up. The cardiologist said he'd wait until I came home. Then he'll do a couple of tests and give me those meds. It's a new drug called Entresto. It's supposed to be a wonderful drug."

"Good lord. Do you still believe it was a good idea to wait?" I nervously asked.

"Yeah, I feel only slightly different. I look forward to trying some new meds. My wind is a little down. Don't go worrying yourself about this. It's all under control."

"Mom? What's your opinion?"

"Your father appears to be doing all right. We don't do the same activities as we used to. But I'll be relieved to get back to Canada."

"I'm going to be watching you, Dad."

"Yeah, yeah, and I'll be watching you too."

Matthew got us moving toward the door, "Great evening, folks. Sorry this is going on with you, Leonard. I've got to get home so my wife can go to work in the morning to support all our bad habits."

I did the obligatory giggle to that.

Matthew added, "I've got the Bronco here, so I'll meet you at home."

Charlie whined, and Dad said, "I'll say goodnight now and take Charlie to do his business."

After Dad sent a quick wave to us as he moved a step away, Charlie ran in front of him.

Mom called to him, "Here, take this flashlight, Leonard."

"K. Thanks. Come on, Charlie, let's go wee."

Upon our arrival home, I begged off a cup of tea, and said that I had to lie down. Matthew went to the living room and turned on the TV. I thought about my dad. I sat on the edge of the bed, head held in my open palms.

What the hell am I going to do? I just can't believe that now I have my father's health issues to worry about. If only Matthew's meds work... Tears formed.

I took stock of the situation, walked into the bathroom to splash water on my face. I told myself to smarten up. *I don't have time to fret about me.* Dad's health issues had to be dealt with. Perhaps

I shouldn't have, but I took one of Matthew's anti-depressants, swallowing it down with water from the tap. *Just this once. Was this a messed-up choice on my part?* After 10 or 11 deep breaths, I changed into my pajamas, and settled down to re-hash my father's hip and heart comments.

Dad might think I was content with the paltry amount of information he had finally revealed, but I'd be texting my reliable sibling, Ruby – the pharmacist – to find out what this heart medication meant. What it meant for his long-term health.

Palm Desert, California

MATTHEW'S JOURNAL

Also, a qualified CPA, Aaron got the job in Palm Springs 20 years earlier. He arrived at my house all those years ago not on the old Honda XL500 motorcycle he'd had since he was 18 but riding a 'new-to-him' 1990 GL 1500 touring Gold Wing. He was physically fit, had worked out back home and was totally able to handle the big bike.

"I bought myself the bike to celebrate three things: my new job; living in the sunny Coachella Valley; and being able to ride enjoyably 12 months of the year. It comes with a numbered plaque and anniversary edition insignia. It's da bomb. Come check it out."

Travis had been little. Jenna stood by Travis as he sat on the bike while we checked the bike out. Jenna grabbed Travis just as we all heard a 'rrr-roar'. He'd turned the darn thing on! Even then, he was a handful!

"Okay, we're probably not getting one," I said, and added, "At least not right now." I could tell by the horrified expression on Jenna's face this was a good call. She relaxed and, while Travis stood awestruck by the bike, she admired the ride.

I was certainly fortunate Jenna got along well with Aaron then and throughout all these years. Now, with not caring about anything, I still had Aaron as a good pal and a good workmate.

As a result of being run down over a year ago, I'd caught covid. I was extremely ill with all the worst symptoms. Fatigue got the best of me, adding to my depression and work performance – rather non performance. Then I was let go.

I peered in the mirror on a day that I even managed to shave. That man staring back from the mirror didn't resemble me, didn't have the expression in his eyes I was familiar with. The sallow face didn't look recognizable – he was hollowed out, just staring at me, glinted cold eyes. I wasn't sure I was even in there. I felt weak, anxious, tired. My head ached all the time. That damn pandemic. This damn feeling of uselessness.

Aaron came by often, at first to help me with work. Once I was fired, he still visited, trying to reach me. He started reading a book to me. I pretended to listen. I knew the boy's story was in Scotland, someone important to him had died and he went off to seek his family, but he ended up on a sea voyage. The voyage gave me time to doze off a little before Aaron called my attention to someone getting killed, and of shipwrecks, deceit and loss. At some point, many days later, somewhere between snoozes and coming back into the story, I heard a good ending, but I can't recall what it was. Each time Aaron stopped reading for the day, I felt a loss – a loss of what, I didn't have any energy to decipher.

Palm Desert, California

12

3 Months Before Matthew's Attempt – July

What Can I Do?

❖ JENNA ❖

WE RARELY GO OUT to visit with friends. Even when the children come to visit, I can see him try less and less, unable to succeed in displays of interest in what they're talking about. He's tired all the time because his sleep habits have shifted to pacing during the night and needing long naps during the day.

My chum and fellow teacher, Milena Sanchez Garcia, has noticed, but I speak only a little about what goes on in our home.

Our neighbours, Kathy and Todd, asked, "Where's Matthew? He used to be out doin' the yard work, fiddlin' and fussin' every weekend." I was sparse in my reply, and they accepted my minimal explanation of his recovering from covid and being despondent from losing his job.

I'd made excuses to Travis and Ashley about their father for a long time, but I noticed the glances that passed between them.

"Your dad is more tired lately from last year's flu. It won't let go."

Each of them originally seemed to have decided not to press me, perhaps in order to save me the embarrassment of explaining something I couldn't explain. Lately, I've told them what they need to know.

"Now being let go from *Smooth Image Surgery* has depressed him more. We're trying to get him past these feelings of not caring." Ashley said sulkily, "No kidding! He doesn't care at all."

"Don't think that way. He just isn't himself."

A little more contrite, she said, "I want him to improve. I want him to be as he always was a couple of years ago. Happy, funny." She looked away before adding, "He's not himself, and I've heard him say things to you. Not cool."

Travis made an awful sour face. "He's definitely not himself! He's not like our dad."

I'm well aware that Matthew's not himself. "The meds were working for awhile, but he seems to have regressed. I'll get him back to the doctor." *I hope that's possible!*

It had been unfair to keep them in the dark about their father's health, as I felt deeply that it had been unfair I'd been kept in the dark about my own father's health. *Obviously, they knew anyway. They'd have to be blind and deaf not to see and also hear what he's been like. Ashley had said she heard him say things to me, and she'd said, "Not cool."*

—⚘—

The problem with my father's health does weigh heavily on my mind. I've had multiple contacts with my siblings. Robert didn't know anything. Dad had kept a tight lip on his heart issues. Now Robert knows, he's communicating with our twin sisters as well.

My first text to Ruby in March, the night Dad had been mildly forthcoming about his medication change, got a quick response.

> Dad finally said something to you. Thank God! Mom confided in me so I could help her decipher the medications.

> He didn't tell me. Mom did! And he was angry with her, but she held firm. I still don't

> understand what you meant by Entresto. You said he would also be taking Forxiga. Why two? He didn't mention two. He's still holding out.

And with that foundation, I began to find out over the next several months what my father was going through. Dad didn't say more than he had to, and Mom simply didn't recognize all the implications of the medications. My father indeed had been prescribed those two medications. Entresto and Forxiga (also known as Farxiga) were for congestive heart failure! I felt distress; however, in talking directly with my pharmacist sister, Ruby, I understood this to be an early stage of congestive heart failure. If the medication worked, then he would be healthier than when I saw them in March.

Now I had an additional worry, along with Matthew's rising depression and drinking. I know that my strong personality, my strength to handle situations, had diminished. *Too many troubles. I feel I could end up depressed as well.*

PART TWO

If you don't laugh, you cry.

Palm Desert, California

MATTHEW'S JOURNAL

I was in the hallway looking into the kitchen. My wife, Jenna, moved past the cupboard walking toward me. I glanced at my two adult children who stood at the door with the lunch their Mom had packaged up.

My daughter, Ashley, said, "Say 'goodbye' to Dad for us. He must be tired not to have come down to give us a proper goodbye."

Travis, my son, added worriedly, "Is he okay? Dad was more withdrawn this weekend."

"I know you're disappointed. As I said, he was prowling around the house until the wee hours, contemplating goodness knows what. He must be exhausted. We'll call tonight. If you're home, we can have a little chat. Safe driving to LA through that nasty traffic."

Ashley said, "Love you, Mom."

"Love you, Mom."

"Love you both to the moon and back!"

I yelled, "I'm here. Good-bye."

They grabbed their bags; each gave Jenna a solid hug and then walked out to the street to Travis' royal blue Camaro.

Waving, Jenna called, "Have a good week, sweethearts. Your dad and I will see you soon."

I waved goodbye from the doorstep. They didn't wave back at me. Perplexed, I started to go toward their vehicle. Stopped. I suddenly knew what happened. I glanced at the window of our bedroom and remembered my body lying on the bed, the bottles of pills surrounding me.

"Oh my God, what have I done? How can I fix this?"

Jenna walked past me, stepping into the house and closed the door behind her. As she called out, her voice carried through the door. "Matthew, time for breakfast. I'll bring your coffee to you this morning."

I followed along in a flowing motion it seemed. When there was no response, she grabbed a cup of coffee for me. As she entered the bedroom, I saw her as she stood there, motionless for a moment, her freckles standing out on her now white face. Air seemed to force itself into her struggling lungs. She screamed – a scream of terror and grief, the coffee cup did a downward spiral, crashing to the floor.

She rushed into the bedroom, took notice I was still breathing, clumsily grabbed for the bedside phone and dialed 911 while grabbing the pill bottles.

As she shouted information over the telephone, I remained behind her and stared over at the bed, our bed, tears streaming down my face. I went a little farther in, close to the bed and glanced toward Jenna. I saw the tears running from her green eyes as well.

I reached my arms out to her, but I couldn't touch her.

"Darling," I whispered. "I'm so sorry -- this was so selfish of me. Why can I see things so clearly now and not a few hours ago? How could I have done this to myself, to you, to our family?"

Jenna knelt down beside the bed. As I watched, distanced from it all, she took my hand, stroked the palms, rubbed my fingers, crying and wailing aloud. Then she stood up quickly and shook me, pulled me toward her, trying to make me wake up. She tapped my face lightly. She tapped my face not so lightly.

"Wake up, wake up, wake up. Wake up!! BREATHE! You can't leave me. I know you've been depressed – we've been trying hard to make you better. WAKE UP!"

As she sat down again, I lowered myself, now close behind her, with my arms around her, while I whispered in her ear, "I'm sorry, darling. I'll make it up to you somehow."

"What!" Jenna must have heard the voice from behind her as she was staring at me beside her. She whipped her head around, tossing her auburn hair every which way, then her eyes riveted back to our bed.

"Matthew, did you just talk to me? Matthew, Matthew, come back to me."

The sirens sounded in the distance quickly becoming closer. She leaned over, reached behind my back and pulled me up to a sitting position, taking every ounce of her strength, almost crumbling under my weight.

The fire truck and ambulance drivers arrived, and the paramedics took me from her as she was losing her grip on me, the man she loved. One paramedic grabbed the pill bottles from the table where Jenna had pointed with the finger of her shaking hand. Cardiopulmonary resuscitation was performed to temporarily pump enough blood to my brain until specialised treatment was available.

My chest tightened, shuddered, air passing through me.

At this point as I hovered by, I went blank.

Palm Desert, California

13

During Matthew's Attempt

At That Moment

◆ JENNA ◆

THE PARAMEDICS QUICKLY LAY Matthew on the stretcher, attaching the oxygen mask. Two policemen had also come in, standing to the left side of the door. The paramedics rushed Matthew out the door, and I started to follow helplessly.

The taller policeman said, "Ma'am, we'll meet you at the hospital. We'll have a few questions."

I couldn't even reply. I rushed out the door.

Palm Desert, California

14

During/After Matthew's Attempt

Day-To-Day

❖ JENNA ❖

My mother and father had been distraught they weren't down in their Palm Springs resort at the time Matthew had attempted suicide. They wanted to hop on a plane from Calgary and come right away to be near us, to help however they could. I'd said no.

The children and I'd spent most of the morning standing or sitting at Matthew's bedside, watching and waiting, being in the way of medical professionals. I attempted to call my Mom and Dad, to tell them there had been no change. To hear their voices, to be told by my 'mommy' *"everything will be okay, sweetheart"*. In all honesty, I wished they were here in the Coachella Valley.

Reminiscing about the conversation this morning, I recalled telling my parents, "There is nothing you can do right now."

My dad had earnestly lamented, "But we could be there for you. Your mom is checking flights out of Calgary to Palm Springs."

"I believe I need to say for all our sakes, 'please don't come yet.'"

"Why, sweetie?" Mom, now on the speaker phone with Dad.

"Mom, I don't have the mental capacity to be social right now. Matthew isn't conscious. I just need a couple of days to gather myself. I'll call you right away as soon as something changes, as soon as he wakes up. You don't need to make all that effort to get here."

"Jenna, we'll talk to you tonight."

Tonight. What would happen during this day? Today already felt so exceedingly long. How could it have been only earlier this morning that Travis and Ashley had left from our front step to head back to Los Angeles? They would've gotten right into the early morning interstate LA traffic, received my telephone call, and, in a state of panic and horror, found an exit to turn around to come back to Palm Springs to meet me at the Eisenhower Hospital.

My mind wandered to my talks with the children. I'd called Ashley and Travis shortly after arriving at the Eisenhower Hospital in the ambulance with Matthew unconscious, unresponsive. *Bloody hell, what had he done?!*

I'd gathered myself and said, "I know you can't possibly pull over to chat with me, but I need you to turn around and come back as soon as you safely can."

"But Mom, the morning traffic's deplorable. I have to get to class, and Travis has a job waiting. What's going on?"

They would have had the call on speaker so they could both hear. I tried so hard to be calm, not to panic them in the midst of heavy, heavy traffic. I chose my words to them carefully, "Something happened to your father. No, don't interrupt until I'm done. When I went into our bedroom, your father wouldn't wake up. The ambulance came, and I need you to meet me at the Eisenhower."

"What do you mean 'somethin' happened', that he 'wouldn't wake up.' Mom?" Travis trying not to yell at me.

"Drive safely. Don't panic. Travis, keep your attention on the road, and call me back once you've turned around and are in less traffic. I can't talk right now. I need to talk to the staff here."

Travis called back a little over 15 minutes later, and I told them both on speaker the little that I knew. "Your dad may have swallowed some pills. The staff are doing everything they can to ensure your father recovers. They tell me he received medical attention soon enough. They are very positive about the outcome."

Of course, there had been discussion about my wording, "may

have swallowed some pills." Neither of them satisfied with my explanation or the doctors being positive. Travis had had a friend who took too many drugs, and the outcome had not been positive. Ashley was crying.

"That's bullshit, Mom!" Travis became angry, hurt. "Why would our father try to off himself? He didn't accidentally take too many pills. He's an accountant for God's sake. He can count."

Travis and Ashley had arrived at the hospital at 8:30 a.m., 90 minutes after they'd left our home. Their attention would have diverted to their week ahead as soon as they were off our street. Now it locked on their father. We stood; we sat; we stood; we paced; we asked questions of every staff member who came into the room.

It had taken every bit of emotional strength I had not to beg my parents to come, to come right away. But I had been strong. I'd told them not to come.

I glanced over at my children and admired my son's tall figure, auburn hair with long sideburns. After I pressed the 'end' button after talking to my parents, Travis put his hand on my shoulder and Ashley leaned into me while sweeping her long red and gold hair from her face, her tears wetting my cheek and blending in with my own tears.

As I set my phone down, Ashley murmured, "It would be reassuring to have Grandma and Grandpa Barnes here."

Little did I know as soon as they'd hung up, my mom booked the flights, then called my twin sisters, Joan and Ruby, as well as my brother, Robert. I later learned all of them considered rushing to Palm Springs from their homes in Calgary. Dad talked my siblings out of that, asked them to come get Charlie, their King Charles Cavalier Spaniel, look after the house, get the mail, and that he and Mom would call or text several times a day to update them.

My mom and dad had flown in, then cabbed it to their RV Resort. About that same time, I called them again. I hadn't been able to reach them. I had my suspicions as to what they'd done.

Dad answered, "We're in Palm Desert now, at the Resort. How's the situation?"

"There's no change. Thank you for coming. I couldn't ask you to come but thank God you're here."

"No pressure, Jenna," Mom assured me. "We're here. We'll do whatever you want, but now we're closer when you need us. I'm certain everything will be okay, sweetheart. I've a feeling." *That's what I'd wanted my mom to say, that everything would be okay.*

After clicking my cell off, I sat in the chair outside Matthew's room and sobbed, relieved they were here, anxiety for Matthew, guilt for any multitude of reasons, then again relief that my parents were here. *They had come!*

During that conversation, I'd told my parents Matthew's parents, Clara, Jack, his brother, Neil, and his wife, Sharyn, had come minutes before. Clara with her sassy dyed blonde hair, cut short in a stiff uplifted sweep to give her a young appearance, arrived looking uncharacteristically harried.

My dad had immediately responded, "We'll let them have their time with Matthew. Glad they're there. After we're settled, I'll give you another call. You call if anything happens, if you need us to talk to."

"Thank you. I love you so much. You're here and that's the best news today."

Ashley and Travis took a few moments to talk to my mom and dad.

Matthew was rarely alone for all the days and nights that followed, everyone quiet, emotional, tears straying down cheeks. We all had that in common right now, any animosity Clara felt for me overlooked. My own mom and dad cared about him, it seemed, as any actual parent would.

As I sat in the visitor chair that I was much too well acquainted with, I felt I could snooze right here. My body became heavy. I stretched again. I didn't want sleep. I wanted to be there when Matthew awoke. The doctor said maybe tomorrow. Otherworldly is a word that came to my mind, the unreality of all that we've been through. Will Matthew remember anything about what he did, about his trip to the hospital, the process the staff did when he arrived? Has he heard any of the words I've said to him, shared my tears?

No, he'll awake, oblivious to what had transpired in his absence. In his absence from my life, me here alone. There's that thought again. *Alone but not alone. He's here, but not here.*

Matthew is still in the state of complete unconsciousness, basically a coma. The medical staff are hopeful that he will follow the pattern with him then moving to the vegetative state and then return of consciousness.

It's evening, and Matthew is still not awake. I've held his hand for hours, but I'm exhausted, and I sit down once again.

I didn't think I slept, but I startled as my head dropped to my chest. The clock said 3:00 a.m., and I had to rub my neck to work out the tight kink in the center. I got up to stretch my back and my legs. *Matthew, wake up!* I hear myself yell this when I found him. I want to yell the same words now, to shake him awake. His hands are warm to my touch, and I held them again for countless minutes. I'm exhausted, but too restless to sit on that wooden chair. *What would the staff think if I curled up beside him and held him? I need him. I need him to wake up.*

I stayed at his bedside all night every night until one evening, a nurse practically ordered me to leave.

—m—

Even though I'd invited Matthew's family to stay with me at our home, they made a good decision to be close to the Eisenhower Hospital and to have their own space to come and go. I'd seen the effect of Matthew's condition weigh heavily on them.

That was one of the most astonishing things I'd seen in a long time. *Clara and Jack holding hands!* They and Matthew's brother, Neil, and his wife, Sharyn, had flown in from Portland, Oregon, taken a cab to the hotel, unloaded their luggage. Without unpacking, they came to the hospital. They'd cab it for a day or two, then use Matthew's Ford Bronco for the duration of their stay.

A phone call to me first to let me know their location and plans. "We're at the Holiday Inn Express & Suites in Rancho Mirage. You know the address? Of course, you do," Jack decided in his deep, commanding voice.

"I've got it all on the GPS. We've been on the 111 before, we've got it figured." This was replying to my inquiry if they might have any trouble getting from the hotel to the hospital. He would be standing in the hotel room – tall, white brush-cut hair, always a stubble beard.

Later, I would learn from Neil that the rooms had all been booked under his mother's name, Clara Hanson. They were bright, casual rooms, each with a sitting area. Free parking, hot buffet breakfast.

Neil's movements were always quick, coordinated. His professional voice as smooth as silk. His off-work voice often flippant, "We probably won't use the outdoor pool, BBQ or exercise room. But you never know, if Matt improves or not, I may need to blow off some steam. Mom picked the hotel. She wanted to stay somewhere close to the Eisenhower, but it had to be decent. She only checked for 15 minutes while Dad finished throwing essentials in a suitcase. I think we can get along good enough. If not, Sharyn and I will crash at your place."

"Neil, that would be fine with me. You know we have a spare room even with Ashley and Travis home. I'm not attempting to control, but it would be good for you to have time with our kids as well if there are any spare moments."

"You're absolutely right. My niece and nephew might need some guidance on the rules of life. We'll play our stay by ear."

Neil and Sharyn moved to our home a week later.

"*Help!*" read his first text message.

Just getting into my Escape, I quickly texted back
What's going on?

Can we please, please stay at
your place for the next week?
Mom and Dad are staying at
the hotel. We need a break.

Of course. I'm on my way to the
Eisenhower. Where are you?

> We're packed, ready to head out.
> Mom and Dad are driving us.
> We've arranged to rent a vehicle.
> Meet you at the hospital to put
> our luggage in your vehicle.
> Drive us to pick up the rental
> after we visit with Matthew?

Yep. See you soon.

I looked forward to having Matthew's brother and wife at our home. It would be incredibly good to have the company and distraction. I liked both of them. They were genuine and easy to get along with. I'd need their sense of humour to get through this. Sharyn was as quick-witted as Neil, her personality bouncy. She'd married Neil after Matthew and I'd moved to California, so I didn't know her as well as I knew Neil. They made a contrasting pair, her hair dark brown, almost black, ebony eyes blazing with intense fire, skin a fabulous olive, and Neil, mousey blond hair, long like Matthew's, eyes blue, skin a pink hue. Slightly shorter than Matthew, his brother was slim boned; Sharyn solid and muscled.

They'd be here on the weekend when Travis and Ashley were home. It would be great for my children to have another visit with their aunt and uncle, something that didn't happen often. *I'll need more groceries.*

Palm Desert, California

MATTHEW'S JOURNAL

When I'd regained consciousness as if from a dream, I had peculiar and unsettling recollections. Had they been real?

I had a vague memory of experiencing panic, realizing I was hovering at the corner of a room – on the ceiling!

What the hell? If that wasn't mind blowing enough, I had seen myself below lying on a cot. No, not a cot – a hospital bed. No! No! No!

Jenna had been beside my bed – then a memory returned of the earlier event, a memory of what I had done before. Déjà vu. But this couldn't be happening. Or wait – this meant I didn't die. I felt that I was going to be all right. Wasn't I? Medical personnel had been scattered about, and machines hooked up. Travis and Ashley stood behind Jenna. Her hands were clasped in prayer. In prayer? Then I noticed the clergy at the foot of the bed. Oh God! Oh Jenna!

Jenna had whimpered, "Matthew, Matthew, can you hear me?"

I had heard her as I lay there. Correction, as I had hovered on the ceiling looking down. Memories had flashed back to me – the events of last night, the events from this morning. Or had it been longer? I didn't know. I didn't think I really wanted to die that night. I'd just wanted something. But what had I wanted? I'd wanted Jenna and the children; I'd wanted things to be easier.

Once I had acted on that choice to end my life by overdose, the scenario could've gone either way. I'd wondered "Have I survived? What did all this mean?" Seeing all the tubes and machines, the fact I was on the ceiling(!), not awake in the bed, and our minister standing there, I was on a two-way street. Which way was I going? I had been vaguely aware of a beckoning light appearing at the end of a long grey tunnel. I remember wondering as I peered through that tunnel, "Should I stay here, or should I surrender to its unmistakeable pull?"

I had attempted to get to the light, but I'd stayed at the ceiling for a long time watching myself below. I'd wondered what would happen to me. I'd tried to move to comfort Jenna and the children, but I had been trapped on that ceiling with no ability to move.

I'd heard Jenna's frantic voice, "I have to call Mom and Dad and Clara and Jack – right now. They need to know."

I recall thinking, "Why am I up here? I want to be with my family." I hadn't understood what I was seeing. For that matter, I hadn't understood why I was seeing anything. I'd decided that I must be alive. I'd watched, aware of the clearing of my airway, insertion of a breathing tube, being administered some sort of medication. I'd felt no pain. Should I have felt pain? I'd watched helplessly as intravenous fluids were put into me. "What was happening? Were they saving me? I loved my wife. I loved my children. I had let them down."

I'd felt faintly cognizant that sometimes I'd been on the level of the bed, but not being aware if I was in my body. I recall that I'd felt emptiness as though a lot of time had passed. Events and people came and went.

From the ceiling, I had seen my mother and father enter the room, Mom crying. They had been alone with me, holding hands. I couldn't think clearly, but that had seemed special to me – my mother and father holding hands.

Then Jenna, Ashley and Travis had been with me at another time. I'd felt hazy, maybe dozing off and on. Was that when I was in my body on the bed?

Then I'd blanked out (again).

Light shines in my eyes. I feel awareness. I'm in the hospital bed. My mind is so sketchy. Those memories haunt me. I feel my eyes opening and closing, but I seem not to have control over their function. I command my eyes to open.

Palm Desert, California

15

Right After Matthew's Attempt

What Is Matthew Hiding?

❖ JENNA ❖

WITH THE TRAUMA WE had in our lives, hair length was a minor, trivial thing!!

To think a couple of weeks before Matthew's suicide attempt, I'd been pondering something so mundane as the length of my hair. The length had grown to five inches below my shoulders, longer than I'd had it in decades. I worn it up in a ponytail at night because my hair annoyed me and scratched my face when I lay down. I reflected often on Ashley's abundance of golden red, luxurious flowing hair.

After four or five months, I realized a large amount of my hair had been coming out on my hairbrush and comb each time I brushed or combed it. On google search, I'd found out hair fell out when put up in a tight ponytail.

After awhile, I'd come to revel in the way it felt against my face when I lay down, soft and warm. Protective. Maybe I needed some security when life around me had turned out to be so insecure, so insecure that I had trouble handling it all.

The belief that my hair might have been falling out because of my own stress hadn't occurred to me until today, days later. My life was full of stress. I constantly fretted about Matthew and my father, but it would've been astonishing for me to worry about myself. My thoughts were of Matthew morning, noon and night, agonizing about him whenever I had to be away from home.

How did we ever get through it? Detached recollections of the time alone at home directly following Matthew's suicide attempt (let's call it what it was) seeped slowly to me. Having been camped out on the living room sofa, I'd remained awake except for catnaps here and there. I couldn't make myself go to sleep in the bed where I'd found Matthew close to death.

Many times, I'd thought of taking another of Matthew's pills. I truly wanted to stop my worries. *I can't. I have to remain strong on my own.* I quietly sang lines from a song my mother often sang, *Could I Have This Dance?* as sung by Anne Murray.

{"I'll always remember the song they were playing..."}

The hospital staff had made me leave after I'd spent days at the hospital, only coming home to shower and get something other than hospital food to eat, something identifiable. I can't conjure up anything that I ate at home, but I'd made an attempt at nutrition.

"Go home. Get some proper sleep," the nurse in charge the third night told me. "None of us want to treat you for exhaustion on top of caring for Matthew. We'll call if anything develops. Don't come back until after 10:00 tomorrow. Doctor Masood will have done his rounds by then. We can give you a report."

I heard them, but I resented being sent home like a teenager. I laid awake, sleep evading me until 4:30 a.m. when I felt myself falling asleep. With every blink my eyelids became heavier. Fatigue nibbled at my senses. I felt my vision become blurred, gray. Then I slept.

"Ring..., ring..."

I had awakened suddenly, but there had been no telephone ringing—no hospital telephoning with bad news. I sensed I'd been dreaming of what had happened the evening before Matthew took all those pills – believing I'd found my husband dead in our bed – but he was alive.

Reliving that night when Matthew received a telephone call from one of his former bosses, I felt panicked. He'd answered that call, and I heard only muffled words from the telephone and Matthew had been responding in monosyllables. His face had been ashen as I glanced over his way. The call ended, but as soon as Matthew hung up, it had rung again. Matthew had too much colour in his cheeks when he hung up from that call, too much emotion.

"Matthew, what were those calls about? You seem troubled."

"Nothing. George Alphonse wanted to check some information with me. Then Aaron called to say George would be calling. I'm going up to bed now. Tell the kids I love them when they get back."

"They're at Robin's house." Distracted, he nodded. *Ashley's friend, Robin – whom Travis had recently been dating.*

At that time, I didn't know what those calls had been about, but I knew Matthew must have been hiding something – from his evasive manner. What I found out later altered my world, had been altering Matthew's world.

Matthew had pretended to be asleep, with the lights off when I slipped into bed.

Then the morning happened. My husband had attempted suicide. And the next days happened, and now I'm alone and I'm awake thinking about his situation at work and had it upset Matthew enough that he wanted to kill himself that night in particular, that it hadn't been the depression by itself. Had there been a final straw in those calls?

I recalled Matthew's parents coming to the hospital the first night he was hospitalized. Clara had been quiet, quieter than I had ever seen her. She whispered loving words to Matthew, stroking his hand gently below where the intravenous was housed. I'd never seen her like this. It pleased me to think she could be a loving mother. Jack stood stoically on the other side of Matthew, a tear running from one eye, his face a crumpled mess. I made an excuse to leave them alone for over an hour. When I returned, they were standing side by side, holding hands.

My God! Disaster brings love and calm, I guess.

Something in Jack's face had changed when he glanced my way, and it made me want to speak with him. Alone. Clara eventually went to the washroom, a sob escaping as she exited the room.

"Jack, is something else the matter besides you're worried sick about Matthew?"

"I don't know for sure. I keep mulling over what Matthew said to me days before this happened. He usually doesn't call because Clara calls a few times a month." His huge, rugged hands were absent-mindedly rubbing together, back and forth.

As Jack hesitated – his booming cynical laugh not evident in any way, he moved away from me, his eyes closing for a moment. I had a hard time being patient, but he continued, "Matthew indicated some documentation had disappeared from the office. He'd neglected to return his key, and the clinic hadn't changed his code. Two terrible coincidences, but they were checking he didn't have these documents in his possession. As a former police officer, I cautioned him to get some legal advice, but Matthew changed the subject."

My mind summoned up the ringing telephone the night before our family disaster, the clinic calling, then Aaron calling. I'd told Jack about this, and he had replied, "Something was up, but we both know it couldn't have been anything that Matthew would've done. I should've said something to you, but Matthew wanted it kept quiet. He refused to discuss it again."

He'd gazed at me with a remorseful expression, a tall man appearing diminished by a guilty conscience, and I immediately had said, "It's not your fault. You're a wonderful father, and you'd been asked to keep a secret." Jack had looked gratefully at me, still wishing he'd pushed Matthew more at that time.

Then I knew that had been the secret Matthew hadn't wanted to tell me – he hadn't wanted to relay to me the reason for those two telephone calls the night before! *Did I need to know? What was the real secret?* Jack and I agreed the conversation had to be broached with Matthew. As we stared at each other, it seemed we were saying the same thing in our minds: "*When* Matthew comes through this."

Jack had said, "The problem's not over. Someone has those documents."

"Matthew either has been involved or became the scapegoat having forgotten to turn in his key." *Who knew Matthew still had his key?*

And had one of my best friends, Cynthia Magee, been aware of all of this? Cynthia had been agitated when I called to tell her about Matthew. After I explained Matthew's medical crisis, Cynthia had said there was something she couldn't discuss with me right then. I'd revealed everything I knew about the situation. Her robust personality had come through with questions about the timing of his suicide. Her pointed questions about Matthew's state of mind were getting me riled. Cynthia was my outspoken lawyer friend – "friend" at this point being questionable.

Irritated, I said, "All right, what's this about? I've told you everything happening. You're keeping something back. Cynthia? I'm not in the mood to play question tag."

"Matthew called me a few days ago, asking for legal advice about his work. I'm sorry, but I can't say anything else to you. Matthew will explain everything when he wakes up."

"He contacted you. Why? Do you know what we're going through right now? What?"

"It wasn't something he meant to keep from you, just a trifling matter."

"Trifling matter?!" That might have been hysteria rising in my voice, and I added, "A couple of days before he tried to commit suicide!"

She was an outdoorsy person, physically fit, but I was sure I could "take her" right now! I was angry, but Cynthia held firm.

"I'm sorry. I wish I could tell you, but I'm bound by client confidentiality law."

She refused to comment further, so, without further adieu, I hung up on her. I'm not proud of that. But, hell yeah, it made me feel good, like maybe I had some control over an uncontrollable situation.

More than once every day I received texts from Cynthia, inquiring about Matthew and any progress. She became a thorn in my side, not telling me anything, but expecting me to relay situations to her. *I'm going to block her.*

Her last email:

> "I know you don't want to hear from me. John Wu asked me to keep track of how Matthew is. We need to know when Matthew can get together with John. Don't cut me off."

What the frickin' hell? My friend Cynthia, a confident, classy and proficient lawyer, had inquired not as a friend. She'd said client confidentiality, but handing Matthew's progress reports to another partner that Matthew and I also knew! *Why was a senior partner in Cynthia's firm getting updates on Matthew's condition? Relating to the telephone calls Matthew received, the calls that Jack had told Matthew to get legal advice on?*

Palm Desert, California

16

During/After Matthew's Attempt

Awake

❖ JENNA ❖

THROUGHOUT THE DAYS SINCE Matthew's suicide attempt, I had copious communications with my siblings, most of which were done through Joan. Ruby and Robert had decided it should be just one of them "bothering" me. I agreed because my mind was too full to concentrate on pleasantries. As I sat on one of the uncomfortable Eisenhower Hospital chairs, my cell chirped quietly twice, signalling it was Joan.
 how is Matthew today?
The same

 how are you, Jenna?
The same – wiped and worried

 love you, sis, hugs
Same

 I became used to the hospital routines, smells, whirring of machines. The scents of antiseptic; wet floors; disinfectants; heated equipment; nurses and staff stepping in and out – snapping on gloves; checking his pulse, temperature, eyes; straightening his sheets; checking reflexes. The hospital routine zoomed around me, a busy whirl of activity day and night. Bits of staff conversation came through the open doorway, telephones being answered, staff paging, a doctor questioning a test result.

All of our family kept their visiting to a minimum, the doctor advising us to only come in two at a time and to give Matthew sufficient breaks so he could sleep. I was the exception. I stayed there quiet as a mouse, just watching him, waiting, wondering. Daily, some improvement occurred. Matthew was moving past the vegetative state with periods of sleep-wake cycles longer, he made facial expressions even though they were not for any apparent reason, just random feelings passing through him. One day, he began briefly moving his eyes toward me. I teared up and stood quickly. He startled as I bumped a table in my haste to hug him.

Finally, on a toasty hot morning, Matthew fully regained consciousness. The sun seemed to shine in the windowless room. It felt like weeks, but it had been only a matter of days. Doctor Masood had indicated complete pleasure when he gave Matthew a thorough going over. I managed to maintain some dignity; however, I wept with happiness, relief. *How would I have ever managed a life without Matthew?*

The massive list of what I would've missed if Matthew hadn't recovered reverberated through my head all night as I sat with him, sat with him sleeping, me blubbering in waves, knowing he wasn't awake to hear me.

I'd been missing the real Matthew for several years: The love from his eyes as he gazed at me; sensation of family history; of belonging right down to our souls to each other; the friendship; the laughter; the connection; his smile making me smile; me making him smile; the continuity of our relationship and marriage; sitting beside him, knowing the man I married was aware and sitting with me; holding hands; the feel of him… My God, the *feel* of HIM.

—∞—

Now I felt the relief that Matthew was going to be all right, that he'd been saved! However, that relief brought with it other feelings.

I realized I was exasperated. Didn't I have the right to feel outraged that he could have done all of this?

I had unanswered questions for a man who had promised to honour me. That meant not lying, not withholding information that would lead to his attempting suicide. *Who was this man?*

He had been an aggressive and angry husband for two years. I hadn't been treated with the care and love that I had been accustomed to. A verbally abusive stranger had taken my husband's place. What would he be like when he was fully recovered? His abusive behaviour had been unacceptable, and I would not stand for it any longer.

I must put my own life back together. We both needed to change, to come together with common goals in our marriage. *And if not? What will my plan be if we can't become the couple that I expect us to be? Will I leave him behind and go on with a life on my own?* I forcibly put that idea out of my head for now. For now, I had a husband who appeared to be recovered from his unsuccessful suicide attempt. For now, my other emotions must be set aside, and my focus on what might happen would need to wait. *I'm ecstatic, relieved, thankful he's alive. My Matthew is alive.*

With that in my mind, I made a mental promise to keep all these feelings to myself, to put on a good front to our family and what friends we had left – as I had done for these past tumultuous years. I needed to maintain a discrete attitude until I could calm down. Yes, I was ecstatic my husband was alive, but I was also infuriated that he could have so callously taken himself away from me, from our children – without having answers to questions as to what had transpired for him to make that messed-up choice of suicide.

He was awake and improving. Our general practitioner, Dr. Masood, kept us all abreast of the situation, good and bad with daily briefings. Mostly his comments were in passing as he attended to his various patients, but he answered our questions with his full attention. At the awake times, Matthew had followed me with those watchful blue eyes. The first day of improvement, he had tears coming from the corner of each eye. When he could communicate verbally, he began with some confusion, was restless and said "I'm tired" repeatedly. He slept a lot, which the nurses indicated was good, that it meant he was healing.

As he became more aware, Matthew wanted to visit with each of us. Travis and Ashley had been by the evening before, coming after their school and workday. Matthew had asked about them again.

"They'll be back on the weekend – three more days – Friday night."

My mom and dad came in every day, worried and consoling, wearing poker faces so as not to upset me, keeping their visits with Matthew short, but being there for me. I needed them.

Aaron visited but relayed he didn't want to intrude on family. He looked despondent, his usual 6'2" height diminished, his broad shoulders slumped. *He's as overwhelmed as I am.*

At a time when I was alone with them, Aaron bent his head of black hair forward, seemingly embarrassed and said, "I didn't do enough to stop this."

"Nonsense," I said fiercely as I put my hand on his arm, making him look at me. "You were our rock."

Matthew's brother, Neil, had been subdued – totally out of character – and I think this threw Matthew off a little.

"You're quiet. Are you ill?" asked Matthew, propped up on two pillows, the head of the hospital bed at lounging height.

At that comment, Neil's personality peeked through, "No, you ass!! I'm fine. You were ill."

"Oh, yes. I guess I was. I'm better now." Taking a deep breath, he added, "I made the wrong choice." He looked very tired and weak. His glance settled on me. "What's the counsellor's name?"

"Dr. Gerstein-Kraus."

"When can I go home?"

"Your Life Counsellor and doctor both said it will still be a number of days. There'll be physical and occupational therapy for a few more days and counselling." I realized I was caressing my heart necklace.

"Oh, with that nice counsellor. What's her name?"
I repeated, "Dr. Gerstein-Kraus."
He appeared to realize he had been told this before, seemed momentarily humiliated. He didn't retain everything which seemed to irk him a little. Neil gave me an apprehensive look, but I gave him a slight nod. We'd been assured this would improve given time and rest.
"I like her. She listens, really listens. When she talks, she makes a lot of sense. Do you like her, Jenna?"
"For sure, Matthew. I like her a lot. We'll see her later this afternoon when you've had a little rest."
"Yeah, I'm tired now."
As he gave a slight cough, I now realized he hadn't coughed while unconscious. They must have given him something for that. *What? Can we have some?*
I gave him a long hug, happy he was doing well – happy that he was alive! I'd be seeing Dr. GK with Matthew at 4:00 p.m.
On the way out, Neil swung his blond head toward me, rolled his eyes and snorted, "Life Counsellor? What the hell? She's a psychiatrist!"

Palm Desert, California

MATTHEW'S JOURNAL

After my recovery, I understood that the answer to those veiled telephone accusations had to be uncovered – the crimes had to be solved, not hidden from. No amount of hiding or suicide would take the blame away from me.

George Alphonse, the Director of Human Resources at my former clinic, Smooth Image Surgery, had made implied accusations that I had taken documents from the clinic either before I left the clinic, or, he said, perhaps afterward I had returned and stolen them. I had, after all, neglected to return my key, and Smooth Image Surgery had not voided my entry code. Of course, any documentation taken from any company was bad, but this was personal medical information from a cosmetic surgery clinic regarding a high-profile person – a woman, a public 'figure' (no pun intended).

I've chosen to write as a means to comprehend what precipitated my actions. My Life Counsellor suggested writing a Journal, something productive. I'll call the victim Tootsie in this Journal, so her identity remains anonymous from my standpoint at least. That stolen file outlined the breast augmentation, her abdominoplasties or tummy tucks, eyelid surgeries, botox facial injections. The company should have been called "You Want It, We Got It". Smooth Image Surgery was a classier name, I had to admit.

The problem for Tootsie probably arose because she had stated emphatically her husband didn't wish her to have the surgery. She confided that her 'companion' had encouraged all these procedures, his being ten years her junior, a hunk also in a high-profile position and also a client. What a pair! They were both frantic that her husband must not find out, that absolutely nothing could go public.

I'm edging toward making it into a book – it would be about everything I'd gone through. Maybe it would help someone else understand, encourage them not to do what I had attempted to do. I can't elicit all my emotions that triggered my suicide attempt. Jenna seems so happy, and I don't think I can discuss those reasons with her. I'm still very confused about how I feel. How the heck do I really feel? Some unsettling thoughts have been popping into my mind. I must get them to stop.

I'm also sidetracked thinking I should write a second book about inconsistencies and how people pretend something that isn't true – something about being a Life Counsellor, but really a psychiatrist. Maybe after this one about how mixed up a life can be and someone in the wrong frame of mind thinks ending that life is the right decision.

So, here I am writing about that night. I'd received the call from George Alphonse. Then when I hung up, Aaron called to warn me he had heard at work I was having a finger pointed at me and George would be calling to 'suss' me out. Aaron's call was too late, but it made little difference. The stage was set that I had stolen a client file from work.

Aaron advised the scuttlebutt reported the client (Tootsie) had been blackmailed for several months by whomever possessed her file! This was a catastrophe for the entire company, now particularly for me with possible charges to be laid. Why hadn't I returned that damn key? Why had my code not been withdrawn by staff? Why had the theft come to light now?

The telephone call from George Alphonse wasn't the first communication from him. The first contact from George had been texts three days before that I had not realized were a finger pointed at me. I thought they were getting in touch with everyone.

"Matthew, there has been a problem here at
  Smooth Image Surgery. A file is missing from the

clinic. Do you have any knowledge of who may have taken it?"

My immediate response had been:

"Absolutely no knowledge!"

George:

"This is just an initial inquiry as we make our way through this investigation. Please keep this quiet for now."

So, I'd called my father. I needed an outside opinion. I couldn't tell Jenna. She would worry too much. I didn't want all the chatter with her the reveal of the clinic theft would entail. My dad would know what to do. Thankfully, my mother was at Neil's that afternoon because she wouldn't have been helpful.

Dad said definitively, "Get legal advice!"

Fifteen minutes later, I called Jenna's lawyer friend, Cynthia Magee, at her law firm "Pemberton, Wu & Magee Law" as a precaution. She said if I wasn't going to confide in Jenna, she would wash her hands of it until I told Jenna. That was when she had me 'hold', came back on the line and told me she was putting me through to John Wu, one of the senior partners at her firm. I'd met him socially a few times. He took down the particulars, and we arranged an appointment – the earliest he had was four days away. At that point I didn't realize how fast it all would escalate.

At 8:30 a.m. two days before my drastic decision, I'd received from George:

"The client has been in again this morning, waiting for me when I arrived. She wants to press charges against us, but not wanting it to go public. Come into the office. Return the key. Your code has been voided. I'll meet you at reception at 10:00."

I returned my key, but there was no affability in George's face, no emotion other than contempt for me. No smooth-talking

George. That was quite a blow after all we had been through, family get togethers, my working there for almost two dozen years. The slimy, greasy facade I'd noticed once he began berating my performance was glaringly evident, his amber eyes flickering over me in distaste before he dismissed me.

Then that debilitating conversation with George the night I took the pills, those damn pills I should never have stashed away. Why did I quit taking the pills as prescribed weeks earlier? It's so clear now. That night, I simply shut down. I couldn't handle it. Aaron's call was that proverbial last straw, advising there had been blackmail, and the clinic had judged I was the likely culprit. My back and my spirit were broken.

When I went up to bed that night well before I made the decision to terminate my life. I'd said to Jenna, "Tell the kids I love them." Then I'd given her a good robust hug and left abruptly. I had to leave her abruptly because I didn't deserve her.

Pacing around and around the house after Jenna was asleep, I thought fiercely about everything happening. My mind kept spinning. "What's going on? My life is falling apart." I berated myself, clarifying that my life had already fallen apart. Then: "I can't continue with all of this hanging over my head. I don't want to deal with my depression or my anger any longer. How many blows can I take before I crumble?"

My choice at that time was to take the pills I'd been saving.

Importantly, now that I was home and truly recovering from my attempted suicide debacle, my current resolution was to find out who had done this thing and to exonerate myself.

I wondered why the police hadn't already been at my home since I was home from the hospital. Who could have done all that and was now framing me? George Alphonse for one! Or anyone in accounting or administration – Aaron!

Not Aaron. No, I shook my head. Where did that thought come from? Of course, not Aaron.

Palm Desert, California

17

Winter

That Is So Selfish

❖ JENNA ❖

THE PSYCHIATRIST, DR. GERSTEIN-KRAUS, at the hospital had been able to induce Matthew to talk and to reveal what his thought processes had been. He had totally rejected intervention previously, but he appeared to trust this doctor, being honest with her. I believe Matthew had scared himself and was able to see what had been happening. She wasn't in fact called a psychiatrist. She is a Life Counsellor, and Matthew seemed taken with her methods.

She explained, "Psychiatrist is too harsh a word. It triggers preconceptions and prejudices among my patients."

I studied her to make my own assessment, noting her manner toward Matthew, deep blue compassionate eyes, her mouse-brown hair down to her shoulders, swept back with a barrette holding it in place. As the appointment went on, I was impressed.

She did more talking than Matthew the first two sessions; however, as he eased into the rhythm of sharing his innermost thoughts, I'd found reasons to be relieved he knew, knew deep inside himself that he wouldn't ever attempt that again. We'd been briefed in full how parasuicide was a gesture, but Matthew had received the same intensive intervention as a suicide attempt.

His apologies were profuse and heartfelt. He cried as he re-lived his emotions before the attempted suicide. We were instructed to call it a 'medical incident'.

My priority was Matthew. The School District made it easy for me to take the time off to be home for Matthew and care for him full time. I had a four-week period where I could be with Matthew at the hospital, at his Life Counselling sessions and, then, at home with him.

With my parents being at the Palm Estates RV Resort, I had their help to find a cleaning lady and in-home nursing care. Mom was ideal at helping me vet the in-home nursing care for Matthew since she had been a nurses' aid. I felt strongly that Amelia, the nursing student, should be here so Matthew was not alone with his thoughts for too long. I could see the current change from how he had been for those years prior to his final desperate breakdown and how he appeared now – present and aware.

But would he revert to chastising me, shattering my self esteem once we were alone at home? Should I confide in Dr. GK about Matthew and what I had grown to view as a personality disorder – prior to this depression? Could she help us to ensure that doesn't reoccur? To help me cope.

Mom's thorough cleaning lady, Juanita, became our once-a-week cleaner. Juanita loved the steady employment, particularly in the off-season when the snowbirds had left.

Ashley was at Uni, so she came on weekends to spend time with her father. Travis took several days off to help out when I went back to my teaching job.

—∞—

One morning when Travis and Ashley were with me in the kitchen, Ashley whispered to me, "How could Dad have done that?"

A lone fly had come in through the open doorway, buzzing around as though waiting for my response. I pondered my choices for an answer.

"Darling, I don't have an answer for you, but we have lived a whole lot longer than you. Your day-to-day emotions can't be the same emotions as people our age—."

Travis jumped in, "Mom! What're you talkin' about?"

"Well, we have baggage we don't even think about. I've watched your dad go from his real self to the self-destructive man that tried to kill himself. Everything fell apart for him in his mind. He felt there was nothing left for him to give us, his parents, his buddies."

Travis blurted out, "That's so selfish!"

Every nerve ending in my body turned ice cold, but I held my retort back to say, "I agree with you both, but the person who tried to kill himself was a shell of your father. I now have an understanding of what his mind had to cope with."

I watched, nervously, as Travis turned toward the patio door. The door was open a foot, but I doubted he heard the birds chirping. *He doesn't seem to be aware that Ashley and I are still in the room. What is he visualizing?*

Still facing the outside, Travis queried, "What if it's in our genes? What if I can't hack not knowin' what I want outta life, get more disgruntled with my current job situation? What if her teaching degree becomes too difficult for Ashley, and she short circuits?"

He turned toward me as I said, "Don't even think that. We'll recognize the signs now, and we won't ever, ever let there be something we neglect to talk through."

Travis said to me, "I feel bad for you. You're as broken as we are, probably 100 times more cuz you lived through it day-by-day. We caught glimpses of it on weekends and holidays."

Suddenly, I had another brainwave, "I think you and Ashley should see your dad's Life Counsellor…"

"Why would we do that?" Travis queried, leaning on the counter.

"No, don't argue. You just said something. We all must acknowledge what happened and to find out the triggers." Observing them glance toward each other in scepticism, I added, "To have a platform to build the rest of our lives on. It wouldn't hurt to see her."

Ashley's objection was, "She has her practice here. We're not driving all this way."

"She doesn't live in the Valley. She practices in Riverside Monday and Tuesday each week."

Peering at me sideways, Ashley responded, "Mom, Travis and I will discuss this. It would be best if we could go together."

That hadn't occurred to me. "Set up your appointment and ask what Dr. Gerstein-Kraus thinks about you coming in together." I simply did what Moms do. I grabbed them both, hanging on with all my heart as I noticed the wayward fly retreat back outside.

I felt their pain. I had many thoughts of Matthew's mental state, his selfishness and heartlessness of taking his own life and leaving us all to cope with the aftermath – had he been successful. This was bad enough – trying to piece together the puzzles of what his decision had meant.

"We all must stand behind your Dad, whether you're in agreement with his actions or not. Love your father, not his actions." *And, boy, did I have to tell myself the same thing. Over and over!*

As my two children came over to me again, leaned in, I cried tears of relief and love for them. I'd stressed, worrying about how they would feel when the hospital stay was over, pondering when we'd believe the danger of Matthew repeating his suicide attempt was less. The nursing student I'd hired would also keep an eye on Matthew. I still had a job to go to. Even though I'd been given four weeks off, I was now back at work for the remainder of the school year.

Since I didn't want to make a mistake, Amelia, the nursing student's major was in Psychiatric Nursing.

For myself, I wanted to be certain everything would be fine. Wondering about Matthew's emotional state had been one concern. However, I had his legal woes to be apprehensive about as well. We hadn't had news from John Wu of any activity by *Smooth Image Surgery*. No police involvement as yet. When would their office take steps to regain the file? When would the police come for Matthew? What evidence did they have?

Assuming we'd hear of any activity from John Wu first, that the clinic's lawyers would advise John, we were semi-confident we'd know what was going to happen a few hours in advance. Would that give us a chance to prepare ourselves, mentally and emotionally?

My feelings went up and down like a roller coaster – one moment secure all would be well – the next moment like a child in a storm. *How resilient were we?*

Matthew had been holding up, but I caught him staring out the window often. I asked him the last time why he did that, and he hesitantly whispered, "I'm checking for an officer with handcuffs." We exchanged looks of concern as I reached to rub his shoulder and left my hand lingering there.

Palm Desert, California

MATTHEW'S JOURNAL

My Life Counsellor told me in the hospital, "It's not unheard of to have an out-of-body experience upon a 'medical incident' like yours." Medical incident indeed! I bloody well attempted to kill myself, but let's sugar coat it to make it more palatable. So, we all call it a medical incident.

She sugar coated her degree, knocking it from Psychiatrist to Life Counsellor. My discharge paper from the hospital clearly indicates I must see a Psychiatrist twice a week and the Psychiatrist will decide when once a week or twice a month will be sufficient. Maybe my CPA degree and a couple of other initials behind my name would cause people to feel "more comfortable" if I called myself a Bookkeeper.

The Certificates on her wall state she graduated With Honours from UCLA University of California, Los Angeles with a doctorate in psychiatry, undergraduate degree in pre-med! I believe that is 12 years of education to become a Life Counsellor which is what the engraved sign on her office door says.

In spite of my initial annoyance with the job title, I'd found myself drawn to her. She was caring and good at bringing my reasoning forward. I felt confident and relaxed in her presence. Jenna came to some of the appointments, and Jenna has major trust in Dr. Gerstein-Kraus, Life Counsellor!

After opening up my feelings and discussing what had transpired – my drinking, the pills, I realized my voice was quiet, so quiet as though I was speaking in a miniature room, not an office. I also realized the reason was that I was embarrassed. Jenna had leaned forward, attempting to catch my words. I hadn't wanted her to hear my words – Maybe I could've kept her from knowing simply by speaking so only Dr. Gerstein-Kraus could hear my simplistic reasons. Life was never that simple. Jenna had to know, had to hear what I had concealed from her. I raised my volume, enough for the basis of my decision to be known to Jenna.

The look of sorrow, guilt and then helplessness on Jenna's face had me turn away for a few moments. Jenna gave me those few moments, and then reached for my hand, moved her hand to rest on my shoulder. I twisted back around to meet her eyes, apology written in mine, forgiveness in hers. Together we looked again toward Dr. Gerstein-Kraus.

Dr. Gerstein-Kraus regarded the notes she'd been taking, silent, possibly pondering how she wanted to approach my effort at justification.

Very emphatically, I'd reiterated, "I'm sorry I did this. I… I didn't think—"

Shaking her head, and putting out a hand signalling me to wait, she then spoke of the difference between a suicide attempt and a parasuicide. Carefully, she explained my parasuicide was a gesture, different from a "true attempt". Her professional opinion was I had no clear intent or expectation of death –or that I could have died. My parasuicide was to be taken seriously, and I was receiving the same intensive intervention as an unequivocal suicide attempt.

"You were lucky. You were both lucky that morning." As she paused and took a breath, she resumed, "Matthew, you've been put on an atypical antidepressant with less side effects. This should cause no tremors, sleep disorder or nausea. Maybe feeling drowsy, dizzy." She'd studied me, obviously appraising my response, "Have you had any of these effects over the past couple of days?"

At the shake of my head, her analysis turned to what she hoped would happen over the course of her appointments with me.

Ending with an order, "And drinking must only be an occasional glass – one glass!"

I looked over at Jenna and repeated, "No problem. One glass."

I didn't let on to Dr. GK or Jenna that I'd had momentary thoughts of 'Why couldn't I kill myself properly?' mingled a minute later with thoughts that I was happy to be alive. I definitely had times of irrational apprehension about the future, and maybe I should have ended it all while I could. They were momentary thoughts, concerning. Which were my real feelings?

Palm Desert, California

18

Winter

Girls' Night Out

❖ JENNA ❖

"You have a white mustache, Cynthia." Milena chuckled at her revelation to her friend. My best friends were a pair of teenagers when they got together. Boisterous insults were the norm.

"Now you tell me! That hunk in the mystery book aisle gave me the once over. I was flattered. Now, I know he was just wondering what hole I had crawled out of. Thanks a lot."

Cynthia shook her blunt cut blonde hair vigorously to get it out of the way while pressing her lips into her T-shirt to blot the icing from her lips.

"Here, you moron. Take this Kleenex," Milena laughed. "Gosh, for a respectable lawyer, you could learn a thing or two – carry a tissue!"

"Yeah, yeah. You have a drop of icing on your shirt, right over your left boob."

Milena screeched! Then she surveyed herself. "I do not! Darn you! What a child you are."

"Yeah, but it was worth your wrath for that moment of panic on your face," countered Cynthia.

While the two of them faced off, grinning and continued to insult each other, my mind wandered to our standing arrangement to get together for a Girls' Night Out at least once every two months. Sure, there were constant texts, telephone calls and an event with two of us; however, the three of us needed to get together to 'let our hair down' once in awhile.

During the winter season, we loved going to the tribute band concerts in downtown Palm Springs just off Museum Drive and Belardo. Either with these two or with Matthew, I've seen tributes to Madonna, Elton John, Tina Turner, Fleetwood Mac and Creedence Clearwater Revival.

Milena, chin-length curly red hair undulating with the breeze, meteorite-coloured oval eyes flashing pure frustration, brought me back to the present, as she said gruffly, "I am ticked off we missed the tributes for Freddie Mercury and Bon Jovi."

I responded with, "Yeah, I'm disappointed as well. That would've been momentous. It's the ideal outdoor venue!"

Earlier in the winter, we had been to the Fantasy Springs venue to see *Celtic Woman*. Aaron had come to visit Matthew that evening ostensibly to watch hockey. However, it was actually so that I felt more comfortable going out. Amelia, the nurse I had hired, was not part of my back-up plan any longer. She had been a Godsend for the weeks she'd been available to help me.

"That Irish music sounded so good," offered Milena.

Cynthia enthusiastically answered, "You bet! That bagpiper really set the tone for the night, and the orchestra. Wow!"

"Oh my gosh, the fiddler. She sprang around like a leprechaun, dancing and ducking."

"Who's up for a drink at the casino?" I asked, uncertain if I really wanted to be out later than this, but knowing Aaron remained visiting with Matthew.

"Oh, you go girl," Milena came out with. "I am in." And we did.

—∞—

The day after Matthew came home from the hospital, I'd called Cynthia, and told her how I felt about her intrusiveness after Matthew's parasuicide attempt. I didn't mince words, and she apologized for her over zealousness. As best friends do, we made up. She brought Matthew and I chocolates and his favourite kind of toffee two days later, ducking her head a little to show her remorse and then winked at me as she turned her head toward me. The brat.

Later that week, I texted her to ask if she and I could have a coffee downtown. It was a moderately hot winter day, high 80s – no Santa Ana winds gusting.

> If you're free, meet for coffee? I'm
> out. Could use some company.

> Where are you? Happens
> I'm low on caffeine.

> Leaving PS Gift Shop.

> Starbucks, corner of Tahquitz?

> Deal – 15 minutes.

That was the day I'd confided in Cynthia. It hadn't been easy. While we sat in the shade of the awning, over the course of 90 minutes, I slowly gave into the need to tell her about our issues surrounding Matthew's depression and illness. As I glanced across North Palm Canyon Drive, I felt certain she must have picked up signals of the unease in our household, and even though I hadn't revealed anything in words prior to this, Cynthia knew what Matthew's horrifying outcome had been.

As I spoke, I felt sweat pool above the collar of my "I'll Have Mine With Sugar" T-shirt. Fanning myself with a rolled-up napkin and grabbing another gulp of Mango Dragonfruit Lemonade (having already consumed a cup of Espresso Roast), I said, "And then he told me he'd saved his pills. I was wrecked! Completely wrecked he could do that to us, to me."

Cynthia grabbed my hand again with both her hands, squeezing, rubbing my knuckles. She held my hand off and on most of the 90 minutes.

"I understand you couldn't make yourself confide in me. I just want to say I would've been there for you."

I became distracted by a passer-by wearing huge Elton John sunglasses, his hair dyed a bright blue. He headed toward the huge red PS (heart) U decoration along Tahquitz, stopped and took a selfie of himself. I then continued, "It would've been a sign of weakness. No, more than that. It would've meant I wasn't doing something right. I should've been able to change what Matthew was going through."

Sipping her second Costa Rica Narango, she said, "I should've confronted you and made you tell me. I saw you agonising, suffering. I tried to keep you occupied, wanting to ask, but I couldn't demand to know."

"I wouldn't, couldn't let you in. Families are complicated, lots of secrets kept inside the home." I looked inside Starbucks loving the orange, green, blue and yellow chairs throughout the inside area. The wind had begun picking up. It was time to head home.

Cynthia nodded assent, "As a lawyer, I know something about secrets kept inside homes." She gave me an encouraging gaze. I felt she had sensed more of our secrets and hoped I would continue. However, my own desire to protect Matthew and my own sense of self worth didn't permit my disclosure. *I'm too ashamed to tell her.*

We walked our separate ways to our cars, but not before Cynthia grabbed me into a full embrace, and said, "I love you, you know."

"I know, and I do you, too."

In the heat of the 85-degree day, I walked on and sat down for a few minutes on the bench beside the life-size iron Lucy. Lucille Ball, the famous actress from *I Love Lucy*, sat beside me on that iron bench, one iron leg crossed over the other, her left arm flung across the back of the iron bench. I tucked myself in there, my head down, thinking. *It'll all turn out, right Lucy? You and Desi didn't make a go of it, but you carried on. Matthew and I can make it work or we can carry on. Right?*

Straightening myself from the position I'd been sitting in, I walked down North Palm Canyon, toward my car. I passed the old Plaza Theatre. *I've loved that place, and the Fabulous Follies. It was a tribute to Palm Springs.* I muttered out loud, "I hope the fundraising works. I'm going to donate a little money today."

Now that our lives had come to a head with Matthew's suicide attempt, it felt good to confide in my friend. I'd have to work up the needed inner resources to share our story with Milena. *Absolutely unfair to keep her out of my confidence.*

Palm Desert, California

MATTHEW'S JOURNAL

At first, theft of the file was kept secret within the Human Resources Department. Then Aaron reported more clinic employees had become aware, causing some apprehension among staff. I'm worried about what my fate would be since I'm under suspicion. I've heard zippo more. Surely this can't hang on for months.

After I'd contacted a lawyer, I felt I had some insulation around me, meaning he would be able to advise me if anything happened. John had scoped out the situation with George Alphonse, but reported back they were doing the investigation "in house". That was why I felt Smooth Image Surgery was attempting to keep things under wraps so that there was no bad publicity for the plastic surgery company.

John Wu had come to the hospital near my discharge date and met with Jenna and me. Cynthia loomed in the background, asking pertinent questions and taking notes. We agreed with Cynthia to stay with John Wu because he was a renowned criminal lawyer. John advised we not wait for the pseudo investigation Smooth Image Surgery was doing. He felt they may have been trying to whitewash it, so it didn't become public. Or at least to keep it from the public for as long as they could. This would not repair my reputation. He recommended his firm hire a private investigator, and we agreed.

Then he instructed Jenna and me in ways to protect our accounts and reputation.

I certainly noticed his attire, along with his professionalism. He oozed authority. His snake-embossed dress shoes would have given me the heebie-jeebies years ago because of the cost.

And his comments had the same effect. "Be aware that any police investigators can freeze your access to bank accounts or other assets as evidence in this investigation. My firm will help maintain access to your assets." Jenna brought out her notebook, writing down the points John was making.

"Secondly, both of you, maintain your silence as much as possible. You are guaranteed the right to remain silent before and after arrest. If your arrest happens, it is imperative you do not answer questions without Cynthia or I present."

Another note went into the notebook. Jenna squirmed and asked, "If a friend asks us a question relating to this, how do we answer?"

John lifted his head and gave her a sharp glare. "Do you want that person to be able to testify in Court what you said to them? Simply say that while the theft is being investigated, you are under instructions from your lawyer to refrain from answering even though they're a best friend."

Shifting in his seat and then standing abruptly, John said in a commanding voice, "Third point, do not respond to press inquiries."

"Oh, we wouldn't talk to reporters," I announced.

"You think you wouldn't, but if they approach you with a microphone and a camera, you may be inclined to stammer some defense out. Reply 'I have no comment' every single time."

On it went. John discussed interview questions and again advised no police interviews unless he or Cynthia was present. John finished with, "None of this may come to fruition. It may only be investigated within that business. I needed to make you both aware of the possibilities. The end result must be that they charge the real criminal, or you will always be suspected of this crime."

When John had left, Jenna and I discussed those possibilities. Who else could've stolen the information on Tootsie? There were a dozen people who could've accomplished this. Unfortunately,

I was a good suspect. Allegedly (confirmed by the hospital stay and psychiatrist report) mentally unbalanced, without a job so they could believe I needed the funds and angry at my boss for any variety of reasons. Did I have a grudge against Tootsie? Hell no but let that not stand in the way of quick and quiet justice. It didn't matter if I got burned. I was no longer an employee and would make the perfect scapegoat for whomever had done this. Who the hell had done it? Again, an unsubstantiated thought – Aaron? Why did I have that thought? He was my best bud.

―⚏―

I'd called Aaron on my cell while still in the hospital.
"What was on the security cameras?"
"I've been pondering how to get these. I'll find out, covertly."
"Covertly?"
"I don't want to raise suspicions. Don't worry, buddy. I'll get back to you soon."
In the meantime, I'd been on-line on my cellphone, scoping security cameras. I skimmed over some information for Jenna.
"Jamming: This tactic works on cameras receiving wireless signals at a set frequency – Overpower the set frequency with a more powerful signal at the same frequency."
And listen to this:
"A powerful LED flashlight can disable a security camera without ever requiring the crook to be on camera. If someone is out to conduct a bit of illegal business during daylight hours, they can achieve much the same result with a simple laser."
Jenna burst out with, "Oh for God's sake ...! That's too damn easy. Anyone could do that. Do we know what's on the cameras?"
My cell had dinged as if on cue. I brought up Aaron's text.
"Can't talk. At work. Bobbi in Security told me she checked for George all days prior to theft being discovered. Nothing except a quick light, then a shadow at the beginning of the taping one evening. Maybe when it happened. Chat later."

Was Aaron being straight with me? I couldn't tell Jenna the thoughts that regurgitated through my head, thoughts becoming all too familiar.

Aaron is the biker.

Aaron the friend my dad didn't want to hang around my brother and me.

Aaron said what my dad didn't know wouldn't hurt me.

Aaron first bought the dope during university.

Aaron was always the bad boy.

Aaron said we should pick up chicks, pretend we were older.

Aaron when he saw Jenna at the hotel said, "She's hot."

It's Aaron I shouldn't leave alone with my wife.

Could the bad boy have set me up?

Palm Desert, California

19

Early Spring

Life In Pictures

❖ JENNA ❖

"He was dramatic, even as a three-year old," I said as Matthew sat down beside me with several old photo albums he'd dragged off the shelves.

I continued, "Do you remember when we brought Ashley home from the hospital, Travis fell down on the floor yelling, 'Put her back where you got her from!' Quite a display."

Matthew chuckled and said, "Then he fell in love with his sister and wanted to be with her almost all day, every day."

"Here he is with Ashley propped precariously on his knee. He had his arm properly supporting her. Just as you took the photograph, he raised his hand to wave at the camera. I rescued her." I smiled and frowned at the same time.

Matthew, with a dazzling smile that reached his eyes, simply asserted, "Brothers!"

Sitting side by side, Matthew and I gazed at photographs linking our histories to each other and to our families.

Grabbing an album from years ago, I smirked and said, "Puddletown. That's what you called Portland when I came to visit you. And I'm still stunned you proposed to me at *Nicks*, brought out the ring, went down on one knee."

I held a photograph taken on a visit prior to the proposal evening, the one that perfectly depicted *Nick's Famous Coney Island*, a restaurant described as the most iconic hot dog bar.

"We had its famous chili-and-onion-smothered franks," said Matthew. "I bet I still had sauce on my face when I asked you to spend the rest of your life with me."

"Yeah, absolutely! For a single moment I imagined you with sauce on your cheek when the minister asked, 'Do you take this man…, I thought, I will – hot dog sauce and all.'"

Matthew reached for me, and I went into his arms, snuggling into his chest – where I belonged. We both sighed at the same time.

"Okay," while flipping to another album page, I said, "Here are a couple of photographs of us with both Aaron and Neil. They're taken inside the *Cadillac Café*."

Matthew had a smile as enigmatic as I'd ever seen him. I said, "What are you contemplating?"

"We used to try to climb into that pink '61 Caddy before they threw us out. Aaron said it would be a great caper. The owners still let us back in after that."

I added reflectively, "Pink flashing CADILLAC sign, vintage pink Cadillac car inside, walls a pink shade of paint, accented by teak wood." Sensing a niggling for a moment, I tilted my head attempting to bring it forward. "Oh, when you were in the hospital, I had a dream that our wedding was all in pink!"

"Well, that would have been intriguing. Don't you dislike pink?"

Emphatically, "Yes! Everything in my dream seemed so bizarre!" I went on to explain the entire dream.

"Phenomenal! That was one crazy dream."

Glancing at another photo, "We all look so young. And innocent. And happy. See those smiles."

I unsuccessfully attempted to ignore the sensation as my tummy rumbled. I began ruminating about food, "Back then my favourite was the Original Cadillac Burger – bacon, cheese, lettuce, tomato on sourdough." Here I paused, scratching my head, trying to conjure up the other ingredients.

"Mustard sauce and onion marmalade," charged in Matthew, happy with his recall. "Yum."

I lamented, "I'm hungry recalling those restaurants. Let's have hot dogs for lunch. BBQ or the Air Fryer?"

"Air fryer. I'll set it up. Do we have anything for salad?"

"Yep. Want to continue with photo albums after lunch?"

"Yeah, a phenomenal trip down memory lane."

"Let's eat," I said hoping no more episodes of him yelling what he used to yell to me, "What are you doing? Mine isn't ready yet, and you have to wait." I'd always obediently put my fork down and waited for him while my dish went cold. I felt a fool now for always thinking it had been my fault. *Time to set standards of behaviour. I can stand up for myself.*

Matthew seemed to be his old self now. Even though I relished the current loving feelings I perceived radiating from him, I held back a little of myself. I needed the insulation until I knew, knew for certain I wasn't letting my guard down too early. I had let him in too many times and then my psyche had been ravaged again.

I had hated Matthew for at least that last year of his Diablo behaviour. It sounds awful even to my ears, but these are ears that had heard swearing, insults, unkind descriptions of me from Diablo. I had asked him several times if he thought himself superior to me because he obviously thought he could judge me and tell me what to do, when to do it. Of course, I didn't ever get a sensible response from him when he was that devil man. The insults and swearing would just rise to another level.

There were so many times I wanted to leave him. When I originally had thought that it was my fault and that I simply needed to figure out how to get him to love me more, I would just leave for a little while – go to my mother and father's resort when they were in town, call Cynthia or Milena on my cellphone while sitting in my vehicle having run away from the verbal abuse – never telling them I wasn't ensconced comfortably in an armchair in my own living room.

My mom and dad didn't ever seem to need any explanation from me when I showed up, unannounced. I know darn well Mom would scrutinize me occasionally – those times when I probably looked a little more dishevelled than my normal look. But she didn't say anything – no words of comfort. Quite frankly, after the time that my mom disregarded my attempt to engage her in my marital problems, I didn't want to be brushed off again. So, I played the game of having just decided to drop in.

Where will I go? I would ask myself. I wasn't going to move to LA to burden Ashley or Travis with my plight. No point in involving them. I still wanted them to respect Matthew. *Had both of them heard their dad insulting and yelling at me?*

Once I'd analyzed all the facts and watched Diablo Matthew in action for many months, I realized that it wasn't my fault, had never been my fault. My respect for Matthew had dwindled to nil. I felt that I simply existed around him. I played the part of a content wife to him to avoid sudden conflict. Maybe I played the part of a puppy just waiting for the times that Matthew was himself, waiting for a bone, a shred of love, a kind word or two.

Shameful for me to admit was how I felt on at least one occasion when Matthew was having a very traumatic day. I'd felt a momentary feeling of pleasure at his discomfort. *'Yes, you deserve this!'* There was a moment of vindication for me after the way he had treated me for those years.

—⋙—

As it turned out, we didn't get back to the photo albums for awhile. There were more albums to go through, but the rest of our photo lives were on our computers, divided into yearly directories. Some I had printed out, but computers had replaced proper photo albums.

The reason we didn't get to more old photos was that after lunch that day, Matthew brought up the subject of our front yard. He'd been reflecting on a photograph he'd taken the week before and wondered if we shouldn't be putting in more desertscape.

"Unusually, there's been rain this year. Didn't you have ideas last year when I wasn't sharing your enthusiasm?"

"I have some sketches I set aside, somewhere." I went into our little study off the living room. After scrounging around, I brought out some drawings, wrinkled, dog-eared. "This is what I saved."

Picking up our plates and putting them on the counter, Matthew had sat down again and scooted his chair closer to mine and kissed me on the cheek. He slid the sketches closer to himself, touched on the plants I had listed at the edge of the drawing. I loved the interest he now showed. I sighed inwardly, excited we were discussing something for the future.

"What you've listed here are exactly the plants I'd love to see in our yard. We have the Soap Tree Yucca, Fencepost Cactus and Aloe succulents. Your sketches are so real looking."

"Thanks Matthew. Do you have time next weekend? Moller's is my favourite place to shop for plants."

"I do know that and, sure, we should go Saturday to decide. I admire this river rock pattern on your sketch. You've one labelled as pea stone. What's that?"

"They are tiny rocks, really tiny and durable. Hey, I also want to go out to Whitewater Rock and Supply. Next door, Kathy and Todd bought a lot of their rock and landscape materials there. Good prices."

"The water fountain feature they bought from Whitewater was less expensive than in town here as well. Absolutely, let's go there first."

… Palm Desert, California

20

Spring

Desertscaping

❖ JENNA ❖

ON A DAY OFF from teaching, Milena came to check out our desertscape. We were on a walkabout to check out other yards on our street. She was dressed in white split-hem capris with an equally out of place Nantucket Stripe blouse as she took in the chaos in our front yard.

"This is a mess! How can you stand it? I would've gone up to the mountains to get away from this racket and commotion!"

"You're spoiled," I replied – because she was. I wore cut-off denim capris and a bland Costco top, dressed for the occasion – working. Milena and her husband, Antonio Garcia, had gone away for weeks one summer when a landscaping crew had re-done their yard.

"Matthew gets enjoyment from doing this project. You know our cleaning lady, Juanita, right? Well, her husband, Mario, does landscaping, and he's letting Matthew help him. Glance at Matthew's face and tell me you would've gone away."

"God, you are right. Sorry, I was being pathetic. I am pathetic, aren't I?"

"For sure. You are. But you're pretty pathetic. Besides, with how physically fit you are, you could be over there working."

Milena snorted, "Not with these immaculate hands, and it would muss my hair."

"Yeah, your hair. Gorgeous hair."

"I was not fishing, but thanks. Not so weak yourself. We need to go to the gym again though. It has been two weeks."

"Absolutely."

When we got far enough away from the noise, Milena stopped and said, "He is doing well, is he not?"

Milena and I'd had a talk when I revealed everything to her. She also had known things were amiss. It appears everyone had an inkling of our family tragedy but didn't want to pry.

"I can tell you some days I still worry. But there's been no indication Matthew isn't in perfect mental condition. His cough from covid receded with time and great medication. That was a relief."

"I am concerned about *you*. You have been through too much."

"Matthew's taken over his old chores and is a partner in all our household tasks and he's pulling his weight with decisions. Those years definitely took a toll."

Milena came to stand beside me and took my hand. "It sounds as if it is all right now. Are you okay yourself? Now?"

"Yeah, I'm relieved, and I'm finally sleeping." I squeezed her hand. "I have the man I married back. Matthew still wants to see Dr. Gerstein-Krause. We call her Dr. GK. I go with him when he wants me to, but she wants to continue their sessions indefinitely. When I saw her last by myself..." At Milena's concerned glance, I continued, "No need to look concerned. This is spot-on therapy for me as well. As I was saying, when I last saw her, she was overjoyed at how Matthew was doing. She's helping me cope. It's worth every penny."

Matthew's 'medical incident' has saved our marriage, saved me having my own breakdown. I don't know how that worked – him changing.

Pointing to a house three down from us, I said, "There's a mix in our neighbourhood of front lawn and desertscape." I wanted to get away from the 'how are you' topic. I broached a topic she loved. Milena was a successful artist, as well as being the art teacher at our school. "I've seen your paintings of the mountains so many times and checked them out on your blog. I find them stunning for every season."

Her self confidence showed as she simply stated, "Oh, they are indeed. I have two more paintings on the go. One is of the Santa Rosa Mountains and the other depicts the Salton Sea from the tram."

"Oh my gosh! When was the last time I came to your studio? Can I come next weekend?"

She touched my arm and said, "You are always welcome."

We wandered off down the street, comparing other desertscape front yards. Most sidings were stucco in tans or sand, a couple of light sunny yellow. With our tan-coloured stucco and olive-green window frames, I needed some colour added by our plantings. The red tiled terracotta roof had been the basis to complement the main rock colour.

Milena observed, "Your new Bougainvillea and the Ocotillo will matchy match with your red rock."

"Exactly! I want to add Aloe Vera." Passing another yard, I pointed and said, "The mini-Lantana in this yard, for instance, bloom all season with assorted colours."

I could tell Milena was losing interest, and she verified that with, "Enough of this," she whined. "I feel parched. Race you back to your place. Take me inside and get me a drink."

As I did an exaggerated head-to-foot scan of my friend's body physique, I shook my head, "Pretty certain you'd win." Oh darn, and she was off! "Cheater. Wait, slow down."

After a glass of cold water, we sat down with a glass of Gewurztraminer wine each. "Here, check out my sketched plan. A flat rock pathway goes across the middle third of our front yard, first curved one direction for half the pathway and then the curve changes direction, like a smiley face and then a sad face."

"Nice idea. Your drawing is great. Then you kept that pattern for winding rock paths, dodging off like a river and three large boulders piled near your house, centered under your window."

"Rebel Red; Oro Verde; and Grey Rock." Pointing to another part of the sketch, "Mario's picking up the trees tomorrow."

"You are good at this, maybe another career after teaching?" She laughed and uttered a long "uh-huh, uh-huh" and a wiggle of her eyebrows. I chuckled at the notion of another career, disregarding it quickly. *Retired means not doing anything else.*

―∞―

It had been Matthew who got involved first. Crud, somehow, I had become interested in helping with the layout of the rocks, ensuring the river plan was exactly as I wanted it. My drawing incited me to want it to be perfect, so I had taken a stick and displayed in the sand-covered dirt where every pathway was to go.

"No, it needs to be more this way, similar to what I've indicated here."

Matthew drew another line. "I thought you wanted it this way."

Scratching out his line, I drew another one in the dust. "There, like this." I continued with all the rivers I wanted, drawing them in the dust. After the landscape fabric was laid down, Matthew called me out to again show where everything should go. I had taken a shovel full of each type of rock and put a little here and there showing where I wanted the "rivers" to go. Soon, I had put a lot of shovelfuls, then more, until I was satisfied the rock formations were going to go "according to plan."

"We're going out for supper." I announced. "I'm done! Done! Done!"

Matthew grinned sheepishly. "I already booked us into Spencer's at 6:30. It's spring break, but I got us a table."

Taking two steps toward him, I planted a kiss on his cheek. "Oh, hell," puffing my lips out with a "paaaaa". "You have dust all over your face."

"Not where you wiped it off with your lips."

"Look at us! We're a mess. Mario, we're done for the day. Have I made some progress for you or just confusion?"

Mario wore his black hair long, rugged in appearance. He peered around with those almost black eyes at the piles of rock demonstrating where the plans should continue. "It all look fine, boss. All good for today."

—⁂—

At 6:25, we left our Bronco in the trusty hands of the valet in front of Spencer's Restaurant. The two vehicles parked directly in front of the restaurant were a Rolls Royce and a Ferrari. At least our Bronco was freshly washed, as were we. Let me tell you, we arrived here a heck of a sight better than 90 minutes before. Thank goodness for a mudroom off the back door. Showered, hair washed and dried, clothes changed, we were new people. I straightened his tie. He tucked my sweater tag in, and we walked in the door.

Spencer's Restaurant was a welcome break after the day's hard work. As advertised, it was *The Best of Palm Springs*. We hadn't been here often, but it was our absolute favourite.

As the maître de guided us to our table, through the indoor seating, to the seating that let the outside in, I noted the tennis courts just outside the back window. We were inside, yet partially outside. We were surrounded by 12-foot-high glass panels, open to let in delicious warm air, not too hot. Just to the left of us was the outside seating, still totally protected from the wind.

"Will this be suitable seating?" I loved this place! I was in a giving mood. My tip would be generous.

Each teak table was covered in an elegant black tablecloth, tented cloth napkins holding the cutlery, the table center adorned with delicate flowers and a silver creamer set. Glancing around me, I observed the various groupings of people. Seated several feet from us was a younger couple. *Is this their first date or an anniversary? Have they come in from LA for the evening, perhaps taking in a theatre production after their supper?*

Having arrived before us, their meal was being served. While I watched, the man put up his arms, appearing awed at the aesthetically pleasing presentation of his meal. Studying my own menu, I could see he had ordered the Grilled Chicken and Gulf Shrimp Puttancesca, and his table mate had received the Wild Mushroom Risotto. Yum, my mouth watered! They were elegantly dressed. *Quite probably out for a special evening.*

Matthew touched my hand to draw my attention back to our own quest for a special evening.

I took on a self-confident expression as Matthew said, "Earth calling Jenna."

"Have you already decided what you are ordering?"

Just then the waiter arrived asking what we wished to drink.

Glancing for affirmation from Matthew, I replied, "We'll each have a glass of water, mine with no ice. Thanks."

Water appeared promptly on our table. Then Matthew ordered a glass each of Mumm "champagne".

"To celebrate our day, our lives, everything."

Smiling, I reasoned we had a lot to celebrate. One glass wouldn't hurt.

I requested a shared Chinese Style Kung Pao Calamari, House Salad and Honey Brine Center Cut Pork Chop. Matthew ordered the Double Breast of Chicken.

Our wait was short, and the meal being set in front of us smelled and looked heavenly. Sitting with our meal, we discussed the landscaping progress. We both felt it was moving along at a good speed. Mario had promised completion within two weeks. Lots happening in our world of optimism.

"Oh, my lord!" I spouted, "This has been the best meal ever!"

"That's what you said the last time we ate here. It must have been a few years ago."

"We came for a brunch with my mom and dad late last spring," I blanched a little after saying that. *He didn't like to be corrected. Damn it. No more bullshit. Bring it on!*

And then he gave me an amiable smile. "Yeah, I forgot. It was amazing then, too." Matthew said this with a little hesitancy as though he wasn't sure of his memory of the event.

His eyes were kind, not switching to vicious and accusatory, and he hadn't gotten out of control – didn't even look like he'd had to catch himself because we were in public. I wondered how long it would take for me to believe that my husband's personality had changed since his 'medical incident'. I needed to believe that it was possible. I needed to believe that I could relax around him.

Settling down, I willingly reached for my husband's hand, and he covered mine with his. I smiled and said, "Every time we come, we're impressed all over again. Twice a year would probably fit in with our budget."

Dessert was again shared – Housemade Tiramisu. After dessert, a waiter magically appeared, pleasantly inquiring, "Will there be anything else?"

"Yes, please. Marrakesh Mint tea for me."

Matthew nodded. "Make it two."

Promptly little silver pots arrived, steaming and delicious.

"I've got meatloaf, mashed potatoes, snap peas and asparagus in mind for supper tomorrow. No need to plan a meal away. I may come out to the yard again tomorrow to inspect and assist if necessary."

"Jenna, there's no 'may' about it. You'll be out."

"Yeah, I'll be out!"

Palm Desert, California

MATTHEW'S JOURNAL

At the session when I had relayed my meager reasoning why I attempted suicide, Jenna was devastated I had kept this from her. I know now it was just a cry for help, that I'd given up that night.

Afterward, back in my hospital room with the door closed, there were recriminations. Jenna looked so darn pretty with the breeze blowing through my open window, pushing fire-coloured hair across her face. Watching me, she looked pale and almost breakable, tearful.

I'd assured her she needn't be anxious, and I promised not to yell at her and attempted to explain that I'd changed. When I asked her to tell me what she was really thinking, she'd appeared skeptical and she still hesitated.

I said, "I feel calmer after this suicide mistake."

"Well..." Shifting her stance, fidgeting with her heart bracelet, she finally said, "Why wouldn't you tell me what was going on? You'd attempt to take your own life to hide from the truth, not fight for what was right?"

I'd bowed my head.

Still nervous, Jenna came out with the big question, "What about the pills you were saving?"

Hedging, I'd responded, "Dr. GK said that isn't unusual, that someone would stop their meds, that I didn't want to be dependent on drugs, and I was rebelling against the whole situation."

I was making excuses again. I comprehended the words were not adequate for anything she was feeling. She'd just stood there, gazing into my eyes, then looking away through the window at the palm trees that were leaning away during a strong Santa Ana wind. Was she leaning away from me in her mind? I needed to get her back with my next words.

I'd said, "I was wrong for so many reasons – for so many years."

She'd snapped her face toward me, looking hopefully and then away again, possibly contemplating how she felt. And then she touched my fingers with her fingers, moving her body close to mine and we stood there. Not a hug, but bodies just touching. Nervously, I took her hand, her grabbing my hand with her other hand, and peering up at me.

I let out a massive breath that I'd been holding for several moments.

Her arms snaked around my neck. "Let's move forward," she'd whispered.

Jenna seemed so hopeful. I wanted so badly for this to be our new beginning. I wanted so badly to be who she wanted me to be. But could I pull it off?

—⁂—

After extensive discussions about what I had done, explanations of the information as I knew it and the people who were involved, I said, "We need to think of something comical to take away all the tensions of today."

"It definitely has been a tense day," Jenna said sadly.

I'd tried imagining humour in a novel regarding plastic surgery, tummy tucks and the person's name being Tootsie. I wondered aloud if the visual of 'rolls' could be amusing.

Jenna was not into the spirit of my conversation. "But this is real life. Not much comical in what's been happening." Tucking an errant strand of her flowing auburn hair behind one ear, looking lovely in every way, my wife smiled and asked, "Um, I'm wondering if Tootsie was the best pseudonym you could come up with for this innocent woman who is being blackmailed? And 'rolls?'"

I chuckled. "It was spur of the moment. I don't have to explain Tootsie Rolls to you, do I? We've bought enough of them at the confectionery."

Catching onto my dark humour, she said, "That's part of my distaste. How can I ever eat a Tootsie Roll again with that connotation in mind?"

"Then thank me. When you were munching on one – a couple of months ago – you said they were bad for your health. More for me."

"That's unfair. I bet you chose that name on purpose just to get my share of the package of Tootsie Rolls."

"It would've been a good offensive manoeuvre, indeed."

So where does this leave me now? Knowing my weaknesses makes me more aware and capable of helping myself. I have Jenna, my rock. The Life Counsellor facilitated my move to seize a new lease on life. If only those random thoughts of suicide would cease. I did want to remain alive. I did!

Changing my thoughts. I asked myself what have I accomplished in my life? Good education, experience in different positions with my CPA. Jenna and I brought two incredible children into the world. They love me in spite of myself. I was a good father. I was an excellent husband for most of our marriage. I'm excited about writing a book from these Journal entries involving my experience. Importantly, I won't let that bastard of a man I was reappear again. Diablo, she called me years ago – the devil. I'd changed after my near-death experience, but who would believe that the near-death experience could cause it?

Palm Desert, California

21

Early Spring

Still Hurting

❖ JENNA ❖

L%%IFE IS GETTING BACK%% to normal. *Isn't it?!*
I saw my Matthew through the open doorway, happy, blue eyes with a light in them as he called, "Hey Travis and Ashley, you were looking for the Bocce Ball set. Jenna sweetheart, I found it under the old Slip and Slide."

"Terrific, but where can we set it up? Our front yard's vanished. No grass. Mom, where've you disappeared to?" Travis called into our house in his deep 'man voice'.

Walking toward the door hearing his deep and mature voice, so man-like, I smiled inwardly and answered, "Already getting the lemonade made. Travis, help me carry the trays out."

As he came into the house, reaching with those long arms, he said, "Sure, Mom. Lemme grab the pretzels. I'll need a snack after the Bocce Ball workout."

Matthew grabbed the pretzels from Travis, ripped open the bag while viewing our yard.

"I love what we did with the desertscape."

I envisioned our newly landscaped front yard through his eyes. It looked genuinely stunning. Matthew had worked alongside our landscaper, putting in dozens of hours of manual labour himself to get our yard to this gorgeous standard.

The bag of pretzels was grabbed back again as Travis used the opportunity of Matthew looking away. A tug of war ensued with Matthew winning by putting Travis in an armlock. By the time they were done this escapade, I'd grabbed the bag and held it away from both of the manly men. The bag had spewed half the pretzels onto the driveway, and both scrambled to get the larger share of scattered pretzels, hooting like children while elbowing each other.

When they stood up, I was munching on a pretzel. Matthew and Travis blew away the desert sand from their bounty.

"Are you two finished playing *Find the Pretzel*?"

Matthew's response was to come over to me and pretend to cuddle, while attempting to take the bag from me. Travis lurked on my other side. I doled out a few pretzels to each, managing to keep the bag for myself. This repeated a choreographed scene which had played out numerous times years before with various outcomes.

He appeared ecstatic to have the kids home and to be setting up Bocce Ball – like we used to. We stood in front of the garage and turned our attention to where we were going to play Bocce Ball today. Matthew had just suggested setting up Bocce Ball in our back yard.

Kathy, a neighbour who had also been a friend, came out her front door, a brim hat shoved over her bright red hair. Kathy was a no-nonsense former soccer coach mom. As she took a step into our yard, she said, "Hello Hanson gang. I guess you'd better set up Bocce Ball in our yard. Your new desertscape is looking remarkable, by the way."

Kathy's husband, Todd, had brought out a bowl of Cheetos from their house to which Travis gave a hungry gaze. Kathy grabbed two and, while looking at Travis, tucked them into her mouth. This was also a ritual.

I responded to her statement about using their yard for the Bocce Ball game by saying, "Yeah, thanks. Your yard is perfect. I'll grab two more glasses."

She again stuck a couple of Cheetos into her mouth, winked at Travis, then waited a second while chewing and responded, "Do you need me to keep score, like before?"

"Yeah. Got paper and here's a pen. Hey, glad you came out."

Ashley, however, stood back a bit and only came forward at my head tilt and a nod toward the game being set up. *I wonder what's with this attitude.*

After the game, I caught Ashley in the study off the hallway and asked, "What was up earlier?"

I watched as she dipped her mop of hair downward, hiding her face. She was silent for a few moments. Just when I began to ask again, she peeked up through her hair.

Standing straighter, sweeping the hair from her face with one hand, she said, "Well, doesn't it still seem odd to you Dad is 'good old Dad' again? I keep wondering if he's going to leave us." There was so much tension around her mouth, on her face.

At my probing gaze, she sounded uncomfortable, "I know, I know. Yeah, we went to the counselling sessions and sat in on two with you and Dad. I realize in my heart Dad's okay. I see it when we visit."

"I understand. You know I do."

"A bit of me is similar to a little girl, afraid of what monster might lurk under the bed. And my father dying is the monster that lurks there."

"Them saying he stole from *Smooth Image Surgery* and blackmailed a client, it's unwarranted."

At that, Ashley grasped my hand and pulled me to her. She had a tear streaming from each eye, blinking them away, rubbing furiously with her fingers. Otherwise, she held herself together.

"I'm afraid that when I leave here after a weekend he won't be here when I return. I study him, and I'm certain all is okay, but sometimes…" More silence, and she gave off an expression as though searching for confirmation.

"Right, but we must keep on. It's as though he's reborn. I haven't seen him this happy and content for years."

Ashley's look brightened. She beamed and nodded at my comments.

"We often discuss how he feels. The counsellor is pleased with his progress. We have to be vigilant, for sure, but we must enjoy what he is now."

"Mom, I empathize, and I get it. I see the pure joy on his face. I *see* my *father* again. I just have to get over my doubt."

And the doubts continued for many, many months. We all wondered. We all had our moments of uncertainty. Right now, things were excellent. On the other hand, my uncertainty stemmed from years of anxiety. *Has he really changed?*

Palm Desert, California

MATTHEW'S JOURNAL

When I'd recovered from my Medical Incident and felt capable of admitting to myself what had happened to me, I started to read voraciously about "Near-Death Experiences" (NDE) and "Out of Body Experiences" (OBE).

Snippets of one article were encouraging:

"National Library of Medicine https://www.ncbi.nlm.nih.gov/

A recent review of research into the characteristic changes following NDEs found ... a new sense of purpose or mission; heightened self-esteem; increased compassion and love for others;"

What happened to me was mind blowing. In reading about others like me, I felt myself calm down to realize I wasn't clinically insane, as well as clinically depressed. I believed that absorbing what happened to others and what I'd experienced actually helped against my depression as much as the psychiatrist aka Life Counsellor's work with me. Realizing, first of all, what life I would've left behind, the life I would have callously terminated, meant something. I had witnessed Jenna's and my family, as well as Aaron's absolute anguish at my possible death.

I want to get some of my thoughts into my Journal. It was a roller coaster ride as I went back and forth about Aaron and his treachery and my thoughts of suicide – thoughts which frightened me.

"I should have done a permanent job of the suicide."

"Why am I still alive?"

"I am nothing."

"Get it over with."

Most days, I felt more in tune with myself, not angry toward life. But I couldn't consistently shake off those occasional thoughts.

I also repeatedly wondered if Aaron had stolen that file and if he was, indeed, the blackmailer, letting me take the fall. I was familiar with having to take the fall. My thoughts would revert to Smooth Image Surgery management and staff.

"George let me take the fall" I'd mutter to myself. Maybe Aaron was too. Why should I trust him? My father said he'd get into trouble some day. Then I'd contemplate how I'd known him for almost my whole life.

"Shut up," I'd yell inside my head and wonder if Jenna could hear my turmoil.

—∞—

When I first came home from the hospital, my mother and father were there, my mother being quite subdued and not berating me at all. I felt her love. Tears were in the eyes of both my parents. Jenna's parents came to see me at home, falling over themselves being even kinder than their normal selves.

When Aaron came for a visit, he said, "Welcome back, buddy." Then he'd said, "Smooth Image is doing an in-house investigation, Matt. They might just settle on you."

"That's crap!" I hollered, got Jenna running into the living room. "Jenna, Aaron says the clinic is going just after me."

Then Aaron had said, "I've been doing some snooping at the clinic. I've a suspicion or two."

My thoughts were erratic. ((Was he really trying to help?))

But I said out loud, "Okay, I'm glad you're trying to help, but you could get caught."

((Was this friend muddying the waters, going behind my back to do more harm?))

He'd scoffed at me and said, "You must be kidding to ask me to stop."

((Anything to shift the blame on to someone else, if I don't get charged.))

"Who at the company knew you hadn't returned your key?"

((You! I told you I meant to return my key, AND YOU WORK THERE. You knew.))

"I don't know who would've known I didn't return my key. Maybe George?" ((Yeah, George. That would be another possibility.))

"Matt, I'll find out."

((You two-timing fiend.))

Again, I'd catch myself, attempt to stop my thoughts from turning on my buddy. Damn it! I needed this settled. Now!

There was the chance that some incriminating evidence against me might come to light. This is the bad part, a part I hadn't shared with anyone – not even Jenna. The evidence that my lawyer, John Wu, knows about is skimpy. He indicated as much. What he doesn't know is that I did actually use my key to go into my office after they fired me. It seems that George or anyone else didn't notice that I went back in, using a different pass code to gain entry. But – then again – if Aaron does know this – knows because he checked the security tapes himself – then he could be holding this piece of evidence as the last screw to frame me. How can I possibly trust him?

My reason for returning to the office was innocent enough. I had left some personal items in my desk. I wonder why they didn't check sooner to see if I'd left anything. Sure, I could have asked Aaron to pick those items up for me after I was so unceremoniously escorted from the building. But, damn it, it was my stuff they made me leave behind. So, yeah, I went back into the building. It seems like a shithead move to have returned unauthorized and unaccompanied in retrospect, and that illicit visit would turn out to be used against me. Totally!

My position in Smooth Image Surgery allowed me to occasionally assign a code to the External Auditors allowing them to do their audit each year. That was the code I used so that my visit wouldn't be detected. Now, if discovered, I'll look as guilty as hell! But I'm not the only one who knows that code, so it still doesn't exclude others from having stolen Tootsie's file.

Jenna's friends, Cynthia and Milena, had visited on my return home – each taking one of my hands, one on either side. Milena, standing back a foot, touched my shoulder, "Matthew, I am so happy you are home."

Cynthia, giving me a punch in the arm, blinked a few times and said, "Glad you're here at home."

"I'm back home to stay, not going anywhere. I'm overjoyed to be here."

((Was I? Stop!))

Palm Desert, California

22

Early Spring

Memories

❖ JENNA ❖

THE PHOTOS OF OUR children! That was when Matthew really brightened. I mused back to when we had sat with the photo albums in front of us. He loved those memories the photos brought back for him, made the memories real to him, made him real to himself!

Then Matthew had picked up his computer and tapped the photo directories. Gorgeous digital photos, ones we could enlarge to see better. Travis and Ashley at the Cathedral City Hot Air Balloon Festival and Food Truck Fiesta; Ashley dancing to the live music; Travis eating, always eating.

Matthew had smiled, "He loved his food, that kid. He still loves his food!"

"Yeah, and then you fight him for the pretzels, and I win!"

We both laughed at that and then at my photos of the tethered balloon rides – Matthew getting into one struggling to maintain his balance.

"A timely shot. Yeah, I thought you were going to fall."

Then one Matthew caught on camera of me ogling a painting at the art show. I loved that art. Then I'd rested my head on Matthew's shoulder, and he turned to give me a kiss. Of course, I kissed him back.

"Anyone could tell from the photos that we all loved doing hikes at Joshua Tree National Park. If I wanted rock formations for our landscaping, that would be the place to sketch some pictures." I contemplated myself actually sketching.

When Matthew had left to pick up some groceries, I'd continued scanning his computer while sitting at our old oak table, the chair where Matthew had sat, now dislodged from its spot.

I muttered to myself, relieved and happy. "Re-visiting our life in photos was a real boost to Matthew."

After putting both our chairs against the table, I'd taken the computer and plodded into the living room to sit on our sofa. Surrounded by the comfort in our home, I'd re-discovered the directory entitled, "Palm Estates RV Photos". I was delighted to see several photos I'd taken of Mom with her group of friends.

I recalled Mom had said Owen was doing very well after the second surgery to repair the last hernia surgery. Trudy and Owen had joined groups from around Omaha, had become caught up in activities there and were not re-thinking their decision to sell. Trudy had also been doing well, so it was time for everyone to move on.

Coming back to the present, still tingling with the sensations of seeing those photographs while sitting with Matthew and how "present" he was, I realized even with enlarging the photos on Matthew's computer, they didn't grasp the intensity of the Joshua Tree murals we'd enjoyed on our hikes. I'd decided to check my own computer directories as well, although I didn't think my creative side would've been able to harness their intensity.

Scrutinizing more of the photos, a number of which Matthew had taken, I decided I should be assembling a few of these, copying them and making Matthew a memory album. My deliberations ran in that direction as I picked up some photographs of the children at their Portland grandparents' home, out in the garden filled with roses. Clara loved roses. Her flower beds were exceedingly grand with Portland's flower, the rose. As the plan formed completely in my head, I chose the pictures I'd get copied. More photos were on

Matthew's computer, although I also had photo directories on my own computer that I could get printed.

I absentmindedly wondered if Matthew would want pictures of visits to my family in Calgary. I discarded this. *He sees enough of my parents every winter.*

Turning over memories of my last visit to Calgary, I chuckled at the reunion with my girlfriends from home. Home! Strange how after three decades, I could still revert to calling it home, when nothing was home about it except the memories. My home was in the Coachella Valley. Rather Palm Desert, the actual city where we lived.

The reunion with my friends, Lynda and Marilyn, had been super cool. Older and wiser, we three. I'd been tall for my age my whole life. Marilyn and Lynda shorter and similar in their height, both exceedingly pretty. My green eyes, Marilyn's brown eyes, Lynda's blue eyes. For many years we acted like we were sisters – until my belief in Samson cooled that for a while. We'd been a team as schoolgirls.

During my visit, we re-evaluated my episode of pushing both Samson and his girlfriend into the pool. We re-lived our crushes on various boys, one now married to Lynda. What a sucker punch that had been at 14 years old because I assumed him interested in me. I gathered later he only hung around with me to be close to Lynda, a striking blonde and more mature than I at that age.

On my visit, we'd met for lunch at the Calgary Tower in the revolving restaurant, revolving 360 degrees once each hour, giving patrons a panoramic view while having their meal. I'd shared with Lynda and Marilyn a tiny speck of what had happened to Matthew. These were my dear childhood friends, but I still didn't delve into the depths of our inner marriage woes or his despair. Touching on the surface appeared enough for them. They were sympathetic, of course, but it wasn't as though they knew Matthew. A few hours here and there.

I also had a wonderful time during my visit to Calgary catching up with Samson's sister, Wendy. She'd been a good friend over the decades. Samson? Well, he became a lawyer, family law, and married that bimbo, Cherise. We didn't discuss Samson in our letters or later in our emails and texts, except that Cherise had left him after he'd cheated on her. Smart girl. Better late than never. We shared stories of our lives, not touching on Matthew's verbally abusive issues either.

—∞—

My husband has been writing his book about his medical incident. He says writing the book is helping him cope and to heal. I've read some material on 'out-of-body' experiences. Of course, I'm fascinated this happened to my husband.
He saw his mom and dad holding hands while he was unconscious.
"I'll tell you everything about my near-death experiences – soon." He'd stated with emotion, then added, "It was just so mind boggling that I need to let it percolate before I tell you."
When I say, I can read him like a book, I remind myself he wouldn't let me read *his* book.

—∞—

Matthew hadn't been well when I enthusiastically brought up desert scaping our yard last year, attempting yet again to interest him in something. I couldn't get him interested in the yard then – maybe a trite subject, but I had continually struggled to bring his attention to our life, the lives of our children, memories of our lives or my cute little happenings at my school with the students. These were the things he'd loved to be regaled about before his depression. Sadly, at that time, I couldn't even get him interested in me emotionally or physically.
I attempted to stop my mind from roaming back to the past. However, over those two Diablo years, there were also those times that he was actually himself. Then I'd try to talk to him about how he'd been behaving, and his persona shift would start all over again. No, he wouldn't accept responsibility for any of it, pretending he couldn't recall or actually not remembering what a son-of-a-bitch he'd been. I'd have an inner thought, *"Well, he is the son of a bitch, isn't he?* That's where it all would have begun. From Clara.

I was willing to give myself to him again – to let myself be hurt if he turned into Diablo Matthew again. I say I was willing to let myself be hurt, but I was changing. I didn't feel that I was the same puppy waiting for the pat on the head. Sure, I wanted everything to be as it had been before two years ago – as it had been for the previous decades when our marriage had been rock solid. But this time, I had to be a fighter. I had to get back the confidence that I'd had – the confidence I'd had when I pushed Samson into that pool. Maybe it wouldn't be in a day, a week or a month, but I was done being that puppy.

Matthew's depression had also seriously impacted our intimacy. That was always the one thing that had brought us together – sex! What our relationship started from had always been good for us. *Had always been!* I repeated in my head as though to punish myself – *Had been.*

Weeks after Matthew came home from the hospital, I still wondered if our love life would resume in the same manner, back to the days when we first married, when sex was all about us, before the 'what if's' or 'what does the future hold?'

Thrillingly, after weeks of despair, we stood in our bedroom suddenly aware of a shift within ourselves, Matthew walking toward me, closing the gap between us, his expression intense. I felt my breath catch in my throat. *Was this it?* I inhaled with an anticipation in my gut. He took me in his arms, hugging me fervently. Hugs turned to caressing, kisses, awareness of each other, clothes falling onto the floor, hands probing, flesh pressing on flesh, passions rising. As we fell to our bed, the palm trees outside the window pushed-pulled in the wind, picking up speed. As those branches swayed and sighed, we swayed with them, releasing our passions as the trees moved with the wind. As we stared longingly at each other, it was as sexy as it had been decades before.

{"*As we moved together, I knew forever, You're all I'll ever need*"}

Palm Desert, California

23

Early Spring

Family Situations

❖ JENNA ❖

I CALLED MY MOTHER to arrange a hook-up. Matthew had been watching a football game, I have no idea what team. Distractedly, he gave me a quick squeeze. *He seems distracted off and on. He must be okay. I'm sure he's okay.* I'd already told him, "No more yelling."

On my way to my mom and dad's, I thought about our enviable relationship with them. When I'd moved to Portland and then on to the Palm Springs area, it hadn't occurred to me in my wildest dreams I would be able to have my parents nearby for the winter months. I'd stoically left them in Calgary, solemn in saying we'd visit, but eager to start anew with the love of my life. I felt the void often, but my new life stretched appealingly before me. They had each other as did Matthew and me.

Once we sat down with our tea, Mom said, "Your dad wants to go to a movie I don't find palatable. Disgusting! But we're going to see Paul Anka at the McCallum."

"I didn't know Dad enjoyed Paul Anka."

Dad should've gleaned in this mood, Mom would be getting her way – if she talked like this to him! Even though only medium height, she displayed her physically fit, hiker build in the best fashion.

"No, he doesn't, but I do. Paul Anka is in town in two weeks, and we're going, and your dad is going to enjoy it. Or else!"

"Or else what?"

"Well, I don't know, but he better enjoy it. We always do what is more important to one of us, and this is important to me. Your dad is really a teddy bear, a lovable teddy bear, or maybe a kitten. He can purr like a kitten sometimes!"

"I don't need to hear about your love life, Mom!"

"Why? You should be glad your dad and I still love each other after all these years."

"I am, Mom. Thanks for sharing."

Quickly, I wanted to dispose of the image of my white-haired father purring like a kitten!

Taking a breath, I asked, "And Dad's heart? Is he taking his meds? What does he do down here for a doctor? "

And I did. I worried about them. They were both 74 now, and the thought something could happen to them generated horrifying emotions. Maybe I didn't have to stress as often about Matthew and his depression. I did have to worry if the *Smooth Image Surgery* ordeal ended up in trial. Guilty of theft and blackmail! What if he were sent to jail? A stabbing pain meant a headache about to begin.

Life contained endless worries. Matthew's personality disorder and depression had been a huge worry. Dad's health. Matthew going to jail. Where would all this end? I said the words to myself that I had composed: *"Instead of worrying what was or what might be, rejoice in what is."* I'd rehearsed these, as well as *"What's the best thing that can happen?"*

"Mom," I repeated. "Is Dad doing everything he should be doing for his health? Are those medications working for him?"

"Your dad's had telephone consultations with his Calgary cardiologist twice this winter. His legs are swelling a little at the ankle."

"Shit!"

"Umm…" Mom appeared extremely agitated, slanting her green eyes away from me. Those eyes the same colour as mine were hiding something.

"What the hell else aren't you telling me?" *What would I do without them each winter? What would I do if Dad's health worsened? God, so many things going on.*

Mom had glanced out the window, taking a moment to form her answer. "His doctor sent him down here with another drug, Lasix, in the event this swelling did occur. He'll take the Lasix to see if his ankles slim down again."

My heart was racing, and my ears were buzzing at this.

She continued as though I wasn't having an emotional crisis in my mind. "His cardiologist is positive that will make the difference. So, every few days, we'll gauge if he should take the Lasix for another couple of days. He's to email photos of his ankles if they continue to swell."

I became upset, furious at being kept in the dark. *Again.* "How is he?"

"He's more tired this week."

Determinedly, I announced, "I'm going to stay long enough for him to come back from… Where did you say he was?"

Now Mom appeared more anxious. She hesitated and said, "He's over at the Club House setting up for Bingo tonight."

"I'll stay to see him and his ankles."

"Oh dear. That's what I was concerned about. He'll be annoyed I told you."

"I don't give a crap if he's annoyed. I'll check his ankles myself."

I was floundering with the revelation of Dad's ankles swelling. It meant that his heart was not able to pump blood sufficiently.

—⁂—

Sitting with me at La Perlita Mexican Restaurant a week later, Mom dropped a different bombshell.

"Your dad and I've been discussing the pros and cons of selling our park model and what we could do afterward."

The waiter came by, stopping a few feet away, as though she knew by my expression, she dares not interrupt this conversation.

She discreetly moved away to another table.

"Oh, Mom!" Checking myself, I calmed down, "Is it Dad's health?"

"No, the swelling is down. We want to consider what else we could be doing for the next couple of years, is all."

I was in turmoil. My mom and dad were the main stability in my life. Matthew had definitely not been dependable. Ashley and Travis had their own lives. My friends had their own lives. My mom and dad could be counted on – sane, reasonable people. When they were here over the winter, I spent considerable time with them, my rocks. *Could I handle Matthew's issues without them? Never mind worrying about Dad's health. What if they weren't down here at all?* I realized that I'm a grown, 50-something woman who depends on her parents. I was breathing too rapidly, and I had to catch myself before my mom noticed.

Taking one more calming breath, I said, "What are the things you'd be interested in doing instead?"

This time when the young waitress stopped at our table, we ordered a mango marguerita each.

"We know with our yearly costs, HOA fees, insurance, electricity and whatnot that we really have an inexpensive five months here, less than we would pay to come down and rent somewhere. We talked about cruises and the usual things other couples do. We just can't get excited about doing anything else."

As Mom chatted on, looking slightly nonplussed at the subject she had brought up, my mind quickly went over the scenario – *they'd be gone!* They had been what kept me sane all these years of Matthew's moodiness, neediness, his emotional outbursts against me.

A different waiter familiar to me from all my visits to La Perlita brought the drinks and then took our order of Fajitas Mixta. We chose the steak, chicken and shrimp with red and green peppers, onions, rice and beans for our shared lunch.

"You know I'd be lost without you. Obviously, you need to do whatever you set your hearts on. It really has been one of the best parts of Matthew and I living down here having you and Dad come for the winter for all these years. And what would I have done without you while Matthew was depressed?"

"I wanted to let you know we were discussing selling, but no decision's made. We'd make money on the sale."

Thundering thoughts raged through my head as I got a grip on my emotions. I had gone to my parents' resort to revive myself, to convince myself I could return to my own home, and Matthew would be his sweeter self... *They can't leave me!*

"Jenna, you're right though. We were able to help with the load you were going through with Matthew being ill. You went through a lot."

You have no idea all what I went through. What I'm still going through. You thought Matthew was what you saw, a loveable guy. Not the guy who'd be verbally abusive.

My mom gave me a sympathetic glance, clearly aware their decision would affect me.

I made myself smile. "Sure, we're on the other side. I'm glad the depression appears over." *Must be over. Who wasn't being totally honest now? I'm emotionally drained every time I let myself respond to how I truly feel. Maybe Matthew has come through to the other side, but I'm very certain I'm not there yet.*

"I'll be upended if you sell, but you must do what's right for you. You've been there for us." *After all, I did leave them 30 some years ago – for Matthew.*

"We aren't making decisions right now. I'll keep you informed. At this point in our lives, it alters every year. We miss Owen and Trudy. It's the same at home."

Shifting positions, wondering if I should ask, I said, "Speaking of home, do you ever think of selling that beautiful huge house Dad built and moving into something smaller?"

"That subject came up as well. We don't entertain as we used to. The fact your father built it, though, it makes it hard to let go."

After our table had been cleared and I'd indicated the bill should be given to me, I said, "What does Dad think?"

In a quieter tone, she responded, "He's more ready to sell than I am. We have someone come to clean at home as well because I can't possibly do it all anymore. Of course, Robert and Eva come to live there while we're away, but Eva is ready to settle down to one house."

"Robert's always been a free spirit. I'm pretty sure they have a bundle saved up. Working with Dad all these years, he has money. Eva is a nurse. How could they not afford their own home?"

"Before we came here this fall, Eva told him he needs to build one for them. I yakked with her last week. He's relenting somewhat. He brought home some floor plans, and they've decided what neighbourhood she'd like to live in."

"Hopefully for more than a year."

"She's adamant."

—⁂—

That week, Mom and I went to two of our favourite stores in the Palm Springs area, Glossy and Chicos. Aaron had picked up Matthew so they could attend a car show. Ashley's birthday was coming up, and she loved the sparkly shirts Glossy sold. I ended up with two for Ashley and one for me. Mom bought several to take home with her.

Mom drove without paying attention to which street she was on.

"Head north and then turn right onto San Pablo Avenue. Then hang a left onto Fred Waring, yeah."

"Is the invitation still open for your brownies and iced tea?" She pulled the vehicle in, and I grabbed the bags of clothing.

I smiled at her as I took her bags out of the back seat. "Of course."

"I hope Ashley will love these zebra and peacock ones from Glossy, reminiscent of our San Diego trip many years ago. They're hella awesome."

Mom shook her head. "I forgot for a moment 'hella' means very. Did you use that word just to get my goat?"

Diving into another bag, I replied, "Yes." And smiled. She gave me a look. I changed the subject.

"During this shopping spree, you didn't get anything for yourself?"

"Two bathing suits. I may as well leave this one here for next year. Oh, but then if we decide to sell..." Pausing, and looking a little lost, she said, smiling, "If we decide to sell, we'd still need to come back to collect everything. Seriously, I can't conceive life not at the park during the winter. Everyone would miss us."

Laughing, I agreed with her. Deep down, I felt troubled. I couldn't let on how significantly it would affect me. But, my God, I would miss her every day of every winter. I'd have to go home more often, but leave Matthew? No, that wouldn't work. *I can't say a thing to discourage them.*

When my mom left, my mind followed her, visualizing them in their resort. Could I concoct the scenario of myself and Matthew living in a resort? No, not even in 15 years. Mom and Dad, as well as all their park friends, truly enjoyed it. We live right here already. Living in a resort wasn't the place for us. It was the place for people who came for 5 or 6 months. Maybe in a few years, it would be time for Matthew and I to think about a condo instead of our big house.

I started thinking about a condo for Matthew and me. Mom and Dad had real community spirit in the resort, and I considered what atmosphere there would be in a condo. Mom said people would miss them if they moved. *Who would miss us*?

—⚈—

While I washed up after supper, I reflected again how lucky we are that Matthew survived his medical incident. I hummed the song again. {*Could I Have This Dance For The Rest Of My Life?}* I ponder this fifty times a day. Medical incident. That's what we call it. Not attempted suicide, but a medical incident.

And then his boss calling that ill-fated night, almost accusing Matthew of being a criminal.

I muttered angrily, "For crap's sake, who did that? Who took the file? Who blackmailed that client? It wasn't Matthew. I know it. I'm so freaking mad, I could smack someone."

When Matthew came into the room, we discussed our concerns. He sputtered and said, "My reputation had been impeccable, but now, I'm scared of what the outcome could be for me. Well, for us I mean."

He paced the room like a caged lion, then peered out the window. "This is a dreadful crime, theft of a client file, blackmail. Will I be charged soon? How is the investigation by *Smooth Image Surgery* going? What about other suspects? George, Aaron?"

Fiddling with my bracelet, worrying, I asked, "Matthew, maybe George, but not Aaron. Surely. What is your company up to? Why aren't we hearing anything?"

"And what the heck is John Wu's so called private investigator doing? What are we paying for?"

I'd been naïve before to daydream that our life was back to normal. It'd been a pipe dream.

Palm Desert, California

24

Spring

Menacing Telephone Calls

❖ JENNA ❖

"You'll pay for this, fucker. I'll get you! And don't involve the police."

As he turned around, his face was white, and his fingers were still gripping the landline. " She said to me, 'You'll pay for this, fucker. I'll get you! And don't involve the police.'"

"Wait a minute!! How the hell do they have our phone number? Does she have your name? Does she know where we live? This must be stopped before something bad happens."

I was sick of this. No amount of worrying was going to make it go away. *What can we do to hurry our investigator along to prove Matthew innocent?*

"We have to – just have to – find who's behind this blackmail before they hurt us. They could give up or they could get physical. This could go either way."

"Yes, it could," he said as he blew out a breath.

Matthew gently took the "Coachella Valley" coffee cup from my hand, put it down and pulled me close.

"I'm sorry you're involved. I can see you're scared."

Gripping him tighter, I said, "I have a bad feeling. And I'm apprehensive you won't be able to handle all this stress." Checking his expression, I continued. "Are you strong enough to wait for this to work its way out?"

"I really hope so. I do really hope so." He pulled away a little, turning to look toward the phone. "I think I should call our lawyer."

I let go of him, giving him a small shove, grabbed my cup, and said, "I agree. Call John."

On speaker, I could hear Matthew unable to get a word in before John started off like a horse on a racetrack, "I haven't received any word from George regarding the company's internal investigation." Without taking a breath, building up steam, "Nothing from our private investigator, and nada from the police." He inhaled.

As John said those facts to Matthew, I initially felt relief. Of course, I quickly realized that is exactly the wrong attitude. We needed information badly.

Matthew charged in, "That sucks, but I have something to talk to you about. We're getting menacing calls on the landline from that client of *Smooth Image Surgery*. Jenna is scared. I'm nervous."

"I recommend calling the police."

"We'll think about that. I just wanted you to know. Anything else you can advise?"

"Do you have a security system at your home?"

"Yes, we usually use it."

"Keep it engaged at all times." John stopped for a beat. "Cancel the landline!"

We should have listened.

Palm Desert, California

MATTHEW'S JOURNAL

Along with the menacing calls, we were receiving hang-ups—no words spoken. It felt eerie. Jenna and I went to visit both our neighbours, sensing it important to explain our dilemma to them and to show we were in this situation jointly.

Kathy and Todd had been briefed months ago about my being suspected of the file theft and blackmail. Todd had been supportive at that time and quite expressive, "What the hell are they thinking that you could do such a thing? You've worked there for 25 years! Those pricks, making you the culprit, instead of finding the real bastard! I'd make them pay!"

Today, we were at their front door to advise them of the scope of the hang-ups and menacing telephone calls. Their American flag hung limply at their doorway – the wind had died down from earlier this morning. Several juniper trees had recently been watered, with droplets still hanging from the needles. We wanted our neighbours to be aware so they could keep themselves safe in case there was someone coming onto our street to snoop or to do harm and might unwittingly harm our neighbours, but also to ask them to keep an eye on our property.

I originally thought I'd simply write notes for my Journal. Months ago, I had to start typing my thoughts because the written Journal had expanded. My manuscript for a book was going nicely. This is how today's visits went.

We've been isolated. I do not feel I can trust Aaron. At least we have Todd and Kathy for support.

Kathy was annoyed, "For goodness sake, why don't they just let the investigators do their job? We'll watch for anyone who doesn't belong. We'll call the police immediately and let you know. Come in for a cup of tea or something stronger?"

Jenna said, "We need to tell the new neighbours on the other side, Patty and Kim Nguyen, what's happening as well. I hope they're not sorry they bought on this street last fall."

"Come back and tell us how that went."

A nod from Jenna. Feeling relieved at their invitation, we agreed to come back. One down, one to go.

Patty and Kim were both at home. We walked up their sidewalk, looking at the mountains in the distance and admiring the tall palm trees behind their home. Kim answered the door, saying, "Xin chào" which I knew meant "Hello".

Kim, medium height and slim, was wearing blue silky tunic-style top with slim-fitting white pants. Patty was very petite, especially polite and dressed in a double-layered, beaded patterned dress with matching pants.

"Come in," invited Patty.

Realizing they were evidently on their way to an event, we nevertheless were invited in. Sitting on their lovely settee, I explained the situation as best I could. I apologized for the problem this may cause them if someone indeed came onto our street with ill intentions. Both of them expressed concern for themselves and, belatedly, for us. I understood their reticence. They barely knew us, but they were very polite with their concern.

I finished with, "I am innocent of any wrongdoing. I have not committed any crime. The police may get involved soon."

At this comment about the police, they exchanged a look of unease.

"That's a good thing. It means that everything will be cleared up, and we won't have to worry any longer. The real criminal will be punished."

This certainly appeared to lessen their worry. After looking at each other, they glanced back to me, then at the card I had set on their table.

"Yes, we will call you if we see anything."

As we left, I was unsure if Patty and Kim would ever be our friends. Granted, they were considerably younger than us; however, I'd have preferred not to have criminal accusations muddling our relationship with them.

Standing in the kitchen at Kathy and Todd's, eating finger foods, it was a relief to have the explanations over with.

"To finding the creep that's ruining your lives," said Todd.

"I'll drink to that," was my easy reply, tossing back a glass of Sangria Todd had poured. Jenna sipped hers as she watched me. I think she knows that I've started drinking again. I've never been good with stress. This was getting to be too much for me. Just a quick gulp here and there straight from the bottle under my bathroom sink. I'm sure she'll find that one. I have another in the shed. There's alcohol for purchase in every store, and I keep another in my trunk.

I needed to get a gun for protection. But, from where? I knew there was a ten-day waiting period before I would get it. I wanted it right away. Who did I know who could help me? Certainly not Aaron. I'd been watching him. He seemed cagier as the days went by. I needed to buy a gun from someone.

Without waiting to think it through, I said to Todd, "I need to buy a gun."

"Whoa, Matthew. No!" Jenna was having none of that. "Not in our house."

Todd shot me a glance. When Jenna looked to Kathy for support, Todd winked and mouthed, "Later."

I gave him the barest of a nod. As she whipped her head around to look at me again, she may have seen that nod. Whatever! Todd was my man.

Palm Desert, California

25

Spring

Painting Sheep

❖ JENNA ❖

WE'D CALLED TRAVIS AND Ashley to tell them we'd been getting the menacing calls.

"What the fuck?!" from Travis.

"Don't say that word to me!" I ordered.

"Mom, it's come out of your mouth."

"Yeah, but it's not one I like to use, and I don't need to hear it."

Ashley was more restrained when I telephoned her next. "So, what are you doing about it?"

"Not answering the landline often."

Ashley, the problem solver, said, "Did you call the police?"

"Not yet."

"Why not?"

This conversation was a repeat of what I'd exchanged with Travis just before.

"The callers have said not to involve police! Your dad doesn't want to antagonize them more."

"That's stupid."

Exactly what Travis said. But Travis had added, "Get a gun."

I'd shouted, "We. Don't. Need. A. Gun!"

To Ashley, I'd said, "He just doesn't want to draw any attention to himself. They told us, 'No police.' We'd have to explain the file theft and blackmail."

"Cripes, mom. Cancel your landline!"

Not missing a beat, I continued, "We're being vigilant about the security system, and checking out the window a lot."

Both of them called Matthew on his cell to get his view of this development, apparently issuing similar comments to him. We continued to be cautious and alert. Travis and Ashley continued to natter at us.

After a quick cup of coffee together that afternoon, I reminded Matthew that I was going to the resort for a paint class.

"I'll stay here. I have a concept for the next part of this manuscript. I don't want to interrupt my thought process."

"You're okay with me going, leaving you?"

"Jenna, I'm sideswiped about this entire thing. The calls are taking more out of me than I would like. I need to distance myself from everything going on around us and delve into this book."

"Okay but call if you want to talk. Or if you miss me."

I took the security alarm off, and then reset it, leaving.

My phone rang as I closed the car door.

"I miss you," he said.

"I miss you, too."

"Have an enjoyable time painting a sheep."

A giggle emanated from my throat, "You know I'm not painting an actual sheep. Enjoy your book."

I'd taken the bottle of Scotch from under Matthew's sink. It could be stashed in my mom and dad's place. Matthew would know I'd found it, but I was sure he had more, perhaps in the shed where he recently had been "sorting through stuff".

Would I find a gun? I was sickened by the nod I saw Matthew direct toward Todd. Todd could be a loose cannon. Would he do such a thing? I knew they had guns in their house. That didn't concern me. I didn't want one in mine. I wasn't used to guns in everyone's home. It didn't seem prudent, positively not with the emotion Matthew displayed about these telephone calls! *Was Matthew a loose cannon? Then Travis encouraged us to get a gun!*

—⚏—

When I arrived, my mom was making spaghetti and meat sauce for supper and left the sauce cooking in the slow cooker. I slipped the Scotch from my bag and set it on the counter.

"My contribution to your stockpile."

"Oh, that's thoughtful, dear." Then tossing her apron on the counter, she said, "I have to change, then we'll head to the Paint Class in the Craft Room. I'm sure you remember us deciding this, eh Jenna? We're doing a 'copy' painting of two Bighorn Sheep on the Mountain."

"That's why I'm wearing old clothes. I'll be a slop with the paint."

We walked a couple of blocks to the Craft Room. With the gentle breeze on my face, I was enjoying another warm and sunny day. A roadrunner strutted near the fountain as we walked around the corner. I gave it one last glance before we entered, noting the roadrunner appeared not one bit alarmed about us.

One of the park residents, Bonnie Hazaar, a professional painter, had volunteered to host the paint class that afternoon. All the supplies were laid out for us. We'd gladly paid a $7.00 fee for the array of paint, brushes, paint trays and canvas set out at each 'station'.

Bonnie said, "Grab a seat, and let's get started. Keep your eyes on my completed canvas while you take notice of what I'm doing with the outline."

As the class progressed, I felt elated, a welcome reprieve from my life.

Following her instructions, we each poured a one-inch circle of white paint and a tiny dab of black paint beside it, then mixed the black with a portion of the white. I was very intrigued by all of this, revelling in the details of Bonnie's completed Bighorn Sheep painting and the outline of another sitting beside it on her painting stand.

During the evening, we all followed Bonnie's instructions – like sheep. We kept an eye on Bonnie's work, while contemplating and adding the contours. We then improved on our colours of mountains altering our shading, then added the sheep. Paint stroke by paint stroke, our attempts developed into paintings.

I had to admit the next day, I was hooked. I hadn't held a paint brush to paint something for myself since grade school. In my life as a teacher, I had the younger children paint their emotions. *Maybe I'll paint my own emotions today.* I was on cloud nine about that paint class. My sheep didn't entirely look like sheep. My mountains were a little bit spindly, but, oh yeah, I was hooked. *I wonder what Milena will say now.*

Bonnie had said to me, "You're a natural." I scoffed at that, but Mom said that I really caught on fast, and I'd only improve each time I came out. She suggested we pick up supplies for me to dabble with at home.

She promptly said, "You can use that spare room that has stuff you don't need. Matthew has his office. You can have a craft room."

By the time I got home after shopping with my mother, I had more supplies than I would use in the next year – or not. I was happy she'd insisted we go to Michael's craft store to pick up some beginner painting manuals. I devoured those and went to work on three painting projects within a week, letting some parts dry while I started another one. *Fabulous! I feel fabulous.*

Palm Desert, California

26

Spring

Sherlock & Watson

❖ JENNA ❖

THE DOORBELL RANG. MATTHEW answered it and ushered in Aaron.
"Hi, Matt. I came to pick up my bike gloves. I left them in your garage."
"I'll get them."
Matthew turned and walked away, not giving Aaron a second glance. I noticed Matthew stop midstride for a second as though collecting his thoughts. He turned back, smiled a half smile and said, "Good to see you, Aaron." *He's evidently not happy to see Aaron.*
The doorbell rang again. Being nearest the door, I answered it. It was my bestie, Cynthia, displaying an expression on her face which I could only describe as odd. If I hadn't known her so well, I may not have caught it. And then I caught something else. A conspiratorial glance between Aaron and Cynthia, odd because I hadn't realized they had a personal relationship. Odd because I hadn't been told. I quickly backed up and shoved a novel under the sofa. I didn't want Cynthia seeing the trash I'd been consumed in moments before. She spied Matthew's book, something more enlightening and mature, entitled, *The Alchemist*, nodding her approval at Matthew.
Hugging her, I said, "Hi, Cynthia. Great to see you."
"I just thought I'd stop by and catch up. Oh, hello, Aaron." She paused for two beats, and continued, "We came from opposite

directions and just ran into each other. Neither of us knew the other was coming here!"

The fact that this 'quick on her toes' friend is having trouble threading intelligent sentences together also tells me something.

I saw another look between the two of them. I glanced at Matthew, but he didn't seem to notice any interaction between them.

What do we have here? This is not the lawyer Cynthia. This is a flustered woman, quite distracted, not her usual held-together self.

"Well, I'm glad you're both here. Come and have a seat. I can get you some iced tea. You look just a little harried."

Answering an unasked question, she said, "I was in a hurry this morning. I needed to stop to get some groceries." Cynthia studied me, but I wasn't giving any clue I had questions about their behaviour. I gave her a smile and turned toward Aaron. He made a show of checking out our Van Gogh print depicting the sidewalk café at night.

"And where were you this morning, Aaron?"

Turning toward me, he coloured a little on the red side, "I bought snacks and then went into the office...for just a little while."

I slipped out of the room and left Matthew, Aaron and Cynthia to their conversation. I rustled up some iced tea and brought four glasses of it on a tray. I brought two large cinnamon buns which I had cut in half, purchased this morning at the grocery store. The grocery store where I hadn't twigged to the fact until now there may have been a clue I'd missed.

As I had hurried through Albertson's Deli this morning to pick up my sparse list of items, I'd seen Aaron in one aisle and Cynthia had been in another aisle. Although I had been in a rush, I jabbered for a minute in both aisles about what each of us had done this week. They both seemed intent on their grocery shopping, slightly distracted I felt. I didn't tarry, and they immediately turned back to the items on the shelves. After completing my shopping, I was already on my way out the door when I glanced back and noticed the two of them standing in line to pay – side by side, not the usual one behind the other. I waved through the store window, but they must not have noticed. Hurrying out the door with cinnamon buns, ice cream and milk, I left all thoughts of them behind.

Why I hadn't considered it, it escapes me now, but I know there had been something on my mind. *Ahh! I'd been deliberating about a painting I was doing of Cabot's Museum.* And I'd been pondering how to do the reflection in the pieces of glass in those special windows that Cabot Yerxa had found in the desert and inserted into his building, piece by piece – no pieces matching the rest of the window. I'd been realizing I needed to attempt another painting of this same subject because I wasn't experienced enough to get everything right.

It was clear to me now – not just the window and how to do it, but suddenly realizing what I had missed this morning and what I was seeing now.

Slyly I stated, "Cynthia, I love that dress. In fact, I loved it yesterday."

Turning a cute shade of pink and peeking down at her dress as though seeing it for the first time, she acknowledged, "I love it, too. I must have left it on the back of a chair and not realized I'd worn the same dress again today."

Tongue in cheek, I announced in a slightly skeptical tone, "For sure, that must be it."

Matthew interrupted and said, "Jenna, could I speak with you a moment in the kitchen?"

I may have lapsed in my hostess capabilities just now. I meekly followed Matthew into the kitchen, turning to give one last glance at Aaron and Cynthia, confirming my suspicions. Cynthia shrugged her shoulders while Aaron threw her a reassuring smile.

Once in the kitchen, Matthew looked askance at me and remarked, "Jenna, this is your friend you're talking to. I thought you two had made up after that tiff with her during my hospital stay – her calling, but not explaining why. It isn't like you to be questioning Cynthia about wearing the same dress two days in a row."

I checked his expression to ensure there would be no outburst.

"I was merely surprised to realize those two in our living room have likely been together since yesterday. Cynthia has not been to her home. She would never wear the same dress twice in a row. You know how particular she is, always on top of everything."

His eyes darted one way and then the other, possibly discerning if there could be truth in any of this. His eyes slanted downward and then back up to me, a twinkle appearing.

Matthew said dramatically, "Are you serious? I didn't realize they even liked each other. I thought my predicament at work would've brought them together professionally. Maybe you're on to something. So, let's go back into the living room and squeeze our prey."

He then grinned a wicked grin, and he rubbed the palms of his hands together. "Let's go get 'em."

I'm relieved to see that he isn't on the topic of Aaron being the thief and blackmailer. He's certainly been tossing that conclusion around.

Aaron sat on the love seat, swinging one foot – back and forth, back and forth. Cynthia perched on the edge of a wing chair on the opposite side of the living room. Both of them, with their drinks held in their hands, were taking tentative sips.

I, in my 'Get to the punch line' way, said, "Sherlock and Watson have solved a case."

Appearing just a little confused, immediately a little bit wary, Cynthia said, "Matthew's work problem? Super! How?"

Aaron looked a little taken aback and turned a shade of crimson. I hoped it was from embarrassment in this situation, not him thinking we had any information about him being involved in the theft and blackmail. *No, not Aaron.*

I said, "No, that's not it, you two. I've solved the mystery of the dress recurrence."

Then the look of resignation – maybe relief – on Aaron's face. And the lawyer 'not giving away anything' expression on Cynthia's. Once more, they glanced at each other. I saw the slightest nod from Aaron to Cynthia and acquiescence on both their faces.

Aaron inquired, "You don't mind we've been seeing each other?"

Matthew and I both had wanted to make them sweat a little, but Matthew gave up and chuckled. I may have squealed.

Sensing their relief in no longer having to keep this secret from us, Matthew and I both shook our heads. Matthew offered, "I'm delighted."

"Why would you think it would make any difference to us?" I inquired.

Cynthia, retaining a professional expression on her face, replied, "There has been a lot going on in your lives. Partly, it involved us in our professional roles. When we realized we had feelings for each other, we didn't want you to think it would interfere with our effectiveness with solving the theft and the accusations directed at Matthew."

"We're happy for you," said Matthew. In a botched attempt at humour, "With a lawyer in your pocket, you'll get free legal counsel."

Then I noted Matthew glance toward the shed where I suspected a bottle lurked. *That hidey hole will be searched again as soon as our company leaves.*

I added with a false delivery, "I'm happy for you two as well! Let's have another iced tea to celebrate friends."

Palm Desert, California

27

Spring

Snickers!

❖ JENNA ❖

TRAVIS AND ASHLEY HAD come to visit Matthew and me for the weekend. The kids wanted to go to the Kennel Club of Palm Springs January Dog Show and Trials. This event was held at the Empire Polo Grounds the first week every January and had been on my bucket list for a long while.

Matthew was sitting on the sofa as I placed the sheets outlining the dog show event on his lap, "Travis and Ashley want to go to the Dog Show. You're looking bored. Let's take it in today."

"Is that this weekend? Phenomenal!"

Travis called Robin, and, 20 minutes later, the five of us arrived, almost immediately coming upon the judging of English Springer Spaniels. *It's meant to be.*

Robin seemed reverent, "Absolutely magnificent!"

Matthew added, "The ones we love are these show English Springer Spaniels."

I'd been thinking of having a pet for awhile now. We both adored Mom and Dad's dog, Charlie. We needed a dog. Matthew needed a dog. Years ago, we had an English Springer Spaniel, Ringo, an overly large male. Even though Matthew took that dog to training, he didn't ever succeed in getting Ringo to totally listen to commands or curbing Ringo's behaviour.

Travis seemed thrilled, "Wow, hella cute dogs. They aren't gnarly like Ringo. Very well behaved." He smiled while leaning closer, "A taller, longer version of the American Cocker Spaniel."

Matthew said, "They're all well trained. Lord, they listen and watch the owners for their cue. What did we do wrong with Ringo?"

Hoping to convince him, I commented, "We could have a dog. You're retired. I'll be retired soon. This is the ideal time to get another pet. We were both working at that time, and Ringo was just a rangy dog."

As we strolled through the space between the show areas, we chatted to owners and groomers, enjoying each of the dogs. We were given treats to feed the dogs and petted several spaniels. After Ashley had 'ooowed and awed' at the Springers, she wandered off to a booth for clothing. Travis and Robin scooted off to chat with one of their friends. We had some time to talk about whether we were ready for another pet.

Matthew noticed something. He pointed behind one of the tables set up for grooming. An owner had two separate crates. One crate had a Welsh Springer Spaniel and the other an English Springer Spaniel pup.

I whispered, "Here's fate stepping in."

"Oh Jenna! That one's phenomenal."

To the owner, I said, "We're mulling over getting another English Springer."

I felt disappointed at her response, initially. "Jersey isn't for sale, but I have his sister at home. She's going to be sold."

"My goodness. Where do you live?" I knew I sounded worried. "We'd love to meet her. Are you in the Valley?" Panicking, it occurred to me that the 3,200 dogs in this show were from all over the country and from Canada.

"We're in Temecula." Glancing at her phone agenda, "I'll be available on Tuesday if you can make it that day. Her pet name is Snickers."

Relief passed through me like a bolt. Matthew and I stared at each other, both of us ecstatic about this new twist in our lives. I could tell he was saying, "Yes" to me with his eyes.

I twisted away from Matthew's excited eyes and looked toward her, "I can take the last period off school that day. It's Prep Time, and we can be in Temecula by 5:00. Is that going to work for you?"

Again, a glance at her phone, "Perfect for me."

All the way back to our house, we were each enthusiastic about another pet. It seemed that Travis and Ashley were as stoked about that prospect as we were.

—⚘—

Matthew and I drove to Temecula, a city not far from Palm Desert that Tuesday in a state of anticipation. We discussed the pros and cons of having another pet, how wonderfully behaved the pup, Jersey, had been. We knew a dependable veterinarian in the Valley and had made a tentative appointment for Wednesday. We dug out the old dog crate from the upper storage area of the garage, brought it along with one of our older throw blankets. We also had found a leash up there. Didn't we ever dispose of anything? Another project for my retirement.

I didn't want to be disappointed. I didn't want Matthew to suffer the disappointment of not bonding with the pup, not being able to bring her home.

I said, "We must be cognizant it might not work out." He nodded, but he looked determined.

As we exited the SUV on Tuesday, Matthew said, "See the immaculate state of their kennels and grounds?"

The owner of *Why Wait For Spring Kennels* whom we had chatted with, Amanda Brown, came toward the vehicle. "Let me show you around the kennels." Each kennel was clean and stocked with lots of water, blankets and a separate food dish. One of the staff was cleaning out an empty kennel. All staff were welcoming and appeared professional in their WWFS T-shirts and khaki shorts.

And then we saw her. We knew it was her, a pup that sat and

waited for us to approach, dark brown eyes staring contentedly at us, assessing us.

"Here, I'll get her out of the kennel for you to see properly."

As Amanda opened the kennel, letting the pup, Snickers, out without a leash, Matthew inquired worriedly, "Won't she run away?"

"Oh, absolutely not!"

I mean, that pretty much settled it for us. We were both down on our knees stroking a well-behaved pup, snuggling up to her, having her lick our hands and our faces. There was no leaping – well maybe small leaps. I felt like leaping myself I was so thrilled. Matthew's face glowed!

Snickers snuggled her face into Matthew's palm, wiggling her little behind, tail wagging. She rolled over for the tummy rub.

Amanda bent to give Snickers a pat while saying, "Her shots are up to date and, as you can see, Snickers has been socialized and has basic training."

"Oh my, for sure, we can see she's been socialized," I responded.

Matthew glanced at me for a moment before returning his attention to Snickers. In that look, I could see his decision. I felt such comfort in seeing the two of them together. As I crouched down, Snickers rolled toward me and licked my hand. We didn't leave her behind at *Why Wait For Spring Kennels*.

"We would love to take Snickers with us. What would that entail?"

Amanda stood up after giving Snickers another pat. She studied us for a few moments, checking us out, I guess. With a smile on her face, she attached the leash I had brought hopefully with me to this place – this place that would start a new stage in our lives – onto Snicker's collar. "Let's go into the office, and we'll talk."

Documentation regarding Snicker's pedigree and shots were brought out. Discussing our scheduled vet appointment, she advised, "You must get Snickers' next shot before she comes in contact with other dogs. Do you currently have any other pets at home?"

At our response in the negative, she said, "Snickers is used to other animals."

All this time, Matthew had his hand resting on Snickers, checking on her.

"Continue to socialize her. Let's go over those commands now so you know what she is used to. I'll show you how we give treats for her accomplishments."

Money, registration and contract documentation and puppy changed hands. Amanda gave us a bag of dog treats and premium food for Snickers. We had ourselves a pup! She happily went into our dog crate and immediately plopped herself down on the blanket and stared at us with an intelligent understanding look.

Amanda followed us to our vehicle. When we were settled, she said, "We offer a service to former pups. Arrange ahead with us, and we'll kennel Snickers for you. Just call to make arrangements."

"Thank you for everything," Matthew said with an expression of hope and joy.

We shook hands, and Amanda gave Snickers one more pat. "Goodbye, girl. Hope to see you soon."

We sat with Snickers for a long time, letting her get used to the idea that we would be taking her with us. We'd put the back seat down in my Ford Escape. I drove and Matthew turned around repeatedly to ensure Snickers had settled. Again, I noticed his content expression.

A brilliant decision.

Maybe this will calm him enough that he won't need to drink. Dr. GK had instructed one drink while on meds! He obviously couldn't handle stress, and those calls had unnerved him. *Damn it! Grow up!* But I couldn't find all the bottles, and he wouldn't listen to reason, said "I just need a shot every now and then."

I knew I'd find all the bottles, and I'd be calling Dr. GK. *I'll stop this nonsense. He isn't going down that road. He'll be taking Snickers for lots of refreshing dog walks.*

―⚜―

We'd blocked that threatening number thinking the calls would stop. This week, as I walked in the door, the phone rang.

"I'll get it," I said to him, a smile still on my lips thinking about a photo of Joshua Tree that I planned to use to paint from.

"Hello."

"I know what your husband did. Tell him to stop the blackmail and return the files."

With the landline still in my hand, I turned to Matthew. My expression told him enough. He took the phone, listened, and slammed it down in the cradle. "They'd hung up."

We blocked that number quickly as well. We gambled that we had all their numbers blocked. However, another call ten minutes later. Hesitating a moment, Matthew answered.

"Give the files back, blackmailing bastard."

Quickly Matthew countered, "I'm not the one doing this," and he'd slammed the handset down.

As soon as he'd hung up, she called right back. "Don't involve the media or police. Or not another cent. This can't go public with my name." She hung up before he could finish his sentence, "I didn't do it. I'm not…." He sunk down onto a chair. He lowered his chin to his chest and shook his head back and forth. "This can't be still happening. I can't handle this."

Sitting there looking pathetic, I felt sorry for him, but his falling apart wasn't going to stop these calls, nor was it going to fix anything.

I said, "We have to handle it. It's apparent the blackmailer is still collecting money from this unfortunate woman. Maybe they're even blackmailing the boyfriend. They're desperate not to have their name made public."

He peered up at me and regarded me with a thoughtful expression, "That's why they're still paying. It's a woman's voice, not familiar, but I've never met Tootsie. Anyway, I'm changing our landline telephone number immediately."

I hesitated to state the obvious. "If they know our name, changing our number won't help. Maybe we really should cancel the home number. We still have hundreds of businesses and people to advise. We may as well change to having just our cellphones."

"I'll change the landline number. They can't know our name. But where did they get our number from in the first place? Unless Aaron sold me out and gave it to them."

Matthew alternatingly made comments about Aaron being the one that stole the file, and that Aaron was blackmailing Tootsie. Then later, he'd switch and say, "Of course, he didn't. I know Aaron wouldn't do that."

Palm Desert, California

MATTHEW'S JOURNAL

Aaron was a friend during my depression, when I didn't even realize I needed a friend – when I thought I needed no one and that no one needed me. After my suicide attempt, Aaron continued to come around to see me.

We broached the crime I'd been accused of occasionally. Aaron knew I'd taken to drinking to calm myself from the stress of the menacing calls.

"Keep it cool, man," Aaron had said. And he wouldn't drink with me. That frosted me. He hadn't been a saint. "I'm not pissing around being your friend if you don't stop. Jenna needs a husband, not a drunk."

"Leave Jenna out of this. She doesn't need you speaking for her."

"No. She doesn't. She needs you, you dumb ass."

"Hey, don't judge me. You've always been the bad one. It's only until all this shit at work and the phone calls are over."

—m—

While my mental state was deteriorating, the fact that I was doing better physically was unmistakable. When I stared at the mirror while shaving, daily, I saw the man I used to be looking back at me, evidence of my work-out routine. As I stood up taller, turning to get a good view, muscles were showing. I caught myself admiring the physique that I used to have two years ago. I gave a little pump of my arm and mouthed the words, "I'm back!" But immediately I recognized that 'back' meant I needed to stop drinking. Soon, but how? Those calls freaked me out.

Also 'better' meant that I shouldn't still have shocking thoughts occasionally surging to the forefront of my mind. I didn't want to think these things, but I couldn't stop myself. 'I should have finished the job.' 'I shouldn't be burdening Jenna with my depressing issues.' 'She'd be better off without me.' One thought bounded into my mind, 'With a gun, I could finish it.' Todd had found me a gun, so now what?

—⁂—

Aaron had fallen in love with the Julian mountain area after he'd moved to Palm Springs. He rode his motorcycle more often than driving his CR-V, only taking the car for long trips – unless the wind was howling through the San Gorgonio Pass, blowing enough sand to block the roads. In the Valley, the wind hurling through the mountains can hit gusts of 50 mph.

One day he showed up on his motorcycle with an extra helmet, told me to grab some solid boots, brought out extra gloves.

"I've got lunch in the saddlebag. I'm going for a ride. Coming?"

"You bet!"

As I caught sight of Jenna in the doorway, I said, "Off with Aaron. We're going for a ride."

She paused for a moment to gauge if I'd been drinking, then replied, "Spectacular. Where?"

Aaron said, "I want to go to Lake Hemet. Okay with that?"

She grinned complete acquiescence and repeated my comment, "You bet."

On the driveway, Aaron gave me hell again, "Are you sober? You're not getting on this bike if you're not!"

I confirmed that I hadn't had a drink that morning.

"You better be sober, you fool! We're not kids anymore, and you need to grow up! It has to stop – for Jenna's sake if you're too stupid to stop for yourself."

I did enjoy my time with my old friend. But afterward, I thought I should have asked him about his relationship with

Cynthia. She's a good friend to Jenna, and I don't want her hurt.

Aaron could be using Cynthia. Would he be devious enough to get close to Cynthia to find out if there's anything I'm not telling him about the case? That Cynthia could tell him what she and John Wu had found out from the private investigator? Does he notice the difference in my attitude toward him? I want to trust him.

That's why all this is so hard on me. I still want to trust him, but can I? My best pal could have stolen from our clinic, is blackmailing the victim and has framed me for the entire thing. How depraved is that? Then if he's using Cynthia to find out what's happening, he's immoral. Could that be Aaron?

On the other hand, if he has real feelings for Cynthia, that would be a good thing. What if, though, he has done all this, and now has involved Cynthia? Even if he is serious about that relationship, it could jeopardize her entire career.

My mind is boggled. I hate how I need a drink to settle my mind about this and everything else I'm struggling with. My whole life is a mess.

Palm Desert, California

28

Late Spring

I Usually Aim Higher!

❖ JENNA ❖

CYNTHIA AND AARON, ALONG with Matthew and I were having supper at one of the best Mexican Restaurants in the Valley, *Guillermo's*. I knew that Matthew didn't know if Aaron had betrayed him. It was taking a chance going out with them for an entire evening. Matthew was in high spirits about this evening out, and he promised not to ruin it by saying anything to Aaron. *Damn it. He better not.*

With the huge Coachella event upcoming in the Coachella Valley a week away, restaurants and bars were especially full, indicating a lot of pleasure seekers already in the Valley.

Rehashing the "hide the fact we're dating" routine, Cynthia said, "The idea was it was also new to us, having recently realized we were more than working together for Matthew's benefit."

She looked as though admitting this to herself. It was good to see her relaxed, away from work, away from the strain of having to keep a secret. But also relaxed, I think, because she was in a place in her life she'd been uncertain she would experience again.

"The point about us not divulging our relationship to you was we could live in our own little world. Confessing it to you guys meant that it was a thing."

"A thing," Matthew repeated, taking a sip of his Negra Modelo beer. *Dr. GK said one drink. This is the one drink. I'm giving him a chance to prove he can do it. Pretty certain I got all the hidden bottles. I keep checking.*

"Well, that we had intentions toward each other," Aaron replied.

"Intentions toward each other," Matthew repeated needlessly.

"Is there an echo in this restaurant?" Cynthia asked. "We wanted to be sure of our emotions before informing you. Thankfully, you didn't mind us having a relationship."

One more time, Matthew repeated, "A relationship."

She glanced toward Matthew, giving him an overly dramatic expression of exasperation. "Will you stop repeating what I say?"

Grinning from ear to ear, Matthew said, "Got you!"

"Okie dokie, you got me," and she kicked him. I saw it as I bent to retrieve a fallen tissue.

Matthew laughed and quizzed, "Is that how you win your big trials? You just go up to the opposing attorney and kick them in the shin?"

Cynthia smirked while saying, "No, I usually aim a little higher." Then she winked.

We laughed and snorted, laughter tinkling throughout the outside seating area of *Guillermo's*.

After a horn honked over on El Paseo, Matthew resumed, "You know our social circle really shrunk with my depression – with the accusations floating around at work."

Aaron said, "I know exactly. People deserted you like rats from a ship."

But I felt that it was Aaron who had stayed on the ship.

Matthew muttered, "Some friends are indeed rats. Good friends are hard to find."

I wanted to slap him. Apparently, no one heard that comment. At least there was no reaction. *Is he that thick that he believes Aaron could do that? Or am I blind to the fact that even this great friend – to both of us – could be deceitful for money? Not Aaron. It just can't be Aaron.*

Our meal had been cleared away, and we each had remnants of our drinks. No one seemed in a hurry for the evening to end.

"I won't have to wear the same dress two days in a row starting next Saturday," proclaimed Cynthia.

"What?!" I sputtered.

"I'm moving half my clothes to Aaron's. It's a trial, a trial I haven't undertaken since I ended my marriage ten years ago."

I'd interjected, "Wow!" but was immediately interrupted by Cynthia.

"After my kids left home for the second time, I've had the house all to myself."

I quickly conjured up memories of Cynthia's children returning home, appreciating along with her that her daughter and son-in-law had reconciled, and her son had moved back out once he was re-hired.

Cynthia still speaking brought me back to the current conversation. "Living with another adult male human being will be a new experience. Living with Aaron is a trial I'll relish more than my best legal trials."

My gaze transferred to Aaron as he slid his hand over top of Cynthia's, declaring "I'm the happiest I've ever been."

"Congratulations," was all Matthew said.

I could see Matthew was pondering something. Worried what he might come out with, I jumped up to give Cynthia a huge hug. I thought about the bad relationships Aaron had discussed with me, being let down. *Aaron deserves this. They both need the relationship to succeed.*

The waiter arrived with our bill, and Aaron grabbed it and said, "I'm paying. It's been a special night with friends." He gave Matthew a light punch in the arm, forestalling any comment from Matthew. I hoped. *Does he get the vibration from Matthew that it's not right between them?*

"You'll need to be careful with any money you spend, or people will wonder where you got it from."

I mouthed to him, "Stop it!"

Aaron did a quick head turn toward Matthew, a look of confusion on his face. He said, "What's that, Matthew?"

I stepped between them to give Aaron a big hug, saying, "Matthew and I are very happy for you both."

I figured Aaron must hear some of Matthew's mutterings. Is he a good actor? Darn it! I don't want to pay heed to Matthew. It's not right. Aaron is a real good guy. And he's in love with Cynthia. Our private investigator will find who did all this shit.

Palm Desert, California

29

Late Spring

Mothers

❖ JENNA ❖

"Mom, Matthew and I are ready for both of us to be retired."

I stood in our kitchen, supper cooking in the oven, and sipping a cup of coffee, my cellphone propped under my chin. Walking toward the living room, I continued to expound on a situation already familiar to my mother.

"Matthew finding out about that work disaster – that was the final straw. We're ready for the next stage."

Mom sighed and said, "I know, Jenna. I know."

"I'm repeating what we both know, but I'm frazzled. And over 30 years teaching, marking papers, preparing day and week plans for the students all has taken a lot of energy. I want to retire, but I'm caught between two worlds."

My mom's terrific laugh rang out over the phone. "Jenna Barnes-Hanson! You're afraid you won't enjoy being retired, that you'll miss teaching?"

"We're set financially with pensions, Matthew's financial planning and great investments. For sure, it's possible the work accusations could mushroom badly if they do go to court, if he is convicted for wrongdoing. It's emotionally wearing on us."

I had no intention of telling my mom about the harassing telephone calls or Matthew's drinking. That was also wearing on us, on me. That would set her on a tailspin. *She isn't here and doesn't need the worries.*

"You'll be fine. Just relax." I heard a ding, then, "Just let me check this text from your dad. Wait a moment."

I always imagined her smiling as we chatted. My parents loved all their children equally. However, joking as siblings, we've each bragged she or Dad loved us just a little more than the rest. Robert especially insisted as the baby in the family, he was favoured. "And I'm the only boy! They were just practising on you until I came along – the real deal." *I'd heard that a zillion times.* Ruby and Joan said they were special being twins, and I, well I, as the oldest had been loved the longest.

"He took Charlie to the vet for yearly shots. He says, 'all is well' and sends his love. Back to you retiring, though. I love being retired. I did hate the two years we couldn't see you all. Travis calling it the 'damndemic' really fits the entire time."

"For sure. A Damndemic!" I took another sip of my Gold Rush California Blend Coffee, still hot in my cup, drinking in the aroma as well as the flavour.

"We know it's time I retired as well as Matthew, but the part about missing my co-workers, missing the ever-revolving door of new students to teach, the staffroom camaraderie at Palm Valley School, that's all difficult to leave. I'm pulled both ways. It was a hard choice to decide to retire this year."

Another of Mom's chuckles preceded another viewpoint. She would be sitting in her favourite old armchair while on the phone, curled up, one leg under the other.

"Well, it's almost the middle of May so you've more than a month to get your mind wrapped around the fabulous life you'll have. It's time. Matthew needs you to be there with him."

Pacing, I said, "I'm not going to be his shadow and ignore my identity. Matthew made decisions without consulting me. I need my own life and my individuality." I said this determinedly as I folded my long frame onto the couch. "It's time for me to be me!" *Matthew and my relationship has been going well.*

"That's definitive. Okay, write up a plan for what you want out of retirement. Discuss this with Matthew. We treated him delicately for the first while, but he has to understand what you want, to get a perspective on this new situation."

"That seems like a sound idea. You're remarkable, Mom, and I can't wait for you to come down to the desert when I'll be retired and have all winter to spend time with you – you'll wish I was back teaching!"

I could tell Mom was winding up the call and hear a sound of her standing up, the armchair creaking.

"I won't tire of you ever, but I'd best run. Take care of yourself and call me next weekend."

"I'm glad you let me natter about this. Bye, Mom."

I caught myself before I'd said anything else. My mom hadn't indicated anything to the contrary when I'd referred to their being down this winter. *Would they be back this winter?*

I clicked off my cell and stood up. As I turned around, I saw Matthew standing in the doorway. I wondered quickly if I had said something to my mother that would offend him. *He's a big boy. He'll have to handle it.* He appeared relaxed with one corner of his mouth slanted up, a half smile, eyes neutral. *No signs of alcohol in his mannerisms this morning. I told him I'd call Dr. GK.*

I grinned back and, as I walked toward him to give him a hug, I said, "Hi there."

A man stood before me, a man I recognized as the man I married, smiling, strong posture, muscles showing from his workouts and basketball with Aaron and Travis on the driveway. I sighed with contentment. *If only – If only he didn't drink.*

"I'm back from taking Snickers for a walk and heard you hang up. I assumed it was my mother checking up, but she would've called me on my cell. I guess I should give her our new number.

"Yes, I've hesitated to give it out, too. Maybe worried we'll have to cancel this number. It was such trouble telling all the businesses our cell phone numbers, but that was the best choice. Your mom will probably call tonight. It's been two weeks."

"Yeah, maybe she'll forget. My mother can cloak her chatter into pushing her opinion on us or interrogating us about rather personal details."

"Yeah, I want to hear what she and your dad are up to, but she manages to get all the bits of information I had no intention of revealing."

I chuckled and sighed with relief because we weren't always able to talk about his mother like this. Since his medical incident, we'd had lots of time to get our real feelings out about his mother's behaviour and empathize with each other.

Matthew said in a sarcastic tone, "It's not her nature to be demure."

I laughed out loud this time as I bent to pet Snickers. I'm thrilled with this pup.

He patted her at the same time.

"How are you, Snickers? Did you have a good walk?"

At that, she rushed toward our back door. "Whoops! Would you want a treat?"

This distraction worked, and I reached for the treat container. Snickers stood beside me, her tail drumming against my leg.

"Good call, Jenna. That's my girl," to Snickers. Then laughing, he said, "That's my girls!"

—⚘—

Just as we were done supper, a ringing phone sounded from his back pocket.

Matthew grabbed his cell and rushed from the room, saying, "Hello, Mom. Yes, I'm fine. Of course, I'm taking care of myself. Jenna's also taking care of me. Yes, Mom."

As his voice drifted away, I finished drying the remainder of the dishes. She'd be giving him the third degree. Why did Clara have to be brutally assertive? How did she get to be that assertive? I mean she wasn't a sergeant major or a high-up-the-ladder executive. I respected her being a homemaker, a mother, and yet she is as aggressive as a pit bull. That would be overlooked if she would just calm down and let sleeping dogs lie. Matthew and I are dealing with what happened. She should let it go and show more compassion. *At least Portland isn't an afternoon's drive here. Thank God they don't live in the Valley or come down each winter.* I blanched as that dreadful thought skittered across my mind.

Matthew came back into the kitchen just as I was straightening the kitchen chairs around the table. He picked up a dishrag and began wiping down the table, scrubbing harder than necessary. I hoped he didn't scratch the surface away with the force he was using. *Another reason for him to drink, to stop her voice in his head.*

"How's your mother?" I asked him this even though we both know I don't particularly like the woman. To clarify, in the beginning, in my innocence, I felt enthusiastic about having her as a friend, as a mother-in-law, as a comrade in arms. *She said she'd let me know when I was part of 'her' family.* Silly me. I kept trying harder, hoping to gain her affection prior to realizing she loved me being uncomfortable and making me believe I didn't belong.

As Matthew described tonight's array of unsolicited advice, I felt his pain. He has a better stance than he did seven-eight months ago. He stood in front of me, tall – no longer sallow. Touching the necklace Matthew gave me on our wedding day, I wondered *Did Matthew inherit her genes?* His father is more even tempered, a former police officer, used to being in charge, but he knows when to step back and listen.

I have to remind myself not to be as judgemental. Clara and Jack suffered two miscarriages after Matthew was born, before she had Neil four years later. This must've affected her terribly – to lose two children. I didn't want to imagine.

"We had the same sort of discussion we always have. She talks and tells me what to do, and I listen. You know her routine: 'What did you do today? Why did you do that? Why aren't you doing this and this? What medications are you on now? Have you talked to the doctor this week? Why is Jenna retiring? Don't you need the money? She is taking retirement early. Is her retirement fund enough?'"

I'd walked over to him and put my hands on his face to encourage him to look at me. His eyes held mine, but he seemed defeated.

"We're going to be fine. You're going to be fine. She is not fine. Come, let's take Snickers for a walk over to Country Club Drive to *Sherman's*. We'll grab a tea and forget about what she said. We both need the fresh air."

"Snickers will love another walk. I'll get my jacket."

But Snickers and I waited ten minutes, and he hadn't appeared with his jacket. With the heat of the Palm Springs May evening, Matthew didn't need a jacket. He just needed time to himself to get over his mother's call. I gave him another few minutes. After I walked back to the kitchen and poured a glass of water, he appeared. *No smell. Hope he hasn't switched to Vodka just to throw me off. He dislikes the taste.*

I didn't say anything, just took his hand and we all went out the door, into the warm night air, fresh air, fresher than the air which had come out of that cellphone at any rate. Snickers was beside herself with excitement that we were actually opening the door and finally (finally!) going for that walk.

We walked – the first 10 minutes we didn't say a word. Neither of us needed to because we both knew how he felt. This had been ongoing for years. No, it had been ongoing his entire life – she's always on about something. I'm not sure she particularly likes her husband, Jack. I revised my last thoughts. *They were holding hands.*

I said thoughtfully, "Maybe we don't give your mom enough credit. Maybe she's just a nervous wreck and can't handle stress."

"You know that doesn't explain everything!"

I reneged a little, "Granted, but let's just keep that scene in your hospital room in mind sometimes."

"If you can, then I can. But let's talk about your retirement. I'm glad you're retiring. We'll have a super time this summer, innumerable things to see and do."

His eyes showed such enthusiasm so I didn't say I wished I could have some time on my own. Our eyes locked. I became caught up in his excitement, loving this "new" old Matthew even more. Inside my head, Anne Murray sang, {*You're all I'll ever need.*}

"Jenna, I know the daytime summer heat is suffocating, but we can do things early morning or in the evening. We can go to Borrego Springs to see the spring flowers, up to Julian in the mountains, the coast to San Diego, Joshua Tree for hikes. We have the whole world in southern California at our fingertips."

And so, it began. I needed to discuss with him the fact I want to have my own life. But that would be another time, not tonight. Tonight, he needed me, and I'd give him that. Honestly, I'd give him anything right now. *Right now. Things are going well right now.*

Palm Desert, California

30

Summer

Retirement

❖ JENNA ❖

AS THE END OF June approached, I became excited about retirement. No doubt I would painfully miss the students and all the staff. I think part of me always will. The staffroom was a highlight of my day, rehashing what had happened in the classrooms, hallways, the gym.

I also had run the school Chess Club with approximately 56 students each year for 12 years. The children looked forward to Wednesday noon hour Chess Club. Another staff member, Marjorie Andrews, helped me each week during Chess Club. Each year as the children became involved, they helped set up the Chess sets, placing the pieces and afterward putting everything away. We had tournaments each March where all of the staff members would take part as competitors for the students. What a blessing to have this support from the staff. Some of the staff members weren't even good at Chess, but the students were over the moon with excitement about playing against a teacher, secretary, principal or the janitor. Since Marjorie and I ran the Club, it was the highlight of the children's year to play against us, me in particular.

"Can I play against you, Mrs. Hanson?"

I felt anguish at the fact the Chess Club would fold after I left. No one was able to take it on. What I felt most nostalgic about was what several students had said to me after returning from the Christmas school holiday.

"I got a Chess set for Christmas."

"My dad (or my mom) is playing Chess with me."

Those comments will always be my high.

The thing about schools is that those taking part in sports are celebrated by everyone. Those who don't play sports tend to be left by the wayside with no one taking notice of their accomplishments. There was an upcoming final student assembly, and I took it upon myself to inquire of the principal if she would mind if I printed off Certificates for the students who'd played Chess in my Chess Club. She gave dubious consent, with a sideways glance and an eyeroll that indicated she believed this a waste of time and resources.

At the assembly, all the sports students received their recognition and awards. Then I stepped up to the microphone and inquired, "How many students here have ever been involved in the Chess Club?"

As over two-thirds of the entire student population stood up, tentatively at first, then sensing the excitement in the air and the large number of students standing, more stood proudly. I heard the inhale of incredulous breath as everyone realized the number of students who had taken part over the years of Chess Club. I gave each student a laminated Certificate of Participation in the school Chess Club. You know, quite a few of the students looked at this certificate in awe. Some hadn't had this type of attention if they weren't involved in school sports. I was proud of them.

—w—

That evening I approached Matthew with Snickers right at my heels. He'd been typing up revisions for the book about his medical incident, and he was ready for a break.

"Let's go over what we each want out of my retirement," I said initiating the conversation.

"That's easy. I want us to be a complete couple again, doing things together, enjoying this phenomenal Valley with outside trips to

Disneyland, San Diego, Los Angeles, Temecula to try the 150 kinds of Root Beer, going to movies, drinking tea in the afternoons, shopping…"

He ran out of steam at the same time he noticed my expression was not as enthusiastic as his.

As he bent over to rub Snickers' back and give her a gentle rub behind her ear, he peeked back up at me with an understanding expression and said, "What are you considering, Jenna?" I was relieved to see that he appeared intrigued.

"You're writing your book. That's what you were working on just now. That will take plenty of hours each week."

His expression showed a lightbulb effect, "Right, well, perhaps not every minute together. Maybe you'll have to find something to do other than depend on me to keep you company when you retire."

A smile curved on his face. I giggled. This was going better than I had hoped. Maybe I hadn't needed to spend as much time fretful he wouldn't want me to have a life of my own.

"I'm laughing because I need time to myself as well as spending time with you. I have my painting now, and that'll take as much time as your writing will. I love to window shop, even if I'm not purchasing anything. I want to go and do all the things you mentioned a minute ago, but we each need to realize we have our own lives."

Snickers became excited at our conversation, sensing we were happy. She bounced a little as she walked toward me, grabbing a squeak toy as though she wanted to be involved in the conversation as well.

I pretended to take her squeak toy away, and off she ran.

As he smiled and glanced my way, he said, "I was only considering how wonderful being with you would be. I wasn't visualizing I also still want my own time – that I probably need time for myself."

Then as he came toward me, "You knew all that. Of course, you want time to be retired after decades of working. Phenomenal to get this sorted out before you actually retire."

Snickers stood at the door, toy in her mouth, obviously wanting a play time in the backyard.

"Snickers, do you want to go for a walk?"

She answered by prancing and running to bring her leash to me. As I put the leash on, Snickers sat without being instructed, waiting patiently.

"You are a good dog." Wag, wag.

Laughing, Matthew walked toward the door, "I'm coming too."

While holding hands, we walked out the door, Snickers steps ahead. As we neared the front of our property, Snickers went into the command of "Heel" without being told.

"You're such a good dog," Matthew said.

As we moved onto Hovley, the sun may have shown long shadows from the palm trees, but today we only saw a beautiful view in front of us. *Matthew hadn't said anything about believing Aaron stole the file in days. Getting everything sorted out is a big ask.*

Palm Desert, California

31

Summer

I Sprained My Freaking Ankle

❖ JENNA ❖

YEAH, WHAT A KLUTZ I'd been that day, slipping on the new flat rock path Mario had laid out in the front yard. As I lay sprawled on the rocks, I screeched out in shock and pain. The damn ankle swelled right there as I cried out. Matthew came running over, Snickers right behind him, now barking at the commotion. Kathy next door turned with her sprinkler in her hand, taking in the situation.

"What happened? Oh, my God. I got your paving stones wet! Is the ankle broken? Should I call an ambulance?"

"No wait. Sit still," Matthew ordered as he cradled me gently in his arms. "Let me examine it. I've got training."

Crying, "I know."

I sobbed pretty good now, feeling the fool. Snickers stood back, her tail still, worried. Matthew had always been the dependable one when our kids or others were injured playing sports.

"Snickers, come." She rushed beside me, licking my extended hand.

Kathy also knelt by my side as she stroked my hair. "I'm so sorry. I didn't realize my water was getting to your rocks. Or they'd get slippery."

"It's not broken, sweetheart," Matthew said soothingly. "We'll get Mario to change them out as soon as he has time. I'm sure the business will trade them in when they find out what happened. Either way, they're toast."

I smiled, even as tears were dripping down my cheeks. "Seems as though it would be a little hard to chew."

Matthew spared me an expression of confusion.

In response to his quizzical look, I replied, "You said, 'they're toast.'"

"Humour is your best medicine. Let's see if I can carry you into the house. Kathy, can you get the door?" As he hoisted me up, he said, "Have you lost some pounds? You're lighter than when we married."

I turned my face into his shoulder, shivering a little at the pain. "I haven't weighed lately." I had too much on my mind. I hadn't bothered weighing, and I hadn't been eating as much. Some people snacked when they were stressed – not me. Matthew drank when stressed. Again, not me.

Snickers ran inside, turning in circles, still alarmed about the confusion and Matthew carrying me.

"Kathy, thank you. I'll get her to bed, put ice on it and check it out again."

"Sorry you guys. Call or text me later to let me know how Jenna is."

I swivelled my head toward her, "Don't you worry. If they can't take water, they were dangerous from the get-go. One of us will text."

"Sorry again," as she quietly closed the door behind us.

There had also been a gash on my knee that Matthew tenderly patted with a cloth, cleaning the area and disinfected with antiseptic. That brought more tears. Matthew iced the ankle off and on for hours.

"Need more ice?"

"Yes, thanks."

When the telephone rang, we both looked at each other, startled. As Matthew answered, I hoped it wasn't Tootsie. Honestly, I don't know why we didn't just cancel the phone. We used our cell phones normally.

"Hi, Kathy. She's doing much better. Okay, I'll tell her. Thanks. Bye."

Kathy? Thank goodness.

"She says she hopes you're better soon. I'll get the ice."

Matthew was only gone a minute or two, but I still leaned to smell his breath when he returned. *Whiskey. Shit.* I knew not to say a word. I surmised another bottle had appeared under his sink or nightstand. That's about all he had time to travel to and from. *The phone call set him off. He has been pretty good lately.*

Snickers had been whining to get on the bed with me. She knew something was wrong. Normally, she stayed in her padded bed at Matthew's side of the bed.

"Just for this afternoon. She's upset."

Matthew looked fondly over at Snickers as she whined beside the bed. "She was upset that first night after we brought her home, lonely for her mom and siblings. You were firm." Lowering his voice to a whisper, he leaned closer and repeated what I had said that first night and all three nights after."

I smelled the whiskey and a breath mint. *Didn't work as well as he hoped.*

Matthew continued, "You told her 'No, stay.'"

As Matthew patted the bed, I said, "Snickers, come," and Snickers rushed to jump up, by now being just large enough to jump onto the bed.

"Now you've started something," Matthew said. "If you two are doing okay, I'm going to type up some more notes."

"I'm good. Work hard."

He wasn't slurring. Had a couple of swallows to calm himself. Not acceptable though. Darn him. I need to count on him for both of us to get through this. And is he going for another 'chugalug' now?

With Matthew working on his journal – that had turned into a manuscript – I settled in to rest my ankle. I'd been thinking a lot over the past months what my future would be with Matthew or without Matthew. Thankfully, Matthew had not died from his suicide attempt. However, witnessing his reaction to the stress we'd been through and the drinking that had accompanied that stress, I knew I wouldn't stay married to a drunk. Hell, I had stayed throughout the verbal abuse – even then considering where I'd go, what I'd do because I wasn't going to put up with that abuse for the rest of my life. As my retirement approached and with this time to reflect, I mulled over my options.

I loved Matthew. I'd loved him dearly for most of our 30 years together. He'd changed back to his gentle self since his suicide attempt and yet there was something still off. There had been no verbal abuse, no indication at all that he couldn't control his temper, or that he'd take his moods out on me. The drinking – sneaking drinks – was really an issue. He needed to just grow up and handle the stress. Yes, I was certainly affected by our stresses, but I was handling it. As I patted myself on the back, I wondered *am I handling the stress?*

I gave in, torturing myself by rehashing it all once again. I used our lawyer's tactic of raising each finger as I thought.

One: Matthew's illness from long-haul covid, that freaking cough. *Mostly done with.*

Two: His depression. *Is it over?*

Three: Blamed for bad business decisions during the pandemic, then fired. *Ongoing.*

Four: Suicide attempt. *Done. Right?*

Five: My father's deteriorating health; my parents' age. *Ongoing.*

Six: Accused of theft and blackmail. *Ongoing.*

Seven: Those fricking threatening phone calls. *Ongoing.*

Eight: Matthew's drinking and hiding it. *Ongoing.*

Nine: Our marriage. *Is it salvageable?*

Ten: Will my parents sell and leave me alone? *Ongoing.*

Damn, there's more. Do I have to start on my freaking toes to keep track?

Eleven: Travis has indicated to me he wants a different job. *Ongoing.*

Twelve: Matthew's obsession that Aaron was framing him for the file theft and blackmail. *Ongoing? Or was he done thinking that?*

Thirteen: To stay or to leave, depending on most of the above. *Ongoing.*

Fourteen: Yes, and then there's Clara's behaviour. *Ongoing and more!*

And there was something in Matthew's eyes, in his expression many times. It would come and go. I saw defeat and resignation for flashes of time. I'd called him on it, and he'd snap out of whatever reverie he'd been in. He'd smile, tell me it was nothing. *Was he suicidal again?* I'd not been married for three decades not to know he was troubled about something. I knew I'd missed the clues before his suicide attempt, missed the aggravation he'd been suffering with George Alphonse blaming him for the theft. At that time, I thought it was the reverberation of George saying it was Matthew's fault that the clinic was failing during the pandemic – then Matthew being fired. I'd missed there'd been more blame for something that he hadn't done, that I knew he hadn't done.

Okay, I'm not handling the stress. My hair is falling out. I'm losing weight. My appetite has been affected. I've been biting my fingernails. I'm hyperventilating thinking about all this. I feel a quiet desperation within myself. It's growing louder each time Matthew drinks.

He can't handle the stress. His psychiatrist says one drink – he drinks here and there all day because of the menacing calls. But he'll continue to experience stress, and then drink unless he himself decides to stop. I feel this desperation because of the drinking, but also because I can't end the anguish he is experiencing. *I do love Matthew.*

I would stand up to him. He must get his drinking issue resolved. If he couldn't, then I'd decide to stay or leave, but I must be certain before I did. When I was retired, it would be more apparent what my choice would be going forward.

Matthew tried very hard to maintain normalcy. He made the meals, helping me up and down as long as I needed it. I used an old pair of crutches Kathy had rushed over with when Matthew had texted to ask if they had any from when Todd had broken his leg years before.

Snickers got to lie on the bed, nuzzling close to me. I told her over and over, "Just for now. This isn't permanent."

I think she understood. Once I was up and about, she went back to her bed beside Matthew, licking his hand when he dropped it down beside the bed.

All the signs were there that Matthew had come through for me and taken great care of me while I needed him. *He must continue on this path.*

—⁂—

I was relieved the front yard paving stones had been replaced with rocks that had more ridges to them. I watered those rocks one day and took a little hike over the area. My sandals gripped them fine as Matthew watched, having told me he would walk over them to test them out.

"Really, let me do it. You just got over a bad sprain."

"Nope, I won't rest easy until I have them under my feet."

Placidly, he inquired, "I wonder where Ashley got her stubborn streak from?"

I ignored that. Snickers had been following behind me. She loved jumping around on the rocks and running through our bushes. She didn't ever damage anything, so we let her have her freedom. Even if anyone walked past, Snickers simply gazed at them. She didn't run away at all! We marvelled at that repeatedly.

"How can two dogs of the same breed be so different?"

"Alpha, Beta?" asked Matthew.

"Neil would probably have a beta joke about that, beta you something or other!"

That made us both laugh recalling the stack of tall tale books with the Beta fish, the joke gift.

Palm Desert, California

32

Summer

Did Matt Do It?

❖ AARON ❖

As I SAT AT a table in the *Smooth Image Surgery* staff room, chatting with a fellow employee, Harry, I noticed that we were situated beside two Human Resources personnel.

I expressed an opinion to him. "Matt should've returned his key sooner."

As Harry stopped raising his French fry toward his mouth, he closed his mouth and opened it again, a quizzical expression crossing his face, "What are you saying?"

"I'm wondering how to feel. You know Matt was my pal for decades. I'm confused by all this, but it's time for me to face facts."

While Harry chewed his French fry and perhaps chewed over what I might be indicating, he remained silent.

After studying me, he said slowly, "Matthew was an important person in our clinic's success for a long time, though."

"That I know. And I covered for him through a lot of his depression. But he's really let himself, his family and me down. My guess is he let the clinic down as well by gettin' greedy for money or maybe trying to get back at *Smooth Image Surgery* for him losin' his job."

Harry seemed to get into the spirit of our conversation, and he giddily joined in, "Yeah, I know. Sucks, doesn't it that a fella can get himself into that?"

I sadly added, "And Matt had been short of money because he had lost his job due to that breakdown."

"I heard all the rumours too, but I'm surprised that you're 'fessing up to realizing it was your pal, Matthew."

Breathing deeply, I then gave him a despondent look. "Yeah, it was a hard choice for me to make."

PART THREE

Forward and Onward.

Palm Desert, California

MATTHEW'S JOURNAL

John Wu telephoned my cell at 7:00 a.m. I jumped up and beckoned to Jenna as I put him on speaker. We listened, no longer groggy from sleep (or booze in my case).

Smooth Image Surgery put out a News Release requesting information from the public. The Release says that Smooth Image Surgery reports a theft of a client file from their company. The Release asks people to get in touch with the clinic if they have information and giving a telephone number. Anonymous information can also be provided via Crime Stoppers. They announced that Smooth Image Surgery reported that their clients' health records are safe and not compromised."

John Wu advised that this News Release was not unusual, and that Communication Consultants recommend this process to get ahead of a story they thought would break shortly and thus control the narrative.

Unsurprisingly, George hadn't even had the courtesy to call my lawyer to advise him. Thankfully, John always kept abreast of News Releases.

Holy mother! I was steamed! This couldn't be happening.

At a quickly arranged conference at his office, we paid, in trust, an additional retainer his firm requested, putting a dent in our savings. I was foreseeing another expensive pair of shoes in his future.

As we entered his office, taking the seats he indicated, John assured us, "We're working on the flaws in the company's information. This could take months or years to go through the system, giving us time to get ready. We've started the defense strategy for your case."

Jenna and I had perused the internet weeks ago, seeking information on this type of theft. With some foreboding, I asked, "What types of punishment may I expect if this goes to trial, and we lose the case?"

John took his now familiar standing position, ensuring he had our attention for his oration. He lifted his chin and mirrored this in the lift of the toe of one shoe. Then shifting his gaze directly to me, he replied, "White collar crimes may involve several options. Not all cases include jail time; often, however, the penalties focus on the payment of money." At this point, his gaze moved to Jenna, then back to me.

I was dimly aware of someone stopping at his office door and then retreating. I heard a man's voice drifting down the hall, commenting to someone. I was annoyed at the distraction. Apparently, so was John because he scowled at the door.

Carrying on, he said, "Financial penalties could include," now raising the familiar one finger as he spoke, then communicating his points. "Criminal fines. Some white-collar crimes come with an incredibly high maximum penalty." Another finger raised. "Forfeiture – Forfeiture would involve you giving back the file you allegedly have in your possession, of course, and money obtained illegally from the blackmail, so you don't benefit financially." Then, with a flourish, the third finger was raised. "Restitution money to be paid back to the victim to help recoup their losses from the crime. As well, you'd pay their legal fees relating to the offense."

Setting aside the piles of dollar signs running through my mind, I was extremely relieved to have this man on our side. I felt he'd leave no stone unturned to get to the bottom of my case. My freedom was at stake but knew his reputation would also be incentive for him to resolve my untenable situation.

Palm Desert, California

33

Summer

Words

❖ JENNA ❖

GABBING ON MY CELL, I said again, "Milena, fantastic job that you and our staff managed to make my retirement. No one has retired without someone giving a party, but I didn't expect it to happen the night you and I were going out for coffee to 'discuss a possibility of my retirement party.'" I chuckled at the memory. "Good thing I'd dressed up because you said we were going to Lulu's."

"Yeah, good thing you did not show up in dirty sweats from some sort of yard work you had on the go. Or paint all over yourself. I had to say we were going somewhere nice."

"I suspected when you didn't turn toward Lulu's Restaurant. Then you pulled up to the *Purple Room Supper Club*. Very exciting!"

My fellow teacher, Milena, her striking red hair causing heads to turn everywhere we went, managed to make any event a joy.

"Having your mom and dad fly in to see the 'Elvis Tribute' was the icing on the cake. We filled a huge chunk of the *Purple Room*."

"Yes, my parents surprising me was the ultimate! Matthew, Travis, Ashley, Robin, Aaron, Cynthia, your husband, Antonio, and all the staff waiting for us was terrific. And Scot Bruce! Truly amazing as Elvis. Matthew found it thrilling to hear he originally came from the Pacific Northwest. My mom swooned the whole evening. Thank you for that memorable night."

"Now you have been an unemployed bum for a few weeks, how do you feel about retirement? Does it feel different from any other summer holiday?"

"Yeah, well, the last two weeks before school starts and the first month are always hectic times. I'm relieved to get away from that. I'll miss the children and the captive audience in the staff room. You never know who's going to come out with what in the staff room, and I miss the stories of what any of the students did."

"It is time we had another outing, Jenna. There is always something going on here in the Valley. I saw there was a magic act coming to one of the casinos. Let us check into it, but now I have to cut this off. We are heading to San Diego early tomorrow. I love San Diego, but not the traffic."

"All right, Milena. I'll check out the magician, and we'll chat soon. Cynthia called yesterday and I'd love to see her again. Let's make it a girls' night."

"Perfect. Chat later."

The end of work doesn't mean the windup of my work friendship with Milena.

—⁂—

Droplets of rain had turned into a very rare downpour. I'd been planning to drive to Jensen's to pick up some special cheeses for an appetizer. That grocery trip could wait. The roads would be swelling from the rainwater and the water pouring from the mountains into the Valley. Driving could be a small hazard until the water went into the washes throughout the Valley.

I decided to go through my boxes of papers and binders I'd brought home from school. As I neared the end of my pilgrimage through the boxes of my teaching life, I came across a slim folder. *Empty.* Opening it anyway since the folder could be re-used, I realized it wasn't empty. It contained a hand-written item, not in my own handwriting. As I read the title line, the significance hit me.

BE KIND BECAUSE YOU CAN'T REWIND (Or *Think Before You Talk*)

This was the poem from a bullied grade XI student. She'd entered my classroom and closed the door. Crying, she'd asked me to read a poem in her hand as she reached it out to me.

"Can you read this and tell me what you think?"

I'd read it then. Now I sat and read this poem once more, and I was shocked again at what she'd written. I knew bullying at the time from my children and other students who'd come forward.

I'd told her, "Your poem is passionate and disturbing. It's terrible what's happening to you. The poem is well written, describing your own emotions from being bullied." I asked her if she had reported the verbal abuses to anyone else.

"No, I don't want to draw more attention to myself specifically."

I touched her shoulder. "Then what do you think is best I do? I'm so sorry you've been going through this, and I want to help you in any way I can."

"I'm baring my soul in this poem, and I want you to read it at the next student assembly."

"But not from you," certainly knowing she didn't want to be singled out.

Grimacing, she'd said, "No. What I want is that you read it from an Anonymous Student. Maybe those being bullied will remember this poem and stand up for themselves – unlike me."

I'd then looked deep into her eyes, and said, "By writing this poem, you took a big step. You took your pain from inside you and wrote it down. It's always good to get it out there."

She'd given me a tentative smile. I continued, "Keep writing. Keep expressing yourself. I'll read this at the assembly. You'll know you took your own big step."

"Thank you so much, Mrs. Hanson. The poem isn't perfect, but it's the best I could do."

Again, I made certain she looked directly at me, "It's perfect for you and that's all that's important. Keep writing. You're meant to be a writer, I think."

"This poem is from the heart of someone who has been hurt. I need you to listen. I need you to *hear*. Learn something from this poem, whether you are the one being abused or whether you are the one who is the abuser. Take away something positive." And I read. A hush came over the room as I read out the poem to the 750 students in the auditorium.

Be Kind Because You Can't Rewind
(Or Think Before You Talk)

I am sensitive, and too easily become hurt
From proclamations you think it creative to blurt.
You say statements that are fundamentally mean.
To make yourself feel superior you are so keen.

You are a cruel person and challenge those others
Such as me who have a vulnerability in you it stirs.
I should stand back and not indicate you hurt me.
I put forth my brave face so my pain you don't see.

It emboldens more injuries for you to inflict.
You find imperfections that are easy to predict
As soon as you see the chasm of my own weakness.
I must stop internalizing the comments you express.

They should not define my inner judgements of self.
I take opinions to heart affecting my health.
My self-worth should not be mirrored by what you think.
You poisoning my thoughts my thin armour does chink.

Are you also bullied? Do you suffer from abuse?
No matter what your circumstance, there is no excuse.
Causing hurt to others can't make you whole again.
Respect yourself first before you can stop your pain.

The assembled students had been quiet, eerily quiet. Someone had started to clap, and then more until almost the entire auditorium resounded with it. Most of the students had stood up – a sign of respect. I'd seen some tears. Oh, the assembly wasn't seamless. I also saw a few sneers. But the feeling something big had happened was prevalent. I didn't glance toward my student, of course. She'd come to me the next day, crying again – with happiness.

"There's been a different attitude." Smiling. She'd added, "Maybe it'll last. Maybe not, but I feel empowered. Thank you. Please keep a copy of the poem."

At the next staff meeting, the student Guidance Counsellor asked that the poem be put into the school newsletter. After a unanimous vote and permission from my student, BE KIND BECAUSE YOU CAN'T REWIND (Or Think Before You Talk) went into the newsletter.

My student had gone on to university and had excelled at writing. She had a public relations job, occasionally sending me articles which had been published in magazines. That poem would be set aside for Ashley for her teaching career.

As I continued through my boxes, I found everything else to be mundane, the usual keepsakes and papers, and it didn't take me long to put the effects into piles of "Throw Away" and "Keep". There were items that I believed Milena might want or Ashley once she became a teacher.

However, as I sat here now, I felt a profound kinship with that student. I'd been through a few years of emotional turmoil. Matthew had been emotionally damaged, and it wasn't my fault. *Not my fault* reverberated in my head.

My gaze riveted on that lone piece of paper. I read and re-read those words. Call it a revelation or just plain sense, but I knew something had altered deep inside me. *I will not be bullied ever again. It's my turn to stand up for myself.*

Palm Desert, California

34

Summer

Attitude Adjustment

❖ JENNA ❖

DR. GERSTEIN-KRAUSE HAD BEEN an angel in my life. Over a period of time, she had given me the strength to talk about my emotions in front of Matthew. We both sat with her during a visit, and she explained to Matthew what would occur at the session.

"Jenna is going to talk to you, and you are going to listen. You are at the stage where none of this will be a surprise to you, and I believe that you'll be relieved to have this all out in the open." She slanted her body, facing more toward Matthew and said, "I want you to hear how Jenna's words to you sound coming back to you when said with me listening."

And so, I began. "I love you." A tear escaped, then another. "But I want to respect you." Taking a large breath in, I continued telling him the things that he had said to me, things that were totally unacceptable.

"I can't respect you until you show me respect – respect my opinions. Not just when it's easy for you, but even when I am questioning your opinion or interrupting something you're doing. There can be no more Diablo raging fits – no more." I stopped to take another huge breath. "Then I will believe our marriage can be saved – if I no longer have to be afraid of you."

Dr. GK firmly said, "That is verbal abuse, Matthew. You've been abusing your wife."

Matthew looked away, then back at me – full eye contact. As Matthew took my hand, another and another tear found a route down my cheeks. I looked away and then dead on at him, waiting.

He said, "It won't happen again. That I promise you. I'm not making excuses. I was a bastard these past few years. I don't know how I could have done and said the things I did, but I do know that I resolve to never be that way again."

I looked up at him, staring into his eyes. "It better not. Never! And no more hiding alcohol and drinking!"

"I promise this for you and for my own sake."

That made a difference. Him saying this, acknowledging that he had treated me badly, not hiding behind saying he can't remember, or denying it. Maybe I now believe him. But it touched me deeply that he owned up to me that he did that.

A few moments passed before Dr. Gerstein-Kraus cleared her throat. "I'm going to hold you to those promises. I'll be inquiring of Jenna. And to reiterate – No more alcohol in or out of your home."

She stood up, shook our hands. As we reached the door, she said, "I'll expect each of you to make an appointment to see me in one month. Separately."

Palm Desert, California

35

Summer

A New Beginning?

❖ JENNA ❖

When Matthew and I went to see Dr. GK, I was concerned he would resent my making an appointment and him having to attend. I was well aware he hadn't been receptive to past appointments made for him.

I'd prepared myself for the outcome either way. It would have been unbelievably difficult for me to start anew if the appointment had led to him being enraged again. After 30 years of marriage, my heart would have been broken, along with my spirit. If that had happened and my parents weren't going to return to the resort, my life would have been an utter mess. "Forward and Onward" was what I'd said to myself over and over prior to our appointment.

Matthew had been quiet on the drive home. At the end of the appointment, all seemed good. He had appeared very supportive, and we'd hugged as he murmured for my ears only, "This is our new beginning."

Since then, he hadn't uttered one word. I let him have his silence. He was quiet until we closed the front door of our home. The door had clicked shut behind me as I turned around to face my husband. He grabbed me, and we embraced. I was crying. He was crying. Real tears.

"Jenna, I do respect you. You're my everything. You've always been my everything."

At this point, I couldn't stand. I made it to the sofa only with the help of Matthew. He sat beside me as I curled myself forward, head in my hands and cried. Through aching sobs, I said, "You were always my everything, too. I lost you for two years. I was lost."

"You're not lost any more. Most of all, I'm not lost any more."

The lovemaking that afternoon was prolonged and passionate. I could joke and say I swooned, and he crooned, but it was not that. It was what any woman and man who had lost and then found each other would ache for – fresh, yet familiar. *He was my guy!* I remembered having that same thought some 30 years ago when I realized how much I loved Matthew, the night I'd told him about Samson. My feeling toward this man – my Matthew, my guy – was unreserved love.

Talking, making love again, falling in love all over. This was what the next several days were about.

It was a dream come true. I wasn't an idiot. I knew there could be setbacks ahead. I felt stronger than I had in years. Those years were behind me. I could handle what might be in front of me.

—ɷ—

Matthew had snuck up on me while I prepared a surprise for him. I'd thought he was sitting in the back yard, but here he was in the kitchen. Standing behind me. He kissed the back of my neck.

Peering over my shoulder, he said, "What've you got here? I haven't seen this album before."

"It's for you, but it's not wrapped yet. I wondered if you'd want to have some of our family photos in your own album – instead of scattered throughout various albums and masses of them on our computers. I made an album for myself too."

"Jenna, wow! Let me get us an iced tea. Then we can check out the albums."

"Iced tea would be nice." *He knows I'll be happy he was having iced tea.*

We spent an hour comparing our albums, Matthew's with a lot more of his parents – my album the opposite, portraying more of my family. I had lots of me with Ruby, Joan and Robert. Matthew sat comfortably beside me while holding his album, his arm around my shoulder. I leaned into his arm, and he tightened it around me.

"I can't tell you how thoughtful this is. Thank you from the bottom of my heart. This really grounds me." Slightly ashamed looking, Matthew confessed, "I hate to admit it, but I don't recollect some of these photos and am quite hazy about others. Did you know that?"

I changed positions to give him a kiss. "I suspected, and I wanted to give you something you can associate with, pick and choose your own time to absorb them fully."

"You're kind right down to your very bones. I'll sit and check these photos out whenever I want. It's really the right size."

His cell pinged, but he ignored it as he went on to say, "I recollect the times we went to Calgary for Christmas prior to your parents wintering in the Valley," indicating one photo after another of Travis and Ashley sledding, skating and attempts at skiing.

"Attempting to ski is right. Not much success on the hills."

"And the snowmen! Awesome photo of Ashley and the snow woman. She insisted on making a snow woman, including your mom's hat and slippers!"

"She wanted to put one of my bras on 'her', but I drew the line at that one. She did use black paint for the eyelashes and red for its lips. She used the snow woman for a teaching moment to Mom and Dad's neighbour's children, indicating the difference between a snow man and a snow woman. Oh my gosh!"

Matthew took a closer look at the photo of the snow woman. "Becoming a teacher was always in the cards."

"Seriously, though, I'm glad she stayed away from sex ed for pre-school students!"

"Instructional, for sure." His face turned pensive before he said, "Seeing those photos of my mother and father with our children makes me think I should be taking a trip back home. Do you think you'd like to come with me?"

"Of course. That would be a fine idea."

"Snickers can be booked into *Why Wait For Spring Kennels.*"

Ding! He checked his cell and said, "I'll call Aaron back later. I don't know what to think about him, and sometimes I just can't talk to him."

"Oh, Matthew. It has to be someone else. You know Aaron through and through. Don't even consider he'd do it."

"I'll keep an open mind."

Damn! He still thinks it's Aaron. I hope so much that he's wrong. But who?

Back to the photos in front of him, Matthew said, "I loved this trip to San Diego with the kids. Was that the Christmas my parents gave us a $500.00 gift certificate?"

"Yes, you're right. If the Zoo wasn't impressive enough, we also went to the Safari Park."

"That was more than amazing."

Picture after picture depicted our safari, seeing the elephants and rhinos at really close quarters. My favourite showed me feeding the giraffes. Thirteen or so giraffes had come up to the truck when we'd stopped. We were given acacia twigs, leaves intact, told to face away from the giraffe being fed, hold the leaves over our shoulders and not to touch the giraffe! Apparently, it would associate my touch with it brushing up against something and, with it's 70-pound head, would knock me right off the truck. Her eyelashes were extremely long, her face serene, exceptionally beautiful.

Aware of her instructions not to touch the giraffe, I'd nonetheless muttered, "Are you sure I can't touch her?" Being so close to this gorgeous gentle-looking giraffe was so tempting and inviting a touch.

Matthew's favourite photos were ones I took of the moments watching a huge water buffalo coming close to the baby rhino, the whole herd behind it. It was angry and ready to attack the baby, pawing and snorting. We had watched from a distance as a baby rhino faced off against that fierce water buffalo. The little thing would charge two or three steps on its baby legs and the water buffalo would back up. The baby thought itself ferocious. However, unknown to it, its mother had come charging behind it, ready to take on the water buffalo. Re-thinking its stand, the water buffalo loped off with an abundance of snorts.

Ashley had announced, "When I become a teacher, I want to take all my students to a zoo. Palm Desert's Living Zoo is perfect."

Snapping out of my reverie, I saw Matthew pointing to photos of Balboa Park in San Diego, obviously reliving the encounters the photographs brought to him.

"Look at this."

Snickers stood up, wondering what the word "look" was to mean for her.

"Jenna, let's get the kids' schedules and take them back! They can bring their significant others. We'll stay somewhere in San Diego and go to Balboa Park. Phenomenal!"

"That does sound like a plan, Matthew."

"We'll go when your mom and dad can come dog sit Snickers."

Again, she looked excited at her name.

I said to her, "They'll bring Charlie to play with you." Snickers wagged her tail lazily even though she seemed to sense she wasn't going anywhere right now. Maybe she did recognize Charlie's name, being the most clever puppy in the Coachella Valley after all!

—m—

Snickers and Charlie loved each other, playing until one of them sagged. The last one standing still jumped around eager to catch the other's attention, hoping to play. What I noticed was the one that wanted to continue playing seemed to gratefully slump down in a heap, breathing deeply and asleep within seconds.

The first time they met, we had Snickers in the backyard. Mom and Dad had come for a visit, bringing Charlie. Charlie bounded out our back door straight to Matthew as usual. Only, this time, Matthew wasn't alone. Charlie stopped short. "Woof?" A question.

Snickers trotted toward Charlie, and we wondered how this would work. Was there going to be a jealousy thing because Charlie loved Matthew, and Snickers was the usurper? They sniffed each other for a full minute, walking around and around. Snickers licked Charlie, and Charlie ran. We hoped as a playing tactic.

"Ruff, ruff."

"Woof, woof." And then they ran.

They roughhoused for the longest time before one collapsed down, sleeping. That first time, Charlie tired first. Snickers whined for a second, hoping for more play, and then lay down right beside Charlie. They looked adorable. Charlie was shorter than Snickers when standing. Our English Springer Spaniel, with her long legs, was taller even with the large age gap. Lying there, Charlie fit into Snickers frame.

"Don't move," requested Matthew. "I'm taking a picture."

"Send me the photo. Snickers won't be this small for long. It'll be awfully cute to see them as Snickers grows," I said.

Snickers moved closer to Charlie, inching her way to snuggle.

"Oh, how charming. Isn't that marvellous how Snickers is lying so close to Charlie? Snap that one," my mom implored, leaning closer to them.

Dad whispered, "I wonder if Snickers misses her mother."

I had shivers. First, because it was an awesome comment about Snickers missing her mother. But my shivers continued as I thought of how I would miss my own mother and, of course, my father if they didn't return to the Valley next winter.

Palm Desert, California

36

Summer

What the Hell?

❖ JENNA ❖

Matthew glanced at the telephone.

"Well, it can't be one of those threatening calls, so no problem." Matthew answered, "Hello."

"I know who you are, you son of a bitch," a man's voice this time from a different number than those we'd blocked, "You aren't F-ing getting away with this. We're not paying a penny…"

"I didn't steal…"

"We didn't want the police involved. We heard the News Release. End of money to you."

"It wasn't me."

I could hear the man screaming, "And we'll get you for ruining our lives."

Matthew slammed down the phone. "What the hell? We changed to a new landline number. How did they get the new number?" His face blanched.

"What? What all did they say? Are you all right? Matthew, here sit down."

Sitting where I directed him, Matthew grimaced, swallowed hard. He said, "I know who you are, you son of a bitch."

"They. Know. Who. You. Are?" I sat down beside him on the

couch. "Maybe they were lying, just trying to frighten us."

"I'm going on-line right now and cancelling our landline. We'll depend on our cells. Damn it! We should have done that before."

Yes, I had said we should weeks ago. Now what? Will cancelling the landline at last end it, or is this now worse than we thought? Do they have a gun? I can't think that way.

After Matthew cancelled the landline, we simply sat and stared, glancing at each other occasionally. We were both numb. And scared.

That night we'd cancelled our landline turned into a night neither of us slept. I'd glance sideways at Matthew lying still beside me and wonder if we should talk. *How is he doing? How is he doing mentally? He said he wouldn't drink. He told Dr. GK and me that. Can he keep that promise?*

I snuggled up beside him as he turned over and faced me, both our sets of eyes wide open. I could see him from the light streaming through the heavy half-open blinds. He looked shell shocked, as I probably also looked. I started to say something to him, and he moved his hand and put his index finger straight up in front of my lips, touching them.

"Shh-hh, don't talk. Just rest. We might not get any sleep, but I don't want to talk about it until morning."

Laying my head on top of his shoulder, he wrapped his other arm about me, and we stayed like that. I attempted to do as he asked. I attempted to rest, attempted to be calm. In my head, my mind was frantic, frantic that we'd made a wrong choice, my mind shouting at me, *Tell the police. Don't tell the police. Tell the police. Don't tell the police. The police will know about the News Release.* I repeated *tell, don't tell…*

The caller had said multiple times not to involve the media or call the police. We hadn't gone to the police. *Smooth Image* had. They had tracked down our new telephone number. *How safe were we? Where is Matthew's gun? Are we safe with him having a gun in the house?"*

Palm Desert, California

37

Summer

Travis And Ashley

❖ JENNA ❖

WE'D MADE IT THROUGH the night, talking the next morning. All we could do is watch and wait. The landline had finally (!) been cancelled. We used the security system. We used our cell phones. We looked around the street frequently. And we lived our lives. I had a new view of Matthew. He had been scared which made me even more aware that I needn't be afraid of him any longer. *Do they know where we live? Will this stress entice him to drink? I should have more faith in him. We'll get through this.*

At the times we could pretend to forget about that particularly threatening call, our lives went on as usual. I felt Matthew's new focus on writing about his experiences before, during and after his 'medical incident' worked out well for both of us. I mean, he was busy three or four hours a day writing, and I could plan my day around that same time to do my painting. I had felt a creative streak in myself forever, but I can't say I considered myself talented.

I read books by artists, as well as painting every vase, flower, face, building, animal and landscape in each of my growing number of reference manuals. My mom had signed us both up for another paint class in the interim. Bonnie again instructed and full of compliments for my progress. When she suggested my taking a painting class held at a local school, I signed up on my cellphone right during the class! Another and another class followed.

My painting skills had progressed to the point where I could see my renderings becoming very similar to the paintings in my craft manuals. I found painting a horse the hardest to get just right because their coat was short, and the shading had to be flawless. If I painted a dog or a cat, the fur colouring could cover my lack of shading skills. Snickers was a fantastic subject in many of my attempts. I got the hang of her long, flowing coat, copying the lines to my satisfaction.

Countless "good girl", "sit", "stay" were heard in my paint room. More "good girl" comments as I sketched and painted and lots of treats. I went on prolonged walks with her, hoping my treats didn't make her gain weight. That enhanced the health for both of us. Snickers heard a great number of queries like "Do you want to go for a walk?" and "Do you want a treat?" This wonderful, soft, silky, charming, delightful dog had become my best friend. Sure, she was a lot hairier than Milena or Cynthia, but she brought me immeasurable contentment.

I discussed with her more than I had ever revealed to my two-legged friends. Their legs were better, but I yakked all day to Snickers, her head tilted one way, head tilted the other way, licking my hand, and a little "ruff, ruff" when she absolutely understood my laments and gratitude for my current life.

I had originally felt that Matthew needed a dog, a dog to walk, a dog as a companion. He'd had a fantastic bond with Mom and Dad's dog, Charlie, on all our visits. He loved her unconditionally. She snuggled right into him when he sat on the floor. I was finding, however, that I was enamoured with Snickers. She was as much my companion as she was Matthew's, and she adored each of us equally.

—⚬—

Matthew had been cooking with gusto again. He used to love to cook, and his enthusiasm had returned. When I'd taught, there had been days I didn't get home for supper until after 5:30, and he had stepped in then and started cooking a couple of times each week – until he couldn't.

As he stood in front of the stove now, casserole dish in hand, he said, "I don't mind doing this, Jenna. You always have a schedule of meal plans, and making supper seems to give my brain time to shift from writing to mulling over my next plot line." He took hold of my hand and pulled me to him, his breath smelling of garlic and spice when I kissed him.

"I realize I haven't let you read any part of my manuscript yet or even my ongoing journal. Even though the book my journals are turning into is about me, the actual story leads me along, grabbing me and pulling me to add details I hadn't realized I was aware of."

"Fascinating. I'll be thrilled when I finally get a chance to read your story. How many words do you have now?"

"I have 65,000. I have a number of plot lines to go through, and I want to keep it around 80,000." As he turned the burner down, he asked, "How's your latest painting coming along, the one of Joshua Tree National Park and some of the desert wildflowers?"

"It looks amazing, even to me."

"You're your worst critic. When you were last working on it, I peeked in. 'Amazing' is a good word for it. Can I see it now?"

"Of course!"

Robin had come over tonight. They got together whenever Travis came from Los Angeles. I often wondered if he came to visit Robin, and we weren't even aware he was in town. Their relationship felt "fresh" according to Travis even though it had been going on for ten months. They were both getting used to the idea of being a couple – Robin having been Ashley's friend since high school. While attending the College of the Desert for additional classes, she also worked as an administrative assistant at our insurance company in Palm Springs. She seemed a good influence on Travis. I could see that. Travis could be a handful. He had calmed down in the past several months.

At supper of baked chili and Caesar salad prepared by Matthew, we were enjoying the apple pie dessert I'd made. In a side glance, I noticed Snickers under the table nosing around for the dropped garlic toast Matthew had surreptitiously thrown a moment before. He gave Robin a conspiratorial glance; her hazel eyes under arched questioning eyebrows, indicated to me, *should I be involved in this?*

I just shook my head at them, harrumphed and said reproachfully, "We'll never train her."

"She's perfectly trained."

"As a vacuum cleaner."

As we all giggled, Travis announced, "I quit my job."

"What?!" Ashley and I shrieked in unison.

"Got your attention. I told them startin' September, I'll work part time." He first smiled at Robin, and then he glanced toward Matthew who displayed a sly expression.

Seeing that expression on Matthew's face, I inquired of him, "What do you know?"

"Travis spoke to me this afternoon. I can't pretend to be surprised. I agree with everything he's thought through, and I'm proud of our son."

"I'm starting part time at Ramirez Construction Company in LA cuz I enrolled at a College of the Desert course. Here, check this out."

He put the folded, slightly wrinkled College of the Desert brochure at the center of the table. Ashley and I, sitting side by side, pushed our pie remnants away and studied the brochure, *Construction Management Certificate of Achievement.*

I read aloud, "'provides education and training for students seeking employment in Construction or any of the related fields in the building industry where they may be involved in the procurement of documents and construction or renovation of homes, offices, retail stores, and many other building typologies.' What's a typology?"

Travis proudly said, "A system for putting buildings into similar groups. Here, it's building function, form or style."

Ashley, leaning over to see more, continued reading, "'Students earning the certificate may also choose to continue their education toward an associate, baccalaureate, or advanced degree in Construction Management or related major.' This is great! Oh my God!"

"Grandma would wash your mouth out with soap if you talk like that," Travis joked.

Ignoring him, I almost squealed with delight and relief at this decision.

"Travis, this is awesome. College of the Desert here in town. What a great idea. You know how I hoped you'd continue your education. Congratulations."

He'd been extremely unhappy with his current job situation; therefore, the decision diminished any concern I had for him. Obviously, he'd spoken to Matthew. I was relieved this was settled. *He'll come to live in the Valley! To be near Robin? I hope.*

In fact, Travis seemed quite proud of himself. "I'm gonna get hella good management training and who knows where this will lead."

"Atta boy," said Matthew. "Life will only improve with some training and education under your belt. This means you won't always be doing slave labour."

"I might even own my own business like Grandpa Barnes and now Uncle Robert. Maybe I'll move to Calgary for a bit to get experience from a real professional. I'm gonna telephone Grandpa right now to tell him."

Matthew stated, "Your dad and Robert will be proud of him. This approach for Travis shows real maturity. He's planned for his future."

As Travis grabbed his cell and left to make his call, Ashley's gaze went to Matthew. "Did you have anything to do with getting Travis to do this?" Matthew gave a little shake of his head, and she swivelled to glance at Robin, "Did you?"

I'd pondered the same thing about either of them a moment before.

Robin, ducking her face away from my gaze, avoided the question. *Didn't want to be in the middle of something that might backfire if she'd intervened in family decisions?*

Matthew cut in, perhaps to save her, "When Travis showed me the brochure, I told him it was a brilliant idea. Then he told me he'd already enrolled and talked to his bosses. He's realized he's in charge of his own future."

He looked pointedly at Ashley, giving her his most endearing gaze, "As are we all, dearest Ashley."

I wonder if he heard Ashley discuss her worry about his not being here the next time she visited. That was months ago. Still...

After the exciting news about Travis had waned, we moved into the living room. Snickers followed and curled up on the floor, practically lying on Matthew's feet. Gently rubbing her ear, Matthew glanced at me contentedly.

Travis spoke on the cell with his grandfather, sounds of excitement emanating from the study. All of us were contemplating Travis's news and deliberating the changes his decision meant as he returned to the living room.

Beaming as he strode into the room, he recounted, "Grandpa agreed it's a great idea, and I'll have a chance to talk to Uncle Robert this weekend. I'll email him the information. Grandma hovered nearby and, when grandpa explained what the excitement was about, she squealed! She does that, doesn't she? She squeals when delighted. Kind of a cute sound. Mom squeals too."

Defensively, I said, "I do not!"

Matthew grinned, "Yeah, you do!"

As Travis gazed at Robin who had her mouth as if ready to utter a squeal, he said, "Not really cool on anyone our age. It's for old folks."

My look stopped anything else coming from him.

"Sometimes you remind me too much of my brother, young man."

"Uncle Robert's a cool dude!"

His gaze swung back to Robin as she flipped her coal-black hair away from her shoulders. "Squealing might be something I already do," Robin teased him. "You don't know everything about me, mister."

I felt relieved and relaxed these two were dating. She'd always been a great friend to Ashley, and the three of them got along so well. Ashley had stopped talking about a former boyfriend and had mentioned a Nathan Sandoval during her visit two weeks ago. She balked at saying more about him, but she seemed cheerful, smiling more often.

Ashley interrupted my reverie.

"I completed both sets of Reiki courses. I now have my second level Reiki."

That might also account for the happier spirit.

"Hey, that's impressive. Your dad and I've been waiting to get treated by you. Congratulations."

Travis muttered, "Reiki. Robin, you were talkin' about that last week."

"Yeah, I knew Ashley was taking the courses, so I checked it out. I read Reiki is a type of energy healing."

Robin paused when we heard a truck rumbling slowly past, then stopping. I rose and peered out the window, reassured to see it was a neighbour's truck. We all had been alert to any strange sound on the street–on the lookout in case Tootsie *et al* had planned some sort of retribution toward Matthew. Quickly, the five of us had gone to front-facing windows to check out that low-grade rumbling sound. Robin, seeing the reassured expression on my face, went back to her seat and resumed her views on Reiki as though uninterrupted.

"According to practitioners, energy can stagnate in the body where there's been physical injury or even emotional pain. Those energy blocks can cause illness."

Ashley then explained her instructor told them that energy medicine aims to help the flow of energy and remove blocks in a similar way to acupuncture or acupressure.

"When can you give me a treatment, honey?"

"I could do a ten-minute demonstration now if Travis will behave himself."

Travis did an index finger and thumb slash across his mouth, "I'm all ears and eyes, Ashley. And Robin promises not to squeal."

"I don't promise!" she stated, squinting her eyes toward him. I could see a self-confident glint in her expression. *Good for her.*

"Okay mom, you can just sit in the armchair, and I'll demonstrate. Please all be quiet. I need to concentrate."

With Travis behaving himself, I could feel Ashley tense behind me, heard her rub her hands together. I closed my eyes, relaxing.

"I'm smoothing your aura before I begin." She breathed a deep breath and held her hands slightly away from me.

"Now I'll begin." She held her hands gently above my head. I could feel my hair being touched, but she didn't lay her hands directly on me. I'd read practitioners held their hands over specific areas called chakras and it wasn't necessary to touch the person.

"I sense something," I whispered. I felt some heat and knew the energy would be transferred to me. Probably three minutes later, Ashley moved her hands to the area of my forehead. "Your third eye," she said softly, held them there for about three minutes and then over my eyes, moving downward onto different parts of my body. I could tell her hands were not being pulled away from me as she moved from position to position. I felt she had constant contact with me, the warmth not leaving my body.

She said softly, "Just for today, be calm; just for today, have joy; just for today, don't worry. Just for today, have peace." I could feel heat continuing through my body. "This is your throat chakra."

Each being a three-minute time frame, she had moved to my 'heart' chakra as she called it. I said, "It's a calming power."

She did a circular movement over my upper area, saying, "This is to finish off. Did you enjoy that, Mom? That's all I can concentrate on now with the family watching and you not lying down, but I really want to try this on Dad tomorrow."

"I felt the heat. I felt a calming sensation. Ashley, wow!"

Matthew asked, "So what happened during the treatment, Ashley? What were you doing?"

"An energy transfer took place. My hands get warm, sometimes almost hot. The energy transferred is 'chi'. Have you ever heard of Tai Chi exercises? It comes through me to whomever I'm treating, and it also helps me as it passes through."

"That's it." Matthew said. "Dr. Gerstein-Kraus did a talk to me early on in my sessions. She's a proponent of Tai Chi. She may have even said Reiki, but it wasn't anything I'd ever heard before. The term didn't stay with me."

"That would've been a session I missed when I was at work," I said, "But I'm pleased you can associate this form of healing with Dr. GK. Will you let Ashley do a treatment on you?"

"Absolutely. Did you get a title with this course?"

"No, no title, but a double certificate stating I have my Reiki, Second Level. If I went on to get my third level, then I can actually teach other people the techniques. I'm contemplating going for Level III. It would be nice to be able to encourage others to have this ability. I'd also like to set up the spare room at my apartment in LA to take in people that I know or at least are recommended to me so I can help them as well."

Travis came out with, "And make a few extra bucks, get some grip."

"Well, there is that."

Palm Desert, California

MATTHEW'S JOURNAL

As I woke up, I was sweating, my pillow damp, my brow glossy. I could still feel my mother's arms around me. It was just a dream, I thought. Nothing real, but I couldn't shake the feeling I had been there, in my mother's arms, her sobbing, me crying because she was crying.

"My baby, my baby. Matthew, thank God I have you," my mother had sobbed in my dream. Could that have actually happened?

Why? I wanted to know. Why did this feel so emotional – so real? I pondered this while I became more fully awake. As the dream receded and my thoughts focussed, I knew why. "My baby" had been the children she had lost, miscarried each somewhere at about three months.

The first I had known about this was hearing my mom and dad talking when Neil was young. They had said how relieved they were Neil had 'lived'. I was quite young, around four and a half years old. I had worried what it meant. I knew what lived meant as opposed to not. We'd had a 'feral' cat that lived in the garage, became ill and had not 'lived'. I remember that vividly. So, Neil had lived. That word stayed in my mind, and I eventually heard Mom talking to a relative, crying about her lost babies, two miscarriages after me and before Neil. At the time hearing that conversation, I recalled being in my mother's arms and her saying what I had just dreamed. Yet, over the years, my memories had dissipated. Until tonight. At least this is the first time I remembered the dream.

"Thank God you lived!" This now came to me like a lightening bolt. My mother had said that as she stroked my wrist when I was in the hospital. I was not back in my body, but still on the ceiling. Then I must've come back soon after because even though I wasn't awake, I knew she was stroking my wrist. Then she had said it again, crying. "Thank God you lived!"

Glancing at the bedside clock, I saw the time was 6:00 a.m., Jenna still asleep beside me. Thankfully, I hadn't disturbed her sleep. I felt desperate to talk to my mother. This was an oddity, but that dream and my thoughts made me incredibly emotional. Mom was always up and having breakfast by 7:30. That was Mom and Dad's routine when he had been a police officer, depending on his shift. But he wouldn't sleep in even on weekends once he made detective. My parents didn't spend the day in each other's company, but that time of each morning they'd have their coffee together in the dining room with a view of Mount Hood, discussing their day ahead for the hour before they went their separate ways.

Even though I decided I'd call my mom, I hesitated, wondering what I'd say.

Without disturbing Jenna, I slipped out of bed, padded to the bedroom door. Before I closed it gently behind me, I glanced back at my sleeping wife. She needed more sleep. She'd spent enough time watching me sleep, ensuring I was rested, ensuring I was okay.

Sipping a cup of freshly made coffee a little over an hour later, I dialed my home telephone number.

"Is everything okay?" a worried exclamation in her question.

"Everything's super, Mom. I was up and I wanted to talk with you."

"Oh? Um, that's nice. I usually call you. It's good to hear your voice. Are you sure everything is okay? We were just having our coffee."

"Let the man speak," pleaded my father, obviously on speaker.

"I'm sorry, Mom, Dad."

"Matthew, what is the matter?" from my mom.

"I'm ... I'm so sorry for letting you down, for attempting to kill myself, for almost taking myself away from you."

"Oh Matthew, you weren't yourself," my mother offered, a verbal gift.

"No, I wasn't. But what I did was unforgivable."

Both at the same time, "We forgive you, Matthew."

My mother continued, "You are our dear son, our first born. We love you."

I paused, for those were not common words from my mother, and I had to take a breath and to savour the emotion of hearing them from her — wanting her words engraved on my heart. I hesitated in relaying more, not wanting to move away from that sensation.

I plunged forward. "Mom, when I was unconscious, I heard you say, "Thank God you lived!"

She took a breath in, another breath in, breathed a heavy breath out. "I did say that." Another breath, a catch in her voice, "You heard me say that?"

"I heard you say that, and..." How would I word this next part? "And I was aware you and Dad were holding hands, while you stroked my wrist below my intravenous."

Then she sobbed. I could hear my Dad comforting her. Did I have my memories skewed? They were comforting each other yet again — like the holding hands. Could my memories be backwards? Could their interactions I'd always remembered as being aloof, resentful, not loving toward each other belong to a teenage boy who had so little life experience? Were my memories faulty? Or did a new love begin once Neil and I had left home, leaving them alone to begin again?

"I love both of you, and I'm sorry. I regret that I attempted suicide. It wasn't my life I wanted to leave behind. It was the me that I had become."

"Matt." It seemed that was all Dad could get out.

"Matthew, life isn't what it should be all the time. Everyone is often unhappy with how things work out with their lives," Mom began.

"That's just it, Mom. You were, are wrong. I'm happy, contented, gratified with my life. I couldn't have been happier with Jenna, Travis and Ashley. Jenna is my soul mate, the love of my life." As an aside, I realized that at least I feel good about myself most of the time, not the suicidal thoughts that had been happening.

My father said, "Matt, I know how much you love her. I see it every time you speak of her and in how you look at her."

There was a pause. Neither of them said a word. Then, a sound, perhaps the rustle of a sleeve against the phone. "I haven't always understood, Matthew." My mother's comment didn't surprise me, but her next sentence made me sit down. "You obviously know I haven't been fair to Jenna. Recently, I've decided to try to alter how I treat her."

Silence for several beats. I needed my breath to slow down. I heard my dad murmur something to my mother, nothing I could hear.

My mother continued with, "I watched her with you and care for you after your incident. I was just resentful of her taking you away from me. I was blinded by jealousy toward her."

"Oh my God, Mom. She'll forgive you. Jenna is an amazing person."

"I know it, Matthew. Your father and I've talked. I haven't let myself take it to heart. You'll see. Next time you come to visit, I'll have my act together."

"Love you both." But I knew my mom was messed-up. Would she, could she follow through and be good to Jenna?

Palm Desert, California

38

Summer

Louie and Dewie

❖ AARON ❖

PERIPHERALLY, I SAW THE two HR employees glance my way and lean slightly to hear more.

"It took me a long time to see Matt for what he is. I've been a good friend to him, but these past few months have shown me a side of him that I didn't know existed."

Suddenly, two shadows fell across our table. A gleeful expression spread across the faces of the two HR personnel, Dewey and Louie. Dewey was really Denise; however, the entire staff in the office called her Dewey, from the Disney characters. What they really needed was an older sibling named Huey to complete the trio of Donald Duck's nephews.

Dewey (Denise), somber, almost sad in expression, spoke first, "In HR, we see a lotta modified documents, lies about references. Now this outright theft of the file, blackmailing. It shoulda been solved months ago."

As he leaned over, supporting his huge body by hanging onto my lunchroom chair, Louie smirked, "Correcto-mungo, sis! I think Matthew has some hold over the bosses cuz we knew he'd stolen the documents and blackmailed that lady."

Turning my face up to his all-to-close face, I provided him with a rueful smile, while nodding. "I think you're right, Louie. Sadly, I think you're right."

My stomach roiled a little at the smell of Louie's breath and being this close to him as he replied, "It's as plain to see as the gnarly nose on your face, Aaron. Have ya noticed him spendin' any more money lately that he shouldn't have?"

"Now that you mention it," I pondered. "Perhaps that trip they plan would be more money than I thought they had."

Harry, my lunchmate again today, seemed quite chipper and raised his voice in a conspiratorial way, "Maybe they're planning to flee! I hear his wife's parents live some place in Canada!"

Lunch break was over, but Louie clapped me on the back as we walked toward the lunchroom exit door, "I'm glad you came around, Aaron. Matthew's gonna get his comeuppance. Soon, I hope." He was smirking as I looked sideways at him.

"I hope that happens, Louie. It's about time this crime was figured out. Matthew has caused *Smooth Image Surgery* and its staff enough trouble."

Louie flashed a look toward his sister, Dewey, and said, "Matthew will get his comeuppance soon enough. We'll see him charged I'm sure. Then we can forget about Mr. High and Mighty and his deceit."

Glancing to the other side of me, I noticed Dewey's pensive expression and wondered what she was thinking. I needed to know if she was on side with getting Matthew charged or not. She would be instrumental in my scheme.

Palm Desert, California

39

Summer

Quandaries

❖ JENNA ❖

"We're not selling!"
"Thank God! It's about time you made up your minds. How did it come about?"
On the zoom call, Mom looked animated. She wasn't sitting in her favourite chair. She wandered around the house, the computer losing her a few times.
"I did not want to sell, and your dad stayed on the fence. I made the decision not to sell."
"Mom, you keep walking out of view of the computer screen. Why are you so frenetic?"
"I just could not part with it or them."
"Now you're not making total sense. Please mellow out, and just say what happened."
She took a couple of breaths as though she had been jogging. Maybe she had – in her mind. Then she went on to tell me of the final conversation she and Dad had on that subject.
"We agreed there are countless wonderful memories and fabulous people in Palm Estates RV Resort." As her jaw jutted out, she went on, "I simply couldn't, wouldn't leave all those behind."

My mom sat down, put her feet up, then stood up – still uneasy, "I mean, we can always sell another year. The places get snapped up pretty fast, and we've taken good care of ours. We kept circling back to the enjoyment we've had there over the past years, what we've done, our friends, that I was finally getting to be pretty good friends with Betty. I finally said, 'And yet we talk of selling our stake down there and moving on.'"

"And?"

Here she paused, recalling the scene in her mind, possibly savouring the feeling all over again. *She's had her hair done.* From the computer, I couldn't see any grey as though she'd finally given in and had it dyed. The effect was gorgeous – no streaks or real grey. When she moved her hand to her cheek to rub it, I could see she'd had a manicure.

Coming back to me, she announced, "Then your dad replied, 'That's just it – moving on to where?'"

So, there it was. They had no definitive plans of what to do after. When I described it to Matthew later, I clarified they had gone around and around throwing out ideas of another resort, maybe a house in one of the neighbourhoods they liked, maybe going on cruises, maybe selling their park model and then renting another one so there would be no commitment if something happened to one of them.

Matthew questioned later, "So that was it? Make a decision by not making a decision?"

Laughing, I replied, "Isn't that how it sometimes goes? I do that all the time with little things. Should I start another painting today? Wait long enough to decide and it's too late that day. Anyway, I'm thrilled."

"Of course, you are. What would you do without them all winter? But honestly, I would miss them too. They're family to me."

My Matthew had said those words – that my parents were family to him as well. The next time I called my mom, I told her, and she said, "I knew that. He's always treated us as though we were a second set of parents to him."

"Oh, Mom! He does, doesn't he? Speaking of parents, I probably didn't even tell you Matthew and I took a quick trip to Portland to visit Clara and Jack…"

Matthew had told me of his dream and of their later conversation. I was rightfully a little skeptical of her changing her spots. However, I'd needed to support Matthew, so I'd gone to Portland with him for a visit. *I can do this* I'd told myself. *Again.*

Interrupting my thoughts, Mom said, "What? And how did that go with her, the dragon lady?" During this call, she seemed calm having made that decision not to sell.

"It went well."

I'd already told Mom of Matthew's dream and that Clara had promised Matthew to be nicer to me, and that she'd admitted to him she'd always behaved badly.

"You didn't believe she could change." Her voice showed her own skepticism.

"She put on a show when we were there." I could hardly express my worry about my next disclosure. "The revelation is that Clara said she and Jack are planning to come next winter for a month."

Mom said succinctly, "Oh boy!"

Now I was pacing. "Oh boy is right. Please God, let her behave. That could be an exceedingly long month. On the other hand, I don't necessarily need to see her all the time. Matthew can go over and visit, and I can have them for supper two or three times. We can go out for supper. We can go places, so we don't have to actually visit…"

My mother interrupted again, "Are you hyperventilating already? She hasn't even made concrete plans. Settle down." By now, my mom had sat down and looked contemplative.

"You're right. Why put the egg before the goose, or whatever that saying is?"

"It was 'which comes first, the chicken or the egg?'"

I pushed my hair out of my face, and said, "Right, science decided the egg first because of evolution."

"If you say so. Anyway, there is also putting the cart before the horse. Just take a breath. She isn't in your living room yet!"

Purposely changing the whole conversation, I asked, "How are my siblings?"

"Robert and Eva bought a house out in the Calgary Nose Hill Park neighbourhood. They had to overbid to get that home. I'm glad it worked out for them. They can get to the mountains easily, and the C-train better serves that part of the city."

"The mountains are a highlight for them. I'm surprised Robert didn't build something. That's all he could talk about when they visited last winter. They even had plans drawn up."

I settled into my chair contemplating that building would have taken a year and would've been time away from Robert being able to build other houses to sell.

"Couldn't get any lot out there, and they wanted that particular area. The kids are excited to be able to get to the ski hills quickly in the winter. And, to get to University. We've been to see it, and they move in six weeks."

"That's fabulous. I'm happy for them. Finally, they can settle into a real home for themselves. Make roots."

"It's marvellous. And your sisters seem to be doing well. No real issues with any of them that I know about, thankfully."

It seemed my siblings were no different from the rest of the world. Troubles came and went, but they all seemed healthy and doing what they needed to do. Absently twisting my heart necklace, I asked the question I'd been avoiding because I was afraid of the answer, "And how is Dad's heart doing?"

Pacing around the room, it could be she too was unsure I should have asked this question.

"He's doing pretty good. The hip is improving significantly."

"Good, but you know I'm asking about more than his hip."

After a little pause, Mom replied, "We discussed with the cardiologist if we should be going down south this winter. He advised your father – looking straight into your father's eyes – a couple of things. I recorded on my phone app what he said to your father, then wrote it out. Here it is. I'll read it: 'You must take your medication as directed; walk, bike, golf, nothing as strenuous as pickleball; no extensive hikes; eat properly; very importantly, no alcohol; weigh yourself at least every two days to ensure no rapid weight gain; take your blood pressure also at least every two days, preferably every day; salt restricted diet; keep watch over potassium.'"

"Watch potassium? It's not good for him?"

"No. Too much could cause kidney failure. I didn't want to tell you all this, but since we will be eating at your place some of the time, you need to know as well. I'm sorry we initially kept you in the dark about your dad's health. We should've told you sooner."

"I'm glad I know now, but for fuck's sake, mom, of course, I needed to know. So do all us kids."

"Jenna, watch your language!"

"I only swear when I'm really upset, angry or afraid."

"Would it be useless to point out you swear too often lately?"

"Yes, it would be useless. It's been a bad couple of years. I'm worried about my father now. You can understand that?"

"Okay, forget I said anything. Just take care of yourself, too. I understand you've been through a lot, darling daughter. I will take good care of your father. The fear of not being able to go down south has really turned him into a rule follower."

"Thank God. I'll find out about this potassium thing, so I appreciate the ramifications. But I have to let you go, Mom. Supper preparation is calling to me."

"Mine's about ready for the oven, but you're in the Pacific Time Zone. After all these years, I forget sometimes. Have a good night."

That conversation had taken another half hour, long enough I did actually have to put off getting groceries for another day because it was time to prepare my lasagna without putting in fresh spinach which I liked to add occasionally. Matthew wouldn't mind the omission, I felt certain. I was just attempting to get additional vitamins and antioxidants into the lasagna.

—m—

Mom's last words to me during our call had been, "I am glad it all worked out with Clara."

I had chosen not to tell my mom what Clara had put me through the evening Matthew and I'd arrived. We had a nice supper of salmon, rice and a cauliflower/broccoli mix. Matthew had taken our suitcase and toiletries bags downstairs when we arrived. During supper, Clara mentioned that her cousin, Maude, had been visiting the week before. Following me down the stairs after supper, she said, "I didn't change the sheets."

"Oh, okay. I'll do that," I replied innocently, wondering if her back felt sore, sympathising maybe this wasn't a good weekend to visit.

"No, you can sleep on those sheets."

What?! That certainly wasn't how I handled company.

I asked politely. I know I asked politely. There would've been no reason to react the way she did after I spoke. I'd asked, "Could we have clean pillowcases?"

Well, that set the stage. She angerly asked if I thought I was better than her cousin. She went upstairs, stomping, threw down a set of pillowcases and slammed the basement door.

Oh man, I've unleased the dragon. What would I say to Matthew when he came down after he'd heard his mom yelling and slamming the door? As it turned out, and she probably knew this, Matthew and my father-in-law, Jack, had gone to get her a pack of cigarettes from the store. I felt shell shocked. This was supposed to be the beginning of a new relationship between Clara and me. I didn't go back upstairs to visit with them that night. Matthew eyed me warily.

I'd said, "I'm tired and not up to visiting anymore tonight."

He went upstairs to continue a visit with them. I didn't tell Matthew that weekend.

No, I didn't want to discuss it with my mother now either. I needed to be shocked, to fume and vent inwardly for awhile. Would my mother-in-law ever accept me into her family? Maybe I needed to stop giving a damn. Whose family was it now, anyway? *Actually,* it's mine. So there! I'm the one with Matthew. I'm the one with her grandchildren.

After speaking to my mother, I immediately switched gears in my mind and texted Ruby. I reiterated all the things Mom had just said to me.

> What is this about potassium? I thought it was good for everyone.

> Spironolactone is an excellent medication for Dad's heart failure. It'll help with the swelling of his ankles, removing excess fluid. Spironolactone can lead to high levels of potassium.

> I can trust whatever you say. Just need all the assurance I can get.

It seemed Ruby then texted both Joan and Robert to ensure that we each had all the available information on our father's heart health.

From Robert:

> Ruby says stop worrying all the time. He's healthier now. Eva and I go over every couple weeks. I have a handle on it. We're all watching him.

I'm grateful my parents aren't selling their place down here. Oh my God, I danced around the kitchen with such happiness. It seemed that I didn't need their place any longer as a refuge to get away from Matthew and his moods; however, I would have missed them because they were special to me. I also knew that I'd be able to keep an eagle eye on Dad all winter. Then I went to my computer and typed "potassium and spironolactone".

Palm Desert, California

40

Summer

Turning Against Matt!

❖ AARON ❖

THE FOUR OF US, Harry, Louie, Dewey and I, were leaving work at the same time. I hung back with them, checking my cellphone. I hoped for my inclusion in the weekly Friday after work bar activity.

"Do you want to come?" Harry asked, peering over to see if I was done fiddling with my phone, "Want to chill with us?"

"Yeah, sure. I'd love a beer or two."

Harry, appearing relaxed, smiled and said, "Or three!"

I waited throughout the hilarity and discussions about everything else. A big goose egg, zero about Matt. Sports, women, movies. No one mentioned a book they had read. Patiently, I added my two cents worth here and there. Two hours elapsed – lots of beers drunk. I wasn't about to rush things if they were still wondering about my loyalty. I finished my nacho order, but Louie was still grabbing and munching. At least his fourth brew in one hand and, having stuffed several nachos in his mouth, he licked each individual greasy finger. Swallowing another chug, he gleefully yelled to Dewey, "I wonder if ol' Matthew will be eatin' prison food any time soon. Aaron, you need ta go to the police and tell 'em what ya' know about that trip and that they might not have the money for it."

About time. Let's get this show on the road. I need this settled.

Dewey, looking a little askance said, "Louie, we don't need to talk about jail time. This is a crime that the clinic can solve. No need to get Matthew into more trouble. He can admit that he did it. With his illness, he might not even remember taking the file."

Now ignoring any response I could have made, thank goodness, he shouted back to Dewey, "Bullshit, Denise, it has to be more'n that. They're getting blackmailed by him."

"Another beer," he gestured sweeping his arm to the waitress as she paused at our table, tray in hand – ready to gather up the glasses and cans on the table. As his hand grazed her upper arm, she backed up a step. "Wassa matter?" he sneered.

"Sir, keep your hands to yourself." Her furious countenance seemed to settle him down for a moment. She looked over at the rest of us, then said, "I'll get your beer. Anyone else?"

"Bring me two!" Louie roared.

Taking our order, she gave Louie one more stare, turned and walked away. A minute later our beers arrived, her keeping a distance from any wayward hand Louie may have intended to put out.

Louie muttered, but I heard him, "Uptight bitch."

His demeanor acquired a darkness. Pretty much chugalugging this fifth beer, he slammed the empty down on the table. I could see he was getting really pie eyed now, slurring, "The clinic needs to get this settled, get Matthew in jail. They've screwed around long enough."

Getting into the spirit, I said, "Yeah, staff are getting riled now the news release is out, worried about their own jobs. We need to nail Matthew."

I kept track of the group's beer intake while restricting my own, maintaining an eye on them all. *We have to move this forward if anything is going to be accomplished.* Harry more or less kept out of it now, just enjoying his food and beverages.

Physically large Louie started on his sixth; diminutive Dewey, her fifth. The more outspoken Louie became and the more I pushed that Matt must go to jail – to have it all settled and done with – the quieter Dewey became. She looked extremely upset and despondent, her own beer consumption no longer keeping pace with Louie.

I said, "Come on, Dewey. Matt would deserve to go to jail if we can get more information on his comings and goings. Let's do some digging' into the timings of his code being used. Let's nail the guy, but good!"

Denise aka Dewey looked at me, really looked at me. She teared up, and she stammered, "I...I don't w-w-want Matthew to be put in j-jail. Months ago, when we were letting employees go, I heard all the talk of it being Matthew's – "

Louie interrupted, "So what! He deserved to be blamed. Someone had to take the heat for losin' the businesses and clients. Aaron's right. The staff are really gettin' antsy this ain't solved."

She muttered a little bit – words I couldn't catch. Continuing on louder, she said, "On more than one occasion, George walked out the door with a terminated employee. He clapped them on the back, 'If only Matthew had done a better job. Sorry to have to let you go because of his inability to handle this situation.'"

Louie roared again, ranting, "He was the Business Manager. He shoulda' managed."

I saw an opportunity to get her aside when Harry had said his wife would be ready for him to come home, whatever that really meant, and Louie slowly got up, stumbled and made his way to the washroom. Harry helped Louie to the washroom door, waved goodbye and slipped out through the back exit where he'd parked earlier.

I took a breath and forcibly said, "Denise, we have to get Matt put in jail where he belongs. He must be put where he can't do this again to some other business." I knew what I needed to say. "Maybe he should go into a mental institution for observation."

She turned to me and said, "What if he didn't do it? I always liked Matthew. He always had a kind word for me. Not everyone does. I know he's married and all, but I fell for him. Oh, shit. I shouldn't have told you that." Outright crying now, she said, "I can't go on like this. I have to go home, but I know I'm over the limit. Louie sure as hell can't drive."

"I won't repeat what you told me, Dewey. I haven't had more than one drink all evening. It just wasn't my night to celebrate with what we must do to get Matt convicted. I'll drive you." I raised my eyes toward the washroom, and said, "Louie's supporting himself on a barstool. I'll drive you both home. If needed, I can help you get your car tomorrow. Just give me the addresses."

She didn't hesitate, almost as if she knew I hadn't been drinking as much or didn't care. Louie had quite a weight to him, and it took a stumbling Dewey and me to get him into my vehicle. I'd planned this eventuality and driven my CR-V, hoping at some point this would occur. Addresses were given. Louie was deposited at home – another step-stumble episode. Thankfully, he lived closest. Dewey returned to the backseat, slouched over, not communicating.

"Aaron, I meant what I said at the bar. I can't go on like this." She went silent. *Was she asleep?* Then a shudder came from the back seat, and sigh, perhaps a sob.

Ingratiating myself a little further into her good books, I said, "It's too bad. Matt was my friend for so many years. If he did it, he must be punished."

This silence is deafening. Have I misjudged her? Surely, I can get her on board here. I need her if this is going to work out for me tonight.

"No! Louie had an idea how to make some quick and easy money." She stopped speaking again. *Was she going to say it?* "I didn't wanna frame Matthew. It just played out that way. George already making Matthew the bad guy with the staff. His being away. His forgettin' to bring back his key."

At this point, my heart fluttered. *Will she tell me more?* I'd guess 90 seconds went past as I fidgeted with my car keys wondering if I should make a sound, afraid to start the engine. Another sigh, a burp, then silence. Finally, I just started the engine and drove. My decision to play the part of a Judas was working. *Come on! Confess the facts.* She was actually crying in the backseat.

After another fractured sigh, she said, "Louie had already stolen the file. He'd already contacted the client. Then Matthew was dismissed, hadn't returned his key. Stupid coincidence. Louie said not to void the pass code for Matthew."

Yes!

"Denise, I had no idea. You've been through a lot, too." Feeling badly for her, I said, "You're wishing you hadn't been involved?"

Now she shouted, "We shouldn't have done anything." Two second later, "We shouldn't have involved Matthew."

"Denise, we're at your place now. Does Louie have the file?"

Instead of answering, she went on to say, "I wanted to stop the blackmailing once they had settled on Matthew's guilt."

This is great. I've got my phone recorder going. Good stuff.

She just kept talking. It felt like she needed to say everything before she burst. "It could have ended. But, no. Louie is so greedy. He's still blackmailing them. He's pretending it's Matthew. He even let slip in one telephone call that he was Matthew. So stupid. He left a message with Matthew's phone number. That doesn't even make any sense. But he'd had a lot to drink, said he didn't care if she contacted Matthew! I was so angry with him. He's out of control with greed and wanting to blame Matthew."

I lied, "Louie seemed like a decent guy before all this happened, but greed can do that to a person." I turned as far around as I could, so that I could study Dewey.

Changing tactics, I said, "I feel badly that Matt is in the middle of all this. I wish we could do something to help our friend, Matthew."

Dewey sighed and said, "It's time." Another belch.

Damn, don't throw up in my car...

"Time for?"

Quickly, she said as though wanting the burden removed from her, "It's hidden in my basement behind the washing machine. Oh, Aaron, I don't want Louie mad at me, but havin' Matthew go to jail, it just can't continue."

I was silent myself for a few beats, thinking. I'd planned so much, but I felt badly for Dewey. She was partly a victim, as well as Matt.

"You could stay out of it for now and not let Louie know you told me. I could call your boss, George Alphonse, and tell him I overheard a conversation, and he needs to sort this out with the two of you. Louie won't recall exactly what he said, and I can use that to say I heard him braggin'. If you really want to. Now that you've told me, though, I just can't let another night go by. Tell me that I can call George, right now with you in my vehicle. I'm so sorry that this happened to you, but you'll feel good about helping save Matt from jail."

"Yeah, I will, but now it's Louie they'll go after. I hope I did the right thing, Aaron. Telling you."

"I know you did, but I can't not report all that's happened tonight." And I didn't have the nerve to tell her right then that I'd recorded her entire confession about their scheme. *Maybe the authorities won't need my cellphone recording.*

—⚏—

I called George and the police. I couldn't trust George. He might let all this get swept under the carpet so he could still blame Matt. I needed it all on record so Matt's reputation would be secure, and they'd not be getting more threatening calls. Dewey was willing to stay with me until we saw George and the police vehicles circle the bay. I didn't want her to have a change of heart and destroy evidence.

By the time the dust settled that night, George had the file, and the police had a written confession from Denise Bixby. The police wanted me in the next morning for a statement, first thing. They wanted my cellphone, too. Louie was picked up the next morning.

Palm Desert, California

MATTHEW'S JOURNAL

I let Jenna down again. I was a mess. Jenna had gone to bed, glaring at me as I drank. "I'm not sitting here with a drunk," she said, sputtering. "Quit blaming Aaron. You don't have any proof. You're paranoid. This was our beginning. Get your act together."

About the same time Aaron would have been working his charm on Dewey, I was at home – a few drinks under my belt – deciding what to do about him. He was a bastard! I had to get him alone somewhere and beat the truth out of him if I had to. He'd stolen the file and was blackmailing Tootsie.

Then he showed up at our home, ringing the bell at midnight.

"What?" I asked him in a surly tone. "What do you want?"

Jenna rushed into the room, "What's happening? Are you all right, Aaron? You're quite flushed?"

"I'm fine, excited to tell you something."

Jenna got Aaron bottled water, and sat down, waiting.

I plunked myself beside Jenna as Aaron told his story to Jenna and me. Aaron – in my good books again – had done it! Boy, was Jenna miffed at me, giving me a triumphant scowl throughout his retelling. It was Aaron, rather than the private investigator John Wu and Cynthia had hired that nailed it down. Aaron had gone "under cover" which, of course, was a loose term considering the culprits knew him well through work at the Smooth Image Surgery clinic.

Jenna said, "That should mean no more threatening telephone calls from Tootsie or Boyfriend Tootsie."

I smiled at Aaron. "You're a hero, Aaron. Thank you so much." I got another glare from Jenna.

((Yes, I'm a shithead.))

"You are very welcome."

As Aaron shifted his gaze from me to Jenna and back to me as though sensing some discomfort in our newly-formed relationship, he said, "Maybe you can lay off the alcohol now."

Stop drinking? Again.

I had to admit to myself Aaron had saved the day. He might have saved me from myself as well. He began to tell me how hard it was to talk against me – concluding with a couple of weeks portraying seemingly total betrayal.

So, who was the bastard now? Not Aaron!

Totally sober, I steadied myself and said jokingly, "I always knew you secretly despised me."

Laughing, he said, "Never, and I owed you big time. Now, really – stop your bloody drinking."

"Yeah."

At his demanding look, I said, "Yes, I will! Right now!" Having placed my glass on the table to show total acquiescence, I went on to say, "You have always been a truly great friend."

((And I haven't been.))

"You kept me grounded for months. Who else would read Kidnapped in its entirety to a lethargic and apathetic friend?"

At the turn of events and feeling my emotions in turmoil in a good way, I cried. No more being the scapegoat. No more being accused of company theft and blackmail. No more menacing calls. My reputation re-established! Our neighbours, our old friends, my work peers would all know that Matthew Hanson was innocent of all they had accused me of, all that they had believed. I could hardly come to grips this was real.

So, I blubbered – inwardly berating myself and acknowledging what it was I had to do to keep everything I had intact – to stay sober. Hearing what Dr. GK had said to me: "No more alcohol in or out of your home."

—⁓⁓—

Tootsie and her rolls were safe from any further blackmail, the husband an unhappy man, the boyfriend dumping Tootsie because of the publicity. Dewey and Louie charged and awaiting sentencing. The courts would probably be more lenient with Dewey because of her help. Two more lawyers got two more clients.

Thank God it was settled! Every time our cell phones had rung, we thought they had found out our cell phone numbers as well. Even though nothing happened to us or our property, the callers had scared the hell out of both of us.

Thankful for having a good friend, I reiterated over and over again what an ass I had been. Aaron, a thief? He believed me, and I had turned on him.

Heartbroken those coworkers had put me through this agony, I had a hard time forgiving them. But I had to forgive myself, too, for being an idiot about Aaron.

Palm Desert, California

41

One-Year After Suicide Attempt

The Beat Goes On

❖ JENNA ❖

WE WENT OVER ALL the facts when Aaron came for lunch the next day. He had been to the police department, given his statement and spent a couple of hours at work. *Smooth Image Surgery* knew the true story, and those horrible accusations were behind us. What a blessing.

"I wouldn't work there again, even if they begged me!" Matthew reiterated over and over. "Not if George Alphonse got down on one knee and begged me."

"Currently, the business is a zoo. The Human Resources Department is rudderless. And Harry told me George Alphonse may be out on his ear."

Matthew and I were ecstatic. George should pay for his treachery.

"Staff have been reporting to the senior doctors who own *Smooth Image Surgery* that George blamed you for no reason – that it was more George's fault for not foreseeing the possibilities of what could happen to businesses as a result of the pandemic."

Matthew snarled, "He should be strung up."

Deciding it was time for a real talk among friends, I walked toward the counter. "I'll pour us a coffee. Matthew and Aaron, the three of us should have a chat about the messed-up choices in the past year – couple of years."

Aaron strode into the study with my contrite-looking husband staring back at me.

Matthew blinked a couple of times, took in a long breath and said, "Good plan. I agree." He nodded, "I'll start from the beginning. We'll talk through them all."

We talked – much coffee replenished.

Aaron stood up and moved behind his chair. "I'm shocked you could have believed such a thing about me."

Also now standing, Matthew looked defiant. "But, Aaron, you've always been the bad boy."

"No, Matt. I haven't been the bad boy for the past 20 years, and you know that."

Aaron was frowning at Matthew, and I wondered what was to come. His look turned a little sour, and he continued, "You want to believe that I'm the bad boy so it can cover for *your* bad behaviour. We're 55 years old. Time to 'Shutdown and Reboot Your Systems', buddy." He actually gave Matthew's shoulder a small shove.

"I found your gun. Travis has it."

Aaron did a double-take looking at me and then swirling around to look at Matthew. "What the hell? Matt?"

"I went next door and managed to convince Kathy to tell me you had a gun."

"Kathy had no right to tell you."

Aaron blasted out with, "Matt, you were not in an emotional state to have a gun!"

"Guns are fine, but Aaron's right. You weren't in the emotional state to have a gun."

"Damn right, Matt."

Turning toward me with concern, Aaron asked in a tight voice, "Are you going to stay with this guy? One more chance. Or are you done?"

I looked at Matthew. He looked from his friend back to me, obviously startled by Aaron's words.

I hadn't answered the question. I thought of all our good years, those bad years, his promises and his broken promises. As I also stood, moving a step away from where Matthew was standing, I balked.

"Are you done acting like a sniveling baby who needs a soother – only in your case, a bottle to suck on?"

"That's harsh."

"So is being single after 30 years of marriage. I'm ready to choose it if you don't grow a pair of balls."

Absolute silence, yet I hadn't heard Aaron leave the room, now only noting the click of the front door as it closed.

"Jenna?"

"How many chances?"

"None. Maybe I have been using Aaron's old bad boy scenario as a crutch for mine."

"Next time you're stressed, what will happen?"

"I'll get through without drinking."

"I won't even give you a goodbye. I'll set up my own life. I have it all thought out. I love you, really love you. I need you, but I need a life with you without booze, without Diablo."

I stood still. I wasn't going to give an inch.

As Matthew glanced at our etched wall mirror, reflecting the two of us standing several feet apart, I watched his chin drop. I still did not move toward him. Oh, I wanted to. I wanted to comfort him, to wrap my arms around him, but I wouldn't. He had messed up again last night, using Aaron as an excuse, always some excuse. This was his choice alone.

His head came up. He would have noted my set features.

"I can do it – no more drinking." I stood my ground. He covered the steps between us. "I won't mess up again." Then those words I'd heard time and time again: "I promise. Stay with me."

"I'll stay, but don't promise me anything this time. Just do it!"

Matthew sat on the couch late that afternoon, drinking a soda, looking off into the distance. He had been there, staring for many minutes. I comprehended that he was seeing his reflection in those windows. Maybe he was seeing himself for the first time in a long time – seeing himself as he really was.

—∞—

"You must turn the page now," said Mom on Zoom when I called to tell them about Aaron solving the crime, the police being brought in, Matthew's innocence solidified.

"Okay?" I know an expression of confusion crossed my face and would've showed on the screen. Mom chuckled.

"Marvellous! Now you need to do something that shows your life is different."

It certainly was different.

"Jenna, Matthew has been cleared of a terrible crime. What can you do to make that dreadful episode completed, finished, concluded…"

I giggled like a schoolgirl. "Slow down, Mom. This time, you're actually hyperventilating. I can see you're really wound up."

Mom yelled to Dad, and they both got on the Zoom call. I was flustered and had trouble relaying again what had transpired. I could see my dad was excited and then he hooted! A smile had spread across his face and crinkled his eyes. I loved seeing them both so happy.

He said, "Best news I can think of. Congratulations. Now everyone understands, really knows he's innocent. Great news."

Mom asked, "How is Matthew?"

"Oh Mom, he was anxious. Now, we have an enormous amount to be grateful for. We've had prolonged talks about the past couple of years. "Pausing for a beat or two, I said, "And, Dad?"

"Yes dear?"

"Dad, what did your cardiologist say on your visit this week?"

His expression changed from excitement about Matthew to a hesitation about my question. I wanted this right out in the open in front of both of them so the whole report could be given. Mom couldn't dodge my questions, and I wanted to hear it from Dad. A breath in, a small smile curving each of their lips.

"It's great news, pumpkin! My medications have cleared up my shortness of breath. My pulse is down, and blood pressure has been stable for several weeks now. Man, I've even lost a few pounds because I'm not retaining water any longer."

"Tremendous!"

"I'm being referred to a Cardiac Function Clinic."

"What's that?"

"This Cardiac Function Clinic will be able to take my calls quicker, and I can email them with any concerns. They have direct access to the cardiologist. There's a pharmacist on staff who is totally familiar with my case. Testing is done there."

"That sounds impressive, but you won't see the cardiologist anymore?"

"Not correct. I'll see him every three months. The Clinic and my cardio guy confer and keep each other up to speed. I still have the blood tests every month. Those go to the Clinic and get reported to the cardio guy."

"Good. I'm satisfied then. But over the winter?"

"I have an echocardiogram – the heart ultrasound – set up for September. After that test, I see my cardiologist. I get blood tests until the first week in November. When the cardiologist sees me, he'll say I'm good to travel. I'm confident."

As I started to close up the Zoom call, Mom said, "Jenna, Charlie says to say hello to Snickers."

When I turned to say, "Charlie says 'hello,'" Snickers lazily thumped her tail at Charlie's name.

I thought again of my mental response when Mom had said our life was different. Yes, it certainly was different! As I quickly went over my list of worries from weeks ago, I felt relief I could mentally put *Done* beside most of them. I'm stronger. I can sense it and love the feeling of being who I really am – competent, resilient. I'm not giving up this feeling of self. Fourteen worries have shrunk to my father's health but trusting his cardiologist; dealing with a belligerent Clara; and keeping an eye on Matthew. I was empowered enough to know I can handle it.

—⚬—

We had been to see John Wu the morning of our celebration, paid the final invoice, gotten a solid handshake – no fingers up to make any points. He'd advised us all details of the case had been handled, police reports filed, and the case closed as far as any charges being laid against Matthew. Adding, "Unless new evidence is submitted." That put a damper on it for one second only. "Just saying," he countered to my groan.

"That won't happen," said a confident Matthew.

John shook our hands, and said, "I'm sure it won't." Pausing, with a gleam in his eyes, he added, "If you want to consider litigation against *Smooth Image Surgery* for everything that they put you through..."

Before Matthew could say a word, I emphatically said, "No. We're done. But thanks for all your service to us."

—⚬—

The celebration of Matthew being cleared of any hint of guilt for the file theft or blackmail, as well as the recognition of everything we had gone through, was held at *The Cliff Restaurant*. We paid the tab for alcohol-free champagne, calamari, entrée and desserts. Our group was the happiest party in the place: Matthew and I, Travis, Robin, Ashley and new guy Nathan, Aaron and Cynthia, Milena and Antonio. Oh, what a night!

We toasted and boasted. Even though the party was for Matthew, Aaron was also the man of the hour.

"Right behind our wedding and our children being born, this is the most wonderful time in our lives," blurted Matthew. "We're blessed to have all that behind us. Toast to the best friend in the world, Aaron."

Drinks in hand, we brought them to our lips and took a sip.

"Right back at you, Matthew. A toast to Matthew!"

Clink, clink, clink, clink, clink, clink, clink, clink, clink, clink.

Aaron said, "Harry from work says he's gonna call you to

apologize for doubting you. At first, he wasn't happy that I duped him, but he came around." Giving Jenna and I each a grimace, he said, "Several others have expressed their need to get in touch with you. I'm not certain you want to talk with any of them."

"I'll talk to them. George has called and grovelled a little, but I'm in no mood to be friends again. Most of the staff don't have my cell number anyway. I just want to get on with the wonder of all of this, not dwell on the past."

"It's true," I ventured. "We have old chums coming out of the woodwork which is nice, but, as Matthew says, 'let's not dwell on the past.'"

I had other toasts to make. I took a deep breath.

"To friends and family; to having the man I married back again." I glanced at Matthew, and he gripped my hand, nodded at me. "To having Matthew's reputation cleared; to having the Life Counsellor tell Matthew to make an appointment every three months or as needed and to email her; to knowing the news and media have covered this story extensively and everyone knowing Matthew Hanson 'is an honourable man.'"

I ran out of breath. As Matthew leaned over to plant a kiss on my lips, I could hear, "To Dad", "to Dad", "to Matthew", "to Matt", "to Matthew", "to Matthew", "to Matthew", "to Matthew", one voice over the other.

Clink, clink, clink, clink, clink, clink, clink, clink, clink, clink.

Matthew, tilted his head and queried, "Is this honourable man thing out of Shakespeare's Caesar?"

"Yeah, I think I channelled Ruby there for a moment."

"Phenomenal!"

Cynthia and Milena had looked at each other and said, "To Jenna." I teared up for these wonderful friends, complete friends. Ashley winked and Travis nodded to me, raising their glasses.

Clink, clink, clink, clink, clink, clink, clink, clink, clink.

They know that I've been through an immense amount, along with Matthew. I gallantly didn't tell any of them my sordid story of

Matthew's behaviour, the toll his attitude and drinking took on me, but they knew. I could see that. I was sorry that Travis and Ashley were aware what a jerk their father had been. Ashley had made me realize with her comment months ago that they had been witness to it. However, I'm proud that I was not the one to relay it to them.

Palm Desert, California

42

What Next?

◆ JENNA ◆

I'd told Matthew how his mother had behaved while we'd been in Portland visiting. I waited until I felt he could take the strain of knowing this. Even though I knew it would be hard for him to hear, he needed to know how things had transpired between Clara and myself.

Matthew approached me, "I don't know how this will turn out while they're down here in Palm Springs."

I gave him a concerned expression, grimaced a little. "We'll do our best to have a great time." Clara had again booked Jack and herself into the Holiday Inn Express & Suites in Rancho Mirage. By the 23rd day of their month-long stay in the Valley, we'd still managed to maintain cordial visits and excursions. They'd also had their own itinerary, so there had been lulls between our interactions.

"We could be on the road to a good relationship, minus her slip up at their home."

"Yes, let's hope my mother has mended her ways. Really changed."

—ɯ—

One evening, I came into the living room with a second glass of Root Beer for myself and handed Clara her third glass of Buffalo Trace Bourbon. I sat down opposite Clara in a wing chair, nervously opened my cell and then pushed it away from my glass. Matthew had driven Jack over to Aaron's to return *Catriona*, the sequel to Robert Louis Stevenson's *Kidnapped*.

Aaron, having grown up as Matthew's childhood friend, had requested Jack stop in for a visit. *It would be an opportunity for Jack to see that Aaron did turn out well – hadn't gotten into trouble. In fact, the opposite had occurred.* The worry Clara and I couldn't get along receded at the same time as the dregs of Clara's second glass. She seemed relaxed.

In a companionable voice, I said, "I'm pleased you and Jack came to the Valley for a stay. You've enjoyed yourself so far it seems?" I had raised the last word so that it became a question. I'd been avoiding loaded questions, hoping not to get an unwanted reaction from Clara. As I crossed and uncrossed my legs and fiddled with my necklace, I realized I looked nervous. *I'm not nervous. We're both being friendly.*

I continued with, "And we're getting along so well." Darn, that wasn't supposed to come out.

"Are we?" Clara asked, her posture stiffening, her voice clipped.

"Of course," was my quick reply. Something in her face caused me sudden apprehension.

"Yes, on the surface, everything is grand. Bottoms up," as she gulped more bourbon. She'd gotten up a minute before and poured herself another glass. I'd been planning not to give her more. She'd come in with her own bottle, knowing we didn't keep alcohol in the house. Clara smiled a smile that didn't reach her eyes. To me, that signalled she might not proceed amicably. At this point, I moved my telephone closer, making an adjustment.

Again, I shouldn't have queried, "On the surface?" *Am I a dunce? Shut up.*

"Listen Jenna, I'll spell it out for you." She put her arm across the back of the sofa as though settling in for a long conversation. A good one, I still hoped, not wanting to admit I had a niggling apprehension.

"I've never been happy Matthew married you." My hopes plummeted. "You're not suitable for him. You're not his type."

Wow, let it all hang out lady. 'Lady' ha!

Still smiling that smile, she said, "You're a lousy mother, a terrible cook and housekeeper. Now you retire and expect my Matthew to pay for your little painting hobby..."

Sitting straighter, I ventured, "Your only concern should be if Matthew is happy."

Swishing her drink in her hand and taking a gulp, I noted an unbecoming sneer materializing on her face as she said, "I don't know how he could be happy – with you for a wife."

Standing up, fuming, I said, "As a courtesy to Matthew and to Jack, I won't let what you say bother me. Matthew fell for all your lies, but not any longer."

Clara spat out. "How dare you talk to me like that!"

"Clara, you need to stop this. Calm down."

"You think I give a damn what you think?" asked Clara, forcefully stubbing out her cigarette. "You've been a thorn in my side for over 30 years. You don't even belong in our family."

I wish I had a pool to push her into.

Still standing, I leaned a little toward her and said in a pseudo-pleasant voice, "That's too bad you feel that way. You don't even realize, it's not me begging any longer if I can be part of your family. It's you who should be asking will you ever be part of my family and will you be part of Matthew's life, part of Travis and Ashley's life, part of any future grandchildren's life."

And then out came Clara's most visceral verbal blow, "I doubt Matthew loves you. He tried to kill himself to get away from you."

I blanched and walked away, tears spilling from each eye. *How could she?* Of course, that comment ran deep. I couldn't deny my husband attempted to kill himself. *Was it to get away from me?*

"Clara!" a voice on the other end of my open telephone yelled.

"What the hell have you done?" shouted Clara.

As I stood silently, she stomped away. I understood she'd be angry. I felt hesitant what would happen next. As she turned around and started back toward me, the door opened, and in stepped Jack and Matthew – the police officer, father-in-law was not happy. His face furious. Matthew had suggested the open telephone for when I believed the conversation might turn. He'd warned Jack, and Jack had agreed, miserable in his concern about the volcano Clara could erupt.

Clara attempted to placate Jack. "Anything you think you heard wasn't what I said."

"Clara, it's time to go back to the hotel."

Clara turned on me, glaring. First, tossing down the rest of her drink, then grabbing her purse, she shoved past me and Jack, striding through the door. Jack turned toward me with his face now ashen. He walked over and gave me a full hug and Matthew a man hug and a quick double pat on the back. He left without saying another word.

"Baby, I'm sorry you went through that. I'll get myself a soda, and we can talk through this. Do you want anything?" At the shake of my head, he touched my shoulder, "Are you going to be okay now?"

"Since Jack's heard Clara's behaviour toward me, I will be." He gave me a quick hug. "I'll be back in a shake."

I wasn't concerned about Clara. She could very well handle herself and Jack, but there would be no more secrets. *I am fine.* Better than fine. She had been a witch, and I couldn't feel sorry for her.

Matthew's brother, Neil, called me two days later.

"Wow, you've got balls, lady! Dad filled me in on the details. Sharyn will be forever in your debt. I'd confided in Dad a couple of times when Mom was over the top with Sharyn, but I've never told him everything. Sharyn reacted with an arm pump when I told her."

"I'm grateful it helped Sharyn. We've chatted about your mother on occasion, so this is a score for both of us – if it works out. Your mom had promised me previously that she'd changed, but she's permanently flawed, sorry to say."

"Maybe this time it'll work. Dad has insisted when they return to Portland, they're going to find their own replica of your Dr. Gerstein-Kraus. They're both going to get counselling so Dad can tell the"

– pausing to laugh – "Life Counsellor what's been going on and ensure Mom doesn't weasel out of this."

"Then it's good news for everyone concerned. I truly do wish your mom the best."

"I know you do. I love her in spite of it all, but I'll love her more when she's improved mentally."

I thanked Neil on behalf of Matthew for calling and texting Matthew as often as he did. "Matthew always gets off your calls with a chuckle in his throat. I loved hearing about your conversations."

"Mom and Dad are off to San Diego for three days if Dad hasn't told Matt that tidbit. It was already on this holiday itinerary. They're going early to change scenery. Mom'll come back with a better attitude. She'll manage the rest of the holiday in control of herself."

"Yes, Matthew told me about the change in plan. Obviously, I'm thankful."

"It's all going to work out, Jenna. You'll see. They finally seem to 'get' each other the past few years. Dad has more patience with Mom. She'll come around."

"Adios amigo."

"Chat later, Jenna."

—ᴡ—

The next week, I watched Clara gaze longingly at my mom and her friends as we were walking away from them at the Resort. Today had been a reconciliation visit for the last time Clara and I were together. Jack had insisted on seeing my mom and dad's Resort. They were here at Palm Estates RV Resort for a couple of hours to investigate the attraction to this lifestyle. Clara had turned up her nose.

"What can they find to amuse themselves with? And the places in which they live -- they're so teeny, the kitchens unbearably modest."

Mom had been gracious even though I'd told her of the Portland episode and had gone into detail about last week's fiasco. The other residents didn't know anything except these were Matthew's parents visiting.

Their visit had been a success. One bit of conversation niggled at me though. When the afternoon and potluck supper were over, I'd heard Clara say to Jack, "I felt strangely comfortable there."

His reply had been, "I loved it. The people are here for pleasure. I could get used to golfing with these guys." His expression portrayed yearning as he listed all the activities. "And just sitting around chewing the fat."

Clara looked thoughtful. *Surely, she wouldn't want to come down for the winter!*

"I was skeptical at first. I hated the idea of all these people around all the time, no privacy – but everyone is here for a good time and friendly. I could get into some of it."

"Clara, I'm interested in doing this."

Thank God I'm already sitting down in the passenger seat. Matthew's eyes widened, and he sent me a 'what the hell' look.

Jack resumed his thoughts, "The pools are appealing. A variety of personalities. Seems fun."

I was desperately fretful they might think of coming to this Resort where Mom and Dad spent the winter. This could be very awkward indeed – *bloody hell, it would be disastrous!*

The daytime weather had been awesome as were most days during the fall/winter season. That had added to Clara and Jack's delight about the park, I supposed.

The *Desert Sun* news had predicted a storm. By the time Matthew and I dropped them off at their hotel, the Santa Ana winds had picked up to a ferocious speed.

Matthew said, "We'll get you safe and sound into the hotel, and we'll head straight home. The roads are a little dangerous during these winds – flying debris."

I'd added, "We'll chat in the morning to find out what you're going to be doing and advise of the road situation."

Clara had proclaimed, "Once the storm's over, we'll be fine."

"Mom, any time there are blasts of wind coming through the pass, at least two roads could be covered with sand, similar to snow blocking roads in a blizzard. The roads could be impassable with the sand the wind brought in."

"Oh!" they both said at once. That surprised them as it did anyone who hadn't witnessed what transpired after a windstorm in the Valley.

"We'll chat in the morning," said Jack.

Palm Desert, California

43

Success

❖ JENNA ❖

I'D WORKED HARD TO learn everything about painting, colours, painting styles. Milena had been a fountain of free advice, and I followed her website and her blog faithfully. I found it relaxing and exhilarating to master the craft of painting and to see the finished product. Milena had helped me set up my own webpage months ago – another step forward.

My paintings initially had been sold at local art shows, as well as through my website. Once a prospective buyer saw my paintings, they'd almost always buy them. I put my prices up, and still they sold. I wanted my paintings – my hard work – to go to a good home. I hadn't lost a sale because of it. I'd kind of work my way around by asking, "Where do you think this will fit in your home?" Stuff like that. Milena said she started out doing that same thing. Of course, I didn't know what wall my beloved paintings were actually hung on at their home or office.

The idea that my paintings were so well liked was fascinating to me. As an artist, I knew my work was good, but I had no idea that other people would love them and be willing to pay the prices I charged.

Today, I telephoned Matthew from *Springs Art Gallery*. I was stoked!

"Matthew, can you talk? Where are you?"

"Heading home from Eddie Bauer at Cabazon Mall. Your call's coming over the Bronco speaker." Snickers perked up at Matthew's voice. "What's up? I sense excitement."

"The Gallery sold two of my paintings for the prices they suggested. Can you believe it?"

"Of course, I believe it. I told you they were outstanding as did everyone else who saw your work. Congratulations. Mimosas – Sprite and orange juice when you get home!"

I giggled. "Yes!"

"It's difficult to think you have to part with something you put your heart into. Which ones did you sell?"

"The one of our landscaping in the front yard! Two snowbirds came in and couldn't take their eyes off it. They want it for over their mantel."

"Oh no! And the other? You wouldn't sell the Snickers and Charlie painting?" Snickers rubbed against my hand holding the cell as she heard her name.

"I wouldn't sell the painting of them curled up together in our back yard. It would break my heart to part with it. I sold the field with horses ambling along up at Lake Hemet."

"I realize you painted them to sell, and I'm glad your work is appreciated. But I can't get used to the idea that we have to part with these beautiful works of art."

As we were having appetizers on the back patio under the moonlight and having a glass of our "mimosas" to toast a successful art show, Matthew said, "I've been through the last read through of my book. *What Was I Thinking?* can be put on KDP Kindle Direct Publishing within a day or two. If there's any interest by the stores in the Valley, I could sell them there. Maybe the bookstore in downtown Palm Springs."

Happily, I responded, "Fantastic." I heard my parcel from Amazon being dropped at the front door.

"That's another celebration. Maybe not another orange juice."

"We've got milk and chocolate cookies…"

"Sold." I laughed. "Another sale today!"

"What did you order from Amazon? Something for me?"

"No, something for me. You won't be surprised I ordered some special brushes for my painting addiction."

As Snickers and I returned with my parcel opened and unpacked, Matthew's expression had turned thoughtful and serious. I set the brushes down and listened to what he was saying.

"In writing this book, I've become interested in an entirely different subject. I think it's another way for my brain to get a rest from the stress of writing my book on the personal subject of suicide."

"I appreciate at times the writing and re-experiencing felt difficult for you. When I read the entire manuscript, I was moved, to tears at much of it." I squeezed his hand. "You masterfully expressed your pain and triumph of survival." Pausing for a moment to control myself. "Also, you handled my emotions and confusion throughout your book accurately."

Taking both my hands, he said, "Thank you. In truth, I couldn't have done any of it without your support and encouragement. I love you."

"I love you, too – really love you. And you're welcome. Tell me what the next project might be."

"Um, well, it's your story, really. You told me about the great grandmother whom you didn't ever meet, and, in about 1920, her bastard of a husband found a new woman, had children with her, and put his own wife in a mental institution and all four children in a Children's Shelter".

"Oh, shit, Matthew. I mean shucks." I reached down to pet Snickers, a distraction from the subject at hand. Snickers snuggled against my palm.

"Shucks? Trying to cut down?"

"Yeah, it's upsetting my mother."

He chuckled. Then he gave me that smile with one side curved up higher than the other, the smile that made my heart do a half flip. I loved this man, *this man.*

I said, "That doesn't sound like a story that would sooth your brain. I love that you can get this out on paper."

He went into his office and brought out some folded sheets of paper. "Here is some of the information you gave me from your mom from his war records."

I read what Matthew had in his hands, and my own hands began to shake. Perhaps they began to shake from the angry flashes of emotion for a man – pseudo great-grandfather – that this letter brought to me. However, partly, I think it was the exhilaration this information could be a family chronicle—that it would portray the life of my great grandmother. I fondled the bracelet, wishing always I could turn back the clock for her, my great-grandmother.

With my hands trembling, I re-read the letters I'd had in my possession for 20 years and gazed at him in admiration.

Looking pleased with my approval, Matthew stated, "Even though I said I'd write your great-grandmother's story, can we work on it together? It's your story to tell, not mine."

"Oh, Matthew, I would love to be part of writing this."

"I want to write this family chronicle for you, for holding our lives together while I fell apart. I would be nothing without you."

"It was a bad time."

"Our sessions with Dr. GK about my random suicidal thoughts resulted in my new medication. I was very messed up back then. You're my soul mate, my inspiration, my life. By writing this family saga, I want to pay tribute to you – for everything you have done – for everything you have made me."

I was speechless for a moment. *Yes, I had helped him during his failures, at least done my best. It had all worked out now. We're both better people.* "Matthew, thank you."

"You deserve to have a good man, and I'm going to be that man. This history will be something you and I will work on together, but it's to show how much you mean to me."

"I have fallen in love with you all over again, Matthew. I think we have a deeper love built on a lifetime of shared good times and bad times. We'll make this work."

That evening after taking Snickers for a walk, I felt closer to Matthew than I had in I didn't even want to think how long. *A freaking long, long time.*

I didn't mind in the least he'd started my family story. I wouldn't have wanted anyone else to do it. With both of us, together with my mom, contributing, this felt ideal. I totally had my real husband back, and tears streamed down my face as I turned away.

—∞—

Last week was another outing with our dearest friends, Aaron and Cynthia. On a Thursday evening, we'd left it up to Cynthia to find a great place to go. As Cynthia pulled into a downtown Palm Springs parking spot, Matthew muttered, "This isn't exactly what I had in mind. Shopping?"

Cynthia countered as she put her new Ford 150 in park, "It's not just 'shopping' Matthew. It's Village Fest. Dozens and dozens of pop-up vendors. It'll be great. Typical Palm Springs."

"Let's get Tamales then. I deserve that if I'm shopping." Matthew obviously felt entitled to have a reward.

Once we all agreed what fast food we wanted, we met at a corner table before our enjoyment of Village Fest was continued. As the warm sun shrunk behind the mountains and stores surrounding us, we ate our supper. Aaron had trotted over to *Great Shakes*. We all spooned up the famous date shakes, slurping up the last drops.

The items we went home with were diverse. Matthew found a fused glass vendor and bought a set of glass jars of every colour for our patio. I found a sun hat that would cover the back of my neck in the summer heat. Cynthia had a collection of bath bombs. And Aaron, well Aaron had bought a bouquet of flowers for Cynthia.

"Crap, is this how it is always going to be?" she said. "I buy something selfishly just for me and you present me with a bouquet of flowers?"

Sniffing them, she smiled what I supposed was a special smile for Aaron, but I caught it. She glanced sideways at me, and turned so I couldn't see her next expression. I could surmise she was whispering as he leaned toward her. They clasped hands as they walked in front of us heading to Cynthia's truck.

"Hey, let's do the Tram ride next time we get together!" I was enthusiastic about this prospect, "Best view of the Valley up at the top of the San Jacinto."

Cynthia turned and piped up with, "Pretend we're tourists. See the Salton Sea."

As Aaron glanced at me, he added hopefully, "We'll have appies in the restaurant. If we get there at the right time, we can see the sun go down. Cool, right?"

Glancing around at the others, I could see a sparkle of interest.

"Tourists. You betcha! Let's do that."

Palm Desert, California

(Three Years Later)

EPILOGUE

❖ JENNA ❖

Tonight, we were having a family get together.

"We are so blessed," said Travis, with Robin tucked in close to his shoulder. "You both went through so much. Mom, you were the rock during the ordeal."

Ashley glanced at me, displaying a perceptive expression.

Sitting in our back yard with appetizers covering the table, our family get together had a glow to it. With evening quickly approaching, I got up to light the two firepits and poured everyone another drink. The coolness tonight made me thankful that a cardigan was snuggled around my shoulders.

Two figures quietly approached from the shadows walking toward the back yard, faces now lit by the distorted light provided by the firepits. Snickers had already jumped up to welcome our new guests, particularly Charlie. An older Charlie ran at a slower gait to meet up nose to nose with Snickers, and the two bounced around each other until Charlie lay down. Snickers plopped down right beside him.

"Sorry we're late. Traffic." My dad set down the platter they'd brought.

"Hors d'oeuvres for tonight's celebration."

Ashley's partner, Nathan, gave a quick shake of his head and said, "What did you just say, Phoebe?"

"Uhhh. Oh, we call them hors d'oeuvres at home. Appetizers. Tonight, we brought several kinds of shrimp. Appies!"

Ashley poked him, and said, "You'll learn to speak some of our Canadianisms."

"Yeah, sure." Skeptically said.

My mom added some small plates and napkins to the array already set out.

I stood up and hugged her. "So glad you got here. We'd figured it was the Friday night traffic." As I bent to get a glass for each of them, Matthew arose to pour some drinks.

After also getting up to give my mom and dad a warm hug, Ashley said, "We're celebrating beginnings." Grinning, "Again!"

Mom turned to Travis and said, "You completed your education and are working a lot, so that's a great beginning."

"Yeah, and I'm doin' well with *Hanson Total Housebuilding*, working throughout the Coachella Valley."

At this point, Dad chimed in, "Good, good. And your Uncle Robert and I are so proud of you, Travis."

Mom moved toward Travis and gave him a hug, "Me too."

"Thanks to both Grandpa and Uncle Robert, the experience I got when I worked in Calgary those months."

"You did well!" reiterated my dad.

Robin sat up straighter, shifting the squirming bundle on her lap. "I'm going in for a half hour."

I rushed to say "You don't have to go in."

"Yeah, she needs changing as well as nursing."

My mom gave Robin and her great grandchild a fond hug. "Tracey is remarkable, Robin. I'll come inside to see her in a bit."

"The guest room has a new dangling toy over her crib," Matthew remarked. "For whenever you come to visit with our beautiful granddaughter."

Travis jumped up and rushed to open the patio door for Robin and seven-month-old Tracey.

"When you go in, Travis, the two of you could check out the photo album that I created with photos of your wedding and Tracey's birth and six-month 'birthday' party."

Travis said, "I'll bring it out. We'll wait until Robin comes back and all look at it together."

I knew Matthew felt gratified to feel my love for Robin and Tracey. Travis and Robin had a lovely wedding two years ago. Best of all, Travis has a genuine and loving mother-in-law and so does Robin!

I remarked, "He is a fabulous husband and father. We're fortunate to have Robin as a daughter-in-law and to have a dear granddaughter."

I gave Matthew a knowing look as we watched Nathan take Ashley's hand. Nathan was always attentive when Ashley showed him old photographs. I said, "This new life of having extended family suits us. It's like having built-in friends."

I knew Nathan was inwardly squirming a little at what he had bought this afternoon while Ashley was at home performing Reiki on a client. He'd told me he'd put the box in his nightstand, a box that contained an engagement ring.

Both Ashley and Nathan taught in LA. I exchanged another glance with Matthew. We'd love to have this tall, broad shouldered, hardworking teacher and lovable guy as part of our family. He attended classes so that he'd be on the fast track to becoming a principal.

"I'll go in to see Tracey," said Mom.

"I'm coming too. We'll be quiet as mice," added Dad over his shoulder.

Opening the back patio door, they shushed each other and scurried in.

"I was thinking of Clara and Jack. Your mom and dad seem to like resort life."

"They report they've the best friends and the best resort in the country near Phoenix." Matthew added, "Not staying in California seemed a phenomenal idea."

I threw him an approving smile at that understatement.

I forgave her, and we get along when we're together. I don't take any crap from anyone anymore. Maybe Clara overcame her personality disorder. She continues to see a 'Life Counsellor' and is on prescribed medication.

After a few minutes, my mom and dad emerged from inside, still shushing each other, followed out the door by Travis and Robin. Robin immediately said, "Tracey giggled and reached for the giraffe whirling toy. She's now cuddled asleep in the blanket we bought during the family San Diego Zoo trip."

"I've brought the baby monitor and the photo album," said Travis, sitting and opening the first page.

Each of our family members peered over Travis and Robin's shoulders as they sat with the album on their knees. There were lots of oohs and aahs.

"It was a fabulous wedding."

"Your dress was marvellous!"

"And the bridesmaids! Ashley, you're gorgeous."

"What about my suit?" asked a disgruntled Travis. "The groom's important, you know. Can't have a wedding without a groom."

Chuckles followed that comment.

Nathan said, "There's truth in that, Travis. It's a good thing you were invited."

Still smiling, I added, "It felt so good to have all our families together."

Ashley said, "Mom, you did a fantastic photograph album. Look at newborn Tracey. I want copies of that one with the stuffed roadrunner."

Looking at all of my extended family, I proclaimed, "Our family is incredible! Look at what we've created. A masterpiece!"

"We've come full circle," Matthew said as he smiled. "A new life has begun for all of us."

"Let's toast to family." I raised my glass of alcohol-free punch. *We forged ahead living our life.*

My mom said, "Our winters down here are fantastic. Leonard's health isn't perfect." He gave her a glare. "However, the medications are doing their job."

"I'm fine, playing golf once a week, enjoying the company of all my buddies in the resort."

"We made the right decision three years ago. I'm delighted in each of our Resort friends and relishing Betty's companionship."

Nathan stated, "Ashley and I can't wait for summer! I think that when all of us are on our Alaskan cruise, we could have a really exciting family time." Nathan gave Ashley's hand a squeeze and they smiled at each other, a smile of love.

"Disney Cruise Line will make it a fabulous trip to take Tracey on," said Robin.

Travis said, "She may be young, but we'll have a hella great time."

Matthew and I'd done some travelling on our own – taken a tour of Europe with *Globus Tours*. Our plan for the future on our 35th anniversary would be touring Scotland with *Lindsays Highland Tours*.

"Milena had mentioned that she, Cynthia and I should go on a tour with *Girl Travel Tours*, "Southern Italy Food & Wine" Campania, Puglia & the Amalfi Coast 12 days. "

Ashley clapped her hands together and said, "Mom, that's fantastic."

I brought out the completed story for *The Mad Mistake*. "This booklet is the culmination of research done by Mom and me. Mom found most of this information decades ago from the Canadian Army Records."

My mom reached for the massive number of pages with trembling hands. "My grandmother's story. At last." She stopped talking, overcome by emotion. "His lust for other women destroyed all their lives."

I went over to my mom and wrapped both arms around her to console her. As I removed the manuscript from her hands, she grabbed onto me shaking her head at the past calamity.

"Thank you, Jenna and Matthew. Thank you for making it right! These deepest secrets are now revealed after such a long passage of time."

"We couldn't have ever written it without you corroborating the facts accumulated over all these years."

My dad took Mom's hand. They stood close together, her head on his shoulder.

Matthew added while looking directly at me, "Jenna's writing style is fabulous, putting her heart and soul into the booklet. We work especially well together – a team!"

I moved to the table, picked up the pitcher and refilled everyone's glass.

Matthew said, "We're going to have an extraordinary life. When you almost lose something, it becomes very precious."

As I raised my glass, I happily said, "Cheers to beginnings!"

Clink! clink! clink! clink! clink! clink! clink! clink!

Thank You

from Moira Darrell

Thank you to my brain "that doesn't shut up" and for the imagination that God gave me. Strangely, I would also like to thank the internet because I was able to check google to verify my memories and facts about places without having to retrace all my previous steps in Calgary, Portland and the Coachella Valley.

I thank the RV Resort that we do actually stay in for a few months each year. Even though no real persons are portrayed in this story, I was able to pull together emotions from interactions with amazing owners and renters that we have become friends with over the years in various parks and resorts. One of the best parts of our life is the months we are able to be in our resort in California. Therefore, thank you to those amazing people from Desert Shadows RV Resort for being exactly who they are.

I thank friends, family, neighbours and acquaintances throughout my life who also have given me the opportunity to feel the love, fun, even sadness that I was able to garner to write both "SELENA AND HER MYSTERIES" as well as "MESSED-UP CHOICES."

To my proofreaders for MESSED-UP CHOICES:

Rod Wiley – He is my "editor," and he gave me abundant insight.

The Writers' Guild of Alberta Manuscript Reader (anonymous) for immeasurable help pointing me in the right direction with many scenes.

Sharon Roddy – Re-read my Final Manuscript – thank you for your words of encouragement.

Regina McCreary of Human Powered Design in Calgary is the person to ask for assistance in putting your manuscript into Epub and Mobi format. She is also a fountain of information for a novice or experienced writer. If you have a question regarding self-publishing, she'll be able to answer it for you!

Thank you to you, the reader. Thank you very much for taking the time to read this book. "MESSED-UP CHOICES" took 20 months to write. I wanted to verify details, so there was thorough research involved. Even though I loved writing these books and may have written them just for myself, the feeling of having someone else see my words and, hopefully, experience the emotions I'm expressing means a considerable amount to me. I am very thankful to you.

If you are not familiar with the Canadian spelling of words throughout this book, I appreciate your patience. Thank you.

And thank you to myself – This was challenging work! Again.

Comments: moiradoubleu@gmail.com

Facebook Page FOLLOW ME- facebook.com/moiradarrellbooks

Please consider leaving a review on the site where you purchased this book, i.e. Ebooks, Amazon.ca, Amazon.com or Goodreads.

All my research for "Messed-Up Choices" is listed following ABOUT THE AUTHOR

Overview for
Selena and Her Mysteries

MOIRA DARRELL's first book published in 2022.

There is more to **SELENA AND HER MYSTERIES** than what you may think when reading the back or hearing a plot synopsis. Hidden in the book description is an entirely different story. When it simply talks about travel, it might not be the travel you're thinking of. When it talks about 'shadows drift by,' they might not be the shadows you think of.

"Honestly, is there nothing that I believed five days ago that actually is what I thought it was?"

Selena Jenkins, a young woman, lives in a huge house - full of mysteries. As doors are opened, mistakes are inevitable. Extraordinary travel takes place, ensuring Selena must mature quickly or be lost in a situation where she cannot stay.

Duplicity is in the wings; friendships grow stronger; love is whispered; shadows drift by; and memories are blurred. Selena's life is complicated as people and events necessitate her to overcome heart-breaking deceit and to make difficult life decisions.

Family mysteries swirl tightly around her, overpowering her thoughts as she searches for answers in unexpected places and circumstances. What she finds will change her life and bring hope for love and, finally, understanding of all the mysteries that shape her past and present.

EXCERPT:

Her Aunt Jenny was crying and saying, "Please, will you come back for another visit sooner?"

Selena did not hear what the young couple answered, but she

clearly heard her aunt's forlorn response. "All right. I will see you there then."

'I will see you there then.' Where would she see them?? Here in Ottawa? Was she going somewhere? Am I going somewhere?

EXCERPT:
Selena found herself sitting on the floor with the folder askew, tears streaming down her cheeks.

"I have no words to even think right now."

Examining the folder to see what else it may contain, Selena found that there were letters from various people and agencies inquiring as to the disappearance, newspaper articles and official documents investigating and, as some years went by, eventually indications that the investigation was closed and incomplete, whereabouts unknown.

Selena felt so many emotions that her mind was clogged. Astonishment, shock, disbelief, devastation, hurt.

"How could someone do that?"

EXCERPT:
"If you're certain – then I've a story to tell you. I said that I usually am honest. On this one instance I wasn't – But only by omission."

At that moment, they were interrupted by the waiter again, re-filling their glasses and asking if there was anything else that he could get for them.

"Thank you so very much. We're both fine here. Everything was delicious." As he walked farther away, Selena looked at Colleen, waiting for her response.

"Now, you give me the tea!"

Laughing, Colleen replied with a bemused expression, "For a long time, I didn't realize that you didn't know."

EXCERPT:
A titillating conversation that had truly grasped Selena's antenna much more sharply than any other conversation had been between

Eric Brisbane, Gavin Perrault and Dr. Robertson, who were all earnestly discussing time travel and the changes in the body's molecules during time travel.

What!!!?? How???!! What's going on here?

Selena had leaned forward trying to catch more of their conversation; however, they walked away while talking. They were out of earshot now.

Selena seriously pondered – "Maybe I could follow them. Now what! I must find out! I wonder if I'll get a chance to find out what's what with those three. If they approach me, what would I say to them?"

Excerpt:

Selena felt so very adrift. Unprompted, one of her old poems slid into her mind:

> You are travelling over the strange wide world,
> Then comes a feeling of being suddenly hurled
> From one cloud to a star in an unexplainable calm
> As though God had taken you in his palm,
> Making you feel safe as if you were asleep
> With thoughts of peace while in a dream so deep.
> Then, far from your most imaginative dreams,
> Comes, so swiftly, such vivid scenes
> Of beauty and splendor – more than you could ever seek,
> So unthought of and, oh, so utterly unique.

Note from the Author

This is my second book, the first being "SELENA AND HER MYSTERIES". An idea of the Selena story had come to me 30 years before, but I had left that 2,000-word segment in a folder for three decades, completing and self publishing it two years ago.

This storyline of "MESSED-UP CHOICES" came to me one evening as I was preparing to go to sleep. An entire chapter of "Matthew's Journal", popped into my head out of the blue. I worried I wouldn't remember it in the morning, so I grabbed my cell phone and dictated into the phone. Since my telephone has a mind of its own when it comes to grammar, spelling and punctuation, it wasn't perfect. Maybe it's my Canadian accent? I was just happy to have it on my cell so I could go to sleep!

There is no similarity between the two books – no repeat storyline, no repeat characters. Character development wasn't as clear cut as it had been with "SELENA AND HER MYSTERIES".

I found in writing my second book, *MESSED-UP CHOICES*, it took a while to become familiar with the characters. *SELENA AND HER MYSTERIES* fell from my fingers easier!

These new characters (people) were reticent at first and had to be drawn out before I was able to get to know each of them well. Once I had them all figured out, Matthew decided to change his entire persona. Well, thanks to Matthew deciding to become an ambiguous, sometimes reprehensible, person, I needed to change Jenna's persona to fit. Aaron, the friend, showed a different side of his character at the same time. Therefore, three main characters had to be re-written. I have to wonder who authors these books? Me or the characters who almost feel like real people by the time I've spent almost 20 months 'living' with them.

The name of Jenna's mother arose because a friend and I were discussing names. We both felt our names weren't common. A day after that discussion, I stopped Phoebe in the street and asked her if she would mind if I used her name as a character in a book. She was pleased. The thing was, at that point, I didn't even have a storyline in mind. Then, this story jumped out at me, so Phoebe is a supporting character.

The name Betty near the end of my book resulted one evening at an event at our RV Resort. Betty Jo, my friend, came up to me with what she imagined was a very angry expression. She said, "I'm really mad at you!" Looking at her and knowing her personality, I twigged onto something humourous. I replied, "You're angry because you aren't mentioned in my 'to-be' book?" She laughed. Well, we both laughed. I said, "I've already made Phoebe the good mother-in-law. I don't think I can make you the bad mother-in-law." Eventually, the character of Betty came into play, and Betty Jo became Betty. No, my character names do NOT represent the real person. There isn't a similarity physique or manner. I'm just using a familiar name. Always the characters have no resemblance to the people I know.

We do travel to the Palm Springs area every winter we can. We stay in an RV Resort. We have stayed in a few RV Resorts over the years. "MESSED-UP CHOICES" does not portray any characters in the Resort where we stay, and we have friends who do not resemble any of these characters. However, there are extremely enjoyable times and events in our real life and fantastic friends. BTW, there is no RV Resort or school currently with the names I have chosen.

Being in the area for several months every winter means I've had the opportunity to visit all the places and restaurants in this book. It's a fantastic area to winter in, with innumerable excursions in the Coachella Valley, the Inland Empire, San Diego, Temecula, up the three surrounding mountain ranges, out into the desert. Oh my gosh, this could be a list of 100. Life in the Coachella Valley is remarkably different from my other life near the mountains of Alberta or my decades living in Saskatchewan.

I have sincere fondness for the accents of people from different areas of the world. Yes, apparently, I too have an accent. The various accents definitely attract me. I wrote in this book terms used by people in different areas and that also brings out a fondness.

I loved writing this book. I was unsure about the subject matter. "Medical Incident" seemed a less shocking term than attempted suicide. I have no idea why the storyline came to me, but, once it did, I needed to ensure it was used. I say, "my mind never shuts up, so I may as well write it down". Then maybe I can sleep…

A few of the subjects in my book happened in small ways to me. When I had one of my babies, I recall being depressed. It's odd to think such a delightful experience of having a child could cause one's mind to turn on itself. One day, I experienced the "light at the end of the tunnel", an overwhelming occurrence. Thankfully, from that day on, that depression was over. Even though I have a 'happy-go-lucky' attitude on life, it doesn't stop me from feeling 'down'.

Write about what you know! I have my second level of Reiki, classes I took so I could help heal myself after West Nile Virus turned neurological. This horrible virus still has its long-term grips on me years later, but most of the symptoms have diminished.

"A Mad Mistake" mentioned in this book is another book I began to write several years ago. It is a true story about my own grandmother. I felt the need to put it into this book as I wanted Matthew to have a future in writing, and that story was a good one for him to get involved in, using Jenna's great grandmother as the main character. Jenna would have been too young for Florence to be her grandmother. One day in the next few years, I might complete "A Mad Mistake" although it takes a real steeling of my will to write about the 'creature' and what he did to my grandmother whom I didn't ever meet, and I feel she needs to have her story told.

The actual "A Mad Mistake" will go on to tell of the child's (my father's) life and how he made contact with his three siblings, a masterful story in itself. Thankfully, many of the children and grandchildren of Florence in these four families had the opportunity to know each other and be a family again after the previous generation had been torn apart by "that creature".

The Creature actually married a third woman after the one he left my grandmother for and to have a child with a fourth woman. Who knows how many others there are? We're still finding relatives through Ancestry over 100 years after Florence was forced into the mental institute by *the creature*.

I have all the facts typed up in my computer. However, once the facts were all there, I ended up beginning to write "MESSED-UP CHOICES" instead. I also have 10,000 words typed up as a storyline for "Journey To Selena". That book would be a prequel to "Selena And Her Mysteries" as well as the after story. Again, it took second place to this current book. Did I say my mind would let me sleep once this second book is complete? Perhaps not…

About the Author

MOIRA DARRELL WILEY is the author's full name. However, she used her first and middle names to write this book because, unbelievably, there was already an author named Moira Wiley!

Moira Darrell was born and lived in a small town in Saskatchewan, then moved to Regina; however, she now lives closer to the mountains in Alberta with her husband and kitty. Some family members are close by; others so far away that it brings tears to her eyes. Such is life.

She has been a daughter, a granddaughter, a sister, a wife, a mother, a grandmother, a legal secretary (22 years), a school admin secretary (12 years), a poet, a hand-sculpting potter in many techniques, dabbled in drawing, painting, has her second level of Reiki (as does Ashley in this current book). Moira is the author of *MESSED-UP CHOICES* and *SELENA AND HER MYSTERIES*.

As a teenager, she loved writing in Composition class and has written several poems, some of which found themselves in her books.

Moira is especially interested in the emotions of her characters (people), the friendships, the relationships, all influenced by people, events, and emotions in her own life. Not that any of these events necessarily happened to her, but the emotions still apply. Both books actually do grab Moira and pull her along with them. She tends to get totally engrossed in the character's emotions as she writes and re-reads segments of her books. She laughs, feels sad, gets a tear in her eye, has anger at a deceit and delight in the happy parts of each book. The characters become like friends. Didn't we all have imaginary friends when we were younger? Well, apparently, Moira still does.

Moira loves nature and nurture, has had many pets – two closely resembling the animals in *MESSED-UP CHOICES*, has loved them all. As she appears in "*SELENA AND HER MYSTERIES*", Moira currently does have a kitty named Caylie Ceilidh Pretty Lady – really. Her English Springer Spaniel, Snickers, now passed away, knew the hand commands described in *SELENA AND HER MYSTERIES* and now is part of her book, *MESSED-UP CHOICES*. Ringo, another English Springer Spaniel mentioned in *MESSED-UP CHOICES*, was her dog. He was a handful and a very overwhelming addition to her young family!!

Moira has volunteered for various groups throughout her life, such as community associations, city zone board, a women's shelter, a housing project, pottery groups and a city arts' committee. She believes in giving to charity by time or donation if you are able.

Live your life to the best of your ability. And "instead of worrying about what was or what might be, rejoice in what IS."

Research

Cabot's Museum (*Author has been here several times*)
    https://www.cabotsmuseum.org/about-us/pueblo/
    https://www.cabotsmuseum.org/

Calgary St. Barnabas (*Author has been here*)
    https://static1.squarespace.com/static/588e65d-737c5818a6a061678/t/5942e693f5e2317702e330ee/1497556639587/walkingtour2.pdf

Calgary Tower (*Author has been here*)
    https://www.calgarytower.com/

Canadian Teachers in USA
    https://www.latimes.com/archives/la-xpm-1985-12-19-hl-30685-story.html
    https://www.latimes.com/archives/la-xpm-1985-12-19-hl-30685-story.html

Celtic Women @ Fantasy Springs - (*Author attended performance*)
    https://coachellavalleyweekly.com/celtic-woman-plays-at-fantasy-springs-december-2-2022/

College of the Desert (*Author has been here often*)
    https://catalog.collegeofthedesert.edu/programs/architecture-environmental-design/construction-management-certificate-of-achievement/

Depression/Treatment/Suicide
    https://www.fda.gov/consumers/free-publications-women/depression-medicines#SSRI
    https://msktc.org/tbi/factsheets/facts-about-vegetative-and-minimally-conscious-states-after-severe-brain-injury
    https://www.ncbi.nlm.nih.gov/pmc/articles/PMC419387/

https://www.betterhelp.com/advice/depression/how-to-know-if-you-are-depressed-11-signs-to-notice-and-when-to-get help/

Fabulous Follies (*Author had been here*)
https://en.wikipedia.org/wiki/The_Fabulous_Palm_Springs_Follies

Hernia Surgery (*Author has had issue*)
https://www.ncbi.nlm.nih.gov/pmc/articles/PMC2999781/

Honda Gold Wing
https://en.wikipedia.org/wiki/Honda_Gold_Wing

Joshua Tree National Park (Author has been here often)
https://www.trafalgar.com/real-word/joshua-tree-national-park/

McCallum Theatre events (*Author has been here several times*)
https://www.ibdb.com/touring-theatre/mccallum-theatre-for-the-performing-arts-562

Nepotism
https://hrmanual.calhr.ca.gov/Home/ManualItem/1/1204

Palm Springs – Coachella Valley (*Author has been several times*)
https://en.wikipedia.org/wiki/Coachella_Valley
https://www.tripadvisor.com/Attractions-g10212293-Activities-c47-oa60-Coachella_Valley_Greater_Palm_Springs_California.html

Palm Desert/Springs/Area (*Author comes most winters*)
https://en.wikipedia.org/wiki/Palm_Desert,_California

Palm Springs Street Fair – some merchants (*Author has been*)
https://codaastreetfair.com/merchant-directory/

Portland Clydes 1990s
https://www.clydesprimerib.com/live-music-portland/

Portland Hollywood Theatre
https://www.pressherald.com/2011/06/16/stress_-try-making-a-film-from-scratch_-in-48-hours_2011-06-16/

Portland Amusement Park 1990s/FREE WILLY
https://en.wikipedia.org/wiki/Free_Willy
https://en.wikipedia.org/wiki/Oaks_Amusement_Park

Portland International Test Gardens
https://en.wikipedia.org/wiki/International_Rose_Test_Garden

Portland Old Town (*Author has been*)

https://en.wikipedia.org/wiki/Portland_Skidmore/
Old_Town_Historic_District
Portland Tourist Information
https://en.wikipedia.org/wiki/
Category:Tourist_attractions_in_Portland,_Oregon
Portland State University
https://www.pdx.edu/academics/programs/undergraduate/accounting
(The) Purple Room (*Author has been*)
https://m.bpt.me/event/5447632
Psychiatrist Degree
https://www.gcu.edu/blog/psychology-counseling/
how-become-psychiatrist
Reiki (*Author has second level Reiki training*)
https://www.medicalnewstoday.com/articles/308772#what-is-it
San Diego Safari and Zoo (*Author has been here*)
https://sdzsafaripark.org/tickets
Shakespeare
https://owlcation.com/humanities/Flower-Quotes-Shakespeare
https://www.poetryfoundation.org/poems/56968/
speech-friends-romans-countrymen-lend-me-your-ears
https://nosweatshakespeare.com/quotes/soliloquies/
Slang
https://californiaglory.com/blogs/articles/los-angeles-slang-expressions
https://higherlanguage.com/nebraska-slang-words-and-phrases/
https://theculturetrip.com/north-america/usa/california/
articles/16-socal-slang-expressions-you-need-to-know
https://www.dominicanabroad.com/new-york-slang-words-nyc/
Theft / Burglary
https://www.skierlawfirm.com/blog/2017/january/
frequently-asked-questions-about-white-collar-cr/
https://www.skierlawfirm.com/blog/2017/january/
frequently-asked-questions-about-white-collar-cr/
https://brinkshome.com/smartcenter/how-to-disable-security-cameras

https://www.laralaw.com/white-collar-crimes/
steps-to-take-before-your-white-collar-crime-arrest/

Vietnamese Clothing
https://www.etsy.com/ca/listing/1190909917/
men-ao-dai-3d-swirl-design-red-blue-or

Whitewater Rock (*Author has been*)
https://whitewater-rock.com/about-us/

Suicide prevention:
https://www.mayoclinic.org/diseases-conditions/suicide/
symptoms-causes/syc-20378048

Made in the USA
Coppell, TX
17 February 2026

71572283R00187